The Psychology
of the Western

The Psychology
of the Western

*How the American Psyche
Plays Out on Screen*

William Indick

McFarland & Company, Inc., Publishers
Jefferson, North Carolina, and London

LIBRARY OF CONGRESS CATALOGUING-IN-PUBLICATION DATA

Indick, William, 1971–
  The psychology of the Western : how the American psyche plays
out on screen / William Indick.
      p.   cm.
  Includes bibliographical references and index.

  ISBN 978-0-7864-3460-2
  softcover : 50# alkaline paper ∞

  1. Western films — Psychological aspects.   2. Western
films — United States — History and criticism.   I. Title.
PN1995.9.W4I53   2008
791.43'65878 — dc22   2008031039

British Library cataloguing data are available

On the cover: Clint Eastwood as William Munny in
Unforgiven, 1992 (Warner Bros./Photofest); weathered boards
©2008 Shutterstock.

Manufactured in the United States of America

McFarland & Company, Inc., Publishers
  Box 611, Jefferson, North Carolina 28640
  www.mcfarlandpub.com

For Sophie

Acknowledgments

I would like to thank to Jim Tate, Professor of English at Dowling College, with whom I created the course "The Western," which was the primary inspiration for this book. The film stills in this book were purchased for book publication at Jerry Ohlinger's Movie Material Store in New York City. A debt of gratitude is owed to the faculty and administration of Dowling College in Oakdale, New York, for their continued support of my research and writing projects.

Contents

Preface

Along with baseball and jazz music, the Western film stands as one of America's greatest lasting contributions to world culture. The medium of film emerged at a time when the Western frontier was all but gone. The legends and heroes of the 20th century that were immortalized in films were based on the mythical era of the Wild West, that brief time in American history between the Civil War and the end of the 19th century, when the land of the frontier wilderness was still open and free, providing the perfect birthplace for the idealized American hero. Just as the antediluvian age was the mythological setting for the Greeks and Romans, and the Dark Ages were the mythological setting for the Northern Europeans, the Western film scenario became the setting for an American mythology and the birthplace of its primary cultural icon — the Western hero. This larger-than-life character found the perfect forum for his legendary adventures on the silver screen, establishing the Western as one of the first and most successful film genres, and also providing generations of American boys with a strong, proud, and often problematic role model for manhood.

The first real feature film ever made, *The Great Train Robbery* (1903), was a Western, and the genre has had many declines and revivals since then. Over 4,000 Westerns, about half of them B-picture serials, were produced between 1926 and 1967, a quarter of all the films ever made. Beginning in 1939, with the popular success of A-picture Westerns such as *Destry Rides Again, Jesse James*, and *Stagecoach*, until 1969, the Western was the most popular and broadly produced action film in Hollywood. The genre has been waning in popularity for the past four decades and has become a shadow of its former self. Nevertheless, sparks of life still twinkle now and then. Twice in the past twenty years, Westerns won Academy Awards for Best Picture

(*Dances with Wolves*, 1990, and *Unforgiven*, 1992); and most recently, a Western (*Brokeback Mountain,* 2005) won Academy Awards for Best Director (Ang Lee) and Best Writing (Larry McMurtry and Diana Ossana). Recent Westerns such as the remake of *3:10 to Yuma* (2007), *The Assassination of Jesse James by the Coward Robert Ford* (2007), and the very modern Western *No Country for Old Men* (2007), display the endurance of the genre. While it inspires little hope of another grand revival, the Western remains a respected genre and an integral part of film history as the principal American film genre of the past century.

During its "Golden Age" in the 1950s, the Western genre developed characters and scenarios that were much more sophisticated and complex than the simplistic hero/villain morality tales that dominated the first half-century of Western films. The Western hero became darker, more conflicted, and shaded with psychological torment and internal conflict. The Psychological Western was born. This book will address two basic questions: What exactly is "psychological" about the Psychological Western? And what are the major psychological aspects of the Western genre as a whole? The book will approach the Western from a mythological perspective, analyzing its characters as archetypal figures and exploring its themes as primal expressions of human drives and needs that perform, on a cultural level, specific psychological functions for its audience.

The myth of the Western frontier is the primary myth of the American nation. It represents the Genesis and Exodus books of American history, the time when America moved westward from a nation of European colonies, pushing the frontier farther and farther until it reached the sea. It was a period in which America defined itself as a nation, established its cultural identity, gave birth to its national heroes, and created its own particular ethos and ideals. The myth traces its history from the original captivity narratives of the Colonial Era, to the aggrandized legends of frontiersman such as Daniel Boone and Davy Crockett, to the frontier epics of James Fenimore Cooper and the dime novels of Owen Wister and Zane Grey. The myth was visualized by great painters such as Remington and Bierstadt, it was brought to life by great showmen such as Buffalo Bill Cody and Wild Bill Hickock, and it was delivered to the masses by traveling Wild West shows and rodeos. In the 20th century, just as the age of the frontier was ending, film became the primary medium of the national mythology. In the first 60 years of film, the Western was by far the most popular film genre. During its heyday in the 1950s, the number of Western films produced outnumbered all other genres combined. The Western mystique ranged far beyond film and publishing, greatly influencing the mediums of television and popular music, as well as American fashion, cuisine, politics — every aspect of American life. Though the Western has shown a steady decline in popularity over the past four decades, its significance is still clear today, because — as yet — no other distinct national mythology has risen to take its place.

Introduction

In studying the Western from a psycho-mythological perspective, we are psychoanalyzing the American Dream. The mythology of the Western frontier, as expressed in both the psychological Western subgenre and in the Western genre as a whole, will be analyzed in this book as both a deliberate and an unconscious expression of American ideals, hopes, fears, and anxieties. The archetypal themes and characters that dwell in the mythical landscape of the Western film are born of the inner conflicts of the American psyche. These conflicts are historical and contemporary, ethnic and universal, spiritual and political, as well as economic and cultural. In its long history, the Western scenario has been used as a backdrop for every American issue, every dramatic structure, and nearly every kind of story that could be told. Though the Western has long lost its status as the central figure in American popular culture, the frontier setting still has mythic significance.

In the century beginning with the end of the Civil War and ending with the escalation of the Vietnam War, the Western arose as the primary mythology of the American people, symbolizing everything that America loved about itself and, in its later days, everything that Americans despised about their own people. We are still living with the repercussions of the Western ethos and the romanticized myth that grew around it: the glorification of gun violence, the idealization of autonomous unilateral action, and the justification of imperialist doctrines. And while it may no longer seem viable as a projection for the collective unconscious of the nation that spawned it, it seems unlikely that another mythology as cohesive and substantial as the Western will arise in the foreseeable future.

In his essay "A Semantic Approach to Myth," Philip Wheelwright illustrates a model in which there are three broad stages in the evolution and development of a myth. Richard Slotkin applied Wheelwright's model to the development of the frontier myth as a whole, beginning with the captivity narratives of the Colonial Era, through the biographical novels about Daniel Boone, the frontier novels of James Fenimore Cooper, the dime novels of Zane Grey, the Wild West shows of Buffalo Bill, and continuing through to the Western films and television shows of the late 20th century. In a much more cursory way, Wheelwright's three stages can be applied to the Western genre. Within this very limited scope, one can see the development of the Western myth within the specific idiom of American film.

Wheelwright's first or "primary" stage is referred to as "mythopoeic." In this embryonic stage of myth development, the myth is still linked quite strongly to the actual historical figures and events that are being memorialized for posterity. Hence, the myth begins with a people's attempt to remember the actual accounts of its own beginnings. As Slotkin (1992) noted: "The primary function of any mythological system is to provide a people with meaningful emotional and intellectual links to its own past." As the birth of the medium of film overlapped briefly with the end of the frontier era, the early years of film reflect an eagerness to record the authentic people, places, and experiences of the Western frontier. Wheelwright referred to these actual details as "artifacts" of the primary myth. They are the "authentic" accounts of what would become legends. The costume and rituals of American Indians, the distinctive vernacular and lifestyles of frontiersmen, as well as celebrated events such as Custer's Last Stand at Little Big Horn, the shootout at the O.K. Corral between the Earps and the Clantons, and the killing of Wild Bill Hickock in Deadwood, Colorado, are all examples of artifacts from the primary myth. Early Westerns of the silent era tended to focus on these artifacts. This focus evolved into formulas, which after perpetual repetition over a course of time, developed into conventional forms and established archetypes. By the end of the mythopoeic era (the first three decades of Western films), the form of the structural myth had become an accepted and integral part of its people's culture.

Wheelwright's second stage is called "romantic." At this point, the metaphor — what the myths represent on a psychological level — becomes more important than the actual artifact. Authenticity and historical accuracy are more or less abandoned in favor of the glorification of the mythic ideal, which is typically embodied in the singular figure of the mythological hero. The romantic stage of Western film, in which the classic Western was born and came of age, will be the primary focus of this book. This stage began in 1939, the year in which the genre experienced a renaissance with the release of classic Westerns such as John Ford's *Stagecoach* and Henry

King's *Jesse James*. These films, and many others like them, glorified the Western hero and idealized the Western code of honor. In the first decade of the romantic stage, there was a tendency to view the hero as a founding patriarch of the American West, a Moses or even Jesus-like figure within the frontier mythology.

In the second decade of the romantic stage, the 1950s, the Western hero took on even more significance, as the primary symbol of American life and the persona of the nation's collective unconscious. The Psychological Western was born. The hero in this new type of Western became more complex. His motivations and methods were called into question by his own conscience. He became a conflicted and haunted figure, a darker and more potent projection of the true conflicts within his people's psyche. As Cawelti noted:

> ... the classic Western shifted its focus from the myth of foundation to a concern with social transition — the passing of the old West into modern society. The hero became not the founder of a new order but a somewhat archaic survivor, driven by motives and values that are somewhat anachronistic in the new social order. His climactic violence, though legitimated by its service to the community, does not integrate him into society. Instead, it separates him still further, either because the pacified community has no need for his unique talents, or because the new society cannot quite contain his honor and his violence. In this situation, the hero increasingly tended toward isolation, separation, alienation.

Wheelwright's third stage, the "consummatory," is described as "a product of a somewhat late and sophisticated stage of cultural development: a post-romantic attempt to recapture the lost innocence of the primitive mythopoeic attitude by transcending the narrative, logical, and linguistic forms which romantic mythologizing accepts and utilizes." In the Western film genre, the consummatory stage is a product of the postmodern age. Films within the genre became self-reflective, focusing on their own part in the formation and perpetuation of the Western myth, and deconstructing the hero to descry his most basic elements, laying him bare for all his faults and weaknesses, and in doing do, revealing the consciousness of the society that created him. It its attempt to understand the myth at a deeper level, there is a renewed focus on realism and authenticity, a concerted effort to get back to the artifact, in hope of regaining an aspect of truth that was lost in the fictionalization of the romantic stage. The consummatory films engage in the deconstruction of the romantic into blatantly bleak and desolate depictions of un-mythic reality. Beginning in the 1960s, realism took the place of romanticism. The psychological Western, which took the first step away from naïve romanticism by humanizing the mythological hero, is followed by the consummatory approaches — the anti–Westerns, modern-day Westerns, elegiac Westerns, revisionist Westerns, and civil rights Westerns — which finish the job by completely stripping the hero of his superhuman qualities. But the deconstruction of the myth, as with the dissection and analysis of any living organism, results in its partial or total destruction. The myth loses its function as the symbols are dissolved in the acid of realism. The hero cannot survive without the nourishing air of romantic idolatry and ethnocentric idealism. In a hero-worshipping culture, if the hero ceases to be revered, then he is as good as dead.

Chapter 1 of this book, "The Mythical Landscape," explores the symbolism of the Western landscape, the major archetypes, and the psychological themes seen in Western films. Some of the dominant Western themes include the significance of honor in the Western hero's character, the ubiquitous conflict between civilized society and the wild men of the frontier, as well as racism and violence. In Chapter 2, "White Knights of the West," the principal archetype of the genre, the Western hero, is analyzed within the context of his various personas: the chivalrous cowboy, the honorable marshal, the lone crusader, and the rebel outlaw. A primary focus of this book is the psychological analysis of the Western hero as a mythical figure, a cultural icon, a human character, and most importantly as an extremely significant role model and father figure for numerous generations of young American males.

Chapter 3, "The Civilized and the Savage," explores the Western archetypes as a metaphor for neurotic conflict within the individual, symbolized by the encounter and integration of savage forces within the wild frontier. Chapter 4, "Western Women," examines the limited but crucial roles played by female characters in the genre. Chapter 5, "Atonement with the Indian," analyzes the changing role of the American Indian in the genre, as a focal point of both racial hatred and cultural guilt for White America. Chapter 6, "Oedipal and Biblical Westerns," focuses on Westerns that have classical mythological themes. Chapter 7 studies the Westerns directed by Anthony Mann, films for which critics in the 1950s originally coined the term "Psychological Western." These films include *Devil's Doorway* (1950), *The Furies* (1950), *Winchester '73* (1950), *Bend of the River* (1952), *The Naked Spur* (1953), *The Far Country* (1954), *The Man from Laramie* (1955), *The Last Frontier* (1955), *The Tin Star* (1957), *Man of the West* (1958), and *Cimarron* (1960). Chapter 8 dissects the Westerns directed by John Ford, the undisputed master of the genre, who more than any other director instilled a sense of tradition and cultural heritage in his "ritualistic" Westerns. In the conclusion, the influence of the Western film on the American consciousness is discussed, as well as the decline of the genre and the emergence of consummatory subgenres, such as the anti–Western and the elegiac Western.

Finally, the pivotal question is addressed: Is the Western dead or alive? Regardless of the future of the genre, the Western film has already assured its lasting impact on our nation's culture, community, politics, and psyche. Even if it dies on the screen, it will still live forever in our memories.

1

The Mythical Landscape

"Myth is history disguised as archetype."
— Richard Slotkin, 1985

When you enter the frame of the Western film, you enter the mythical realm of a historical period that never really existed, except in the imaginations of writers, entertainers, and filmmakers. The closing of the Western frontier towards the end of the 19th century had an incredibly significant effect on the psyche of the American population. It created a lost era, a time gone by that would never come again, an empty space in which history would become legend and men would become heroes. Frederick Jackson Turner, an eminent 19th-century historian, said in his influential "frontier thesis," "The Significance of the Frontier in American History" (1893): "*Up to our own day American history has been in a large degree the history of the colonization of the Great West. The existence of an area of free land, its continuous recession, and the advance of American settlement westward, explain American development ... and now ... the frontier has gone, and with its going has closed the first period of American history.*" In Turner's view, shared by many, the conquest of the Western frontier was the mythical creation period in our nation's history, the era in which America's character, values, and ethos were born. The men who won the West — the settlers, pioneers, soldiers, and cowboys — would become the legendary heroes who would go on to become the iconic role models for generations of Americans to come.

The myth of the frontier hero traces its roots back to antiquity. In many ways, the frontier hero is reminiscent of classical heroes from Greco/Roman and Judeo/Christian mythologies. The classical heroes were either blessed by the gods or were demigods by divine birth. Like the classical heroes, the

11

frontier hero's bravery, dedication to purpose, willingness to sacrifice, and extraordinary abilities — especially in the field of combat — set him apart from other men. In the New World, the frontier myth began with the captivity narratives of the 16th- and 17th-century pioneers. In these stories, men, women, and children abducted by wild Indians wrote of the harrowing brutality and savagery that they experienced at the hands of their captors. The narratives were not hero sagas, but rather Christian morality tales, in which the Indians were portrayed as devils, the captivity as a Hell on Earth, and the captive's redemption as spiritual, rather than physical. The first true hero stories of the frontier were born of the biographical epics of legendary figures such as Daniel Boone, Kit Carson, and Davy Crockett. These highly fictionalized biographies represented the first attempts of American writers at establishing a national hero based on the frontiersman persona. The rugged, independent frontier hero was mythologized into an archetype in 19th-century literary epics set on the Western frontier, usually in upstate New York. James Fenimore Cooper's "Leatherstocking" cycle of frontier novels were the most significant and influential of these epics.

First published in 1826, Cooper's *The Last of the Mohicans* presents the frontiersman as a noble knight-errant. He is in tune with nature and violent only when pushed. He is more comfortable living in the open frontier than in the cities, and most importantly, he does not conform to the laws and customs of civilized society. He answers only to his own code of honor and enforces his own personal brand of justice. The classic Western hero as seen in films, however, would not arise until the beginning of the 20th century, with novels such as Owen Wister's *The Virginian* (1902) and the many books of Zane Grey and other dime novelists. These writers established the cowboy hero as the legendary icon of the West. They dressed him in chaps and a ten-gallon hat, straddled him atop a horse, armed him with a revolver, and set him loose on the Western plains.

The entertainment value of the Western myth was demonstrated by the tremendous success of Buffalo Bill Cody's Wild West show, which was the nation's most popular live show in the late 19th and early 20th centuries. It was only natural that the Western would make the immediate transition from live show to movie show, as the closing of the frontier, the emergence of the Western myth, and the dawn of the film industry all occurred simultaneously. Like all art forms, the Western film in the early 20th century can be seen as a medium that reframed and represented the topical social issues of its time. In an era in which America was struggling with the problems of alcoholism and prohibition, Westerns depicted a world of bawdy saloons filled with whiskey-guzzling cowboys, in which drunkenness was both commonplace and problematic, as an instigator of violence and lechery. While the nation was trying to cope with the unparalleled violence of two world wars, violence in the Western film seemed cleaner, more honorable, and more gallant than the mechanized wholesale slaughter of modern warfare.

At a time of unprecedented nationalism, when America was defining itself as a world power, the Western depicted the dream of "manifest destiny" as a glorious triumph of rugged determination, supreme courage, racial superiority, and the fulfillment of God's will. In the words of Richard Slotkin, the preeminent mythologist of the Western frontier, the land west of the Mississippi was reconceived as "the New El Dorado" by Americans looking back at the seminal events of the 19th century. In retrospect, Americans saw their fathers and grandfathers as the new conquistadors, exterminating and displacing native populations as they raked and raped the "virgin land" for gold, silver, and precious space. The foreword from Cecil B. De Mille's Western epic *Union Pacific* (1939) expresses this mentality in a nutshell:

> The legend of Union Pacific is the drama of a nation, young, tough, prodigal and invincible, conquering with an iron highroad the endless reaches of the West. For the West is America's Empire...

The American Creation Myth

The Western film provides a type of psychological catharsis that goes beyond temporal societal issues. The Western provides its nation with its own book of Genesis — an American creation myth. Like the book of Genesis in the Bible, the American creation myth offers not only a historical interpretation of its ancestral heritage, but a set of morals and values that provide meaning for its successors, and most importantly, a canon of legends to be told and retold for generations to come. From these legends were born a legion of heroes to be worshipped and revered. The hook of the Western genre is that it often aspires to be a historical recollection of the building of America told in an exciting and meaningful manner. The caveat is that the history is inaccurate, and the message is filtered through the values and ideals within the era in which each film was made. What the Western actually provides is a living mythology, an ever-flowing and ever-changing wellspring of tall tales, homegrown heroes, glorified ancestors, and archetypal figures.

In the function of the American creation myth, many Westerns, especially those made during the "Golden Age of Westerns" (1946–1962), create a distinct Biblical feel in their scenarios and settings. The barren desert landscape, the menacing presence of hostile natives, the constant threat of warfare, the perpetual struggle for survival, the absence of civilization, and most importantly, the lack of a governmentally enforced system of law and order, all endow the Western frontier with an archaic atmosphere reminiscent of Biblical times. The pioneer Americans faced the same obstacles that the ancient Hebrews faced when entering the "promised land." The conquering of the indigenous peoples, the creation of order from chaos via the establishment of towns, the taming of the land through farming or ranching, and the taming of the savage elements within people via the enforcement of law and justice, are the dominant themes in both the latter books of the Old Testament and the Golden Age era of Western films.

The conflicts faced by the characters of Western films reflect their mythical setting. In Oedipal Westerns like *Red River* (1948), cattle barons and their cowboy sons inevitably shoot it out over their rivalry for livestock, land, and the love of a woman — just as Laius and Oedipus had it out over their rivalry for the hand of Jocasta and the land of Thebes. In sibling-rivalry Westerns like *Winchester '73* (1950), gunfighter brothers inevitably shoot it out with each other over the love and favor of their father, just as Cain and Abel battled over the love and favor of God, the heavenly father. And just as the latter books of the Old Testament recall the constant warfare over the Biblical territories, in the Western frontier, the land itself is always a source of eternal conflict, whether it is between homesteaders and ranchers, cavalry and Indians, cowboys and Indians, or cowboys and cowboys.

The Mythical Landscape

Upon entering the landscape of the Western film, the viewer vicariously enters an American Eden, a wilderness paradise that is now all but lost. John Ford, the most poetic of the Western directors, shot his films in Monument Valley, Utah, a landscape of mythical proportions, with immense freestanding sandstone rock formations rising a thousand feet high from the desert floor. George Stevens filmed his mythical masterpiece, *Shane* (1952), in Wyoming's Grand Tetons, amid the jagged peaks of snowcapped mountains and the endless broad valleys beneath them. Ang Lee's recent *Brokeback Mountain* (2005) purveys a similarly reverential approach in its depiction of the majestic landscape of the Rocky Mountains and the Western plains.

John Izod, a professor of screen analysis who specializes in applying Jungian psychoanalytic theory to film, believes that the landscape in the Western plays the part that a female love interest would typically play in a film:

Oedipus West. John Wayne (left) as Tom Dunson and Montgomery Clift as Matthew Garth in Howard Hawks's *Red River* (1948, United Artists).

Eros, which would ordinarily attach man to woman, drew the Western male to nature, such was the appeal of the pastoral ideal. This obsessive love leads him to invest the wilderness with feminine qualities. The resulting displacement makes for a dangerous, uroboric courtship of the Earth Mother. It inhibits the proper maturation of the Western hero's psyche and accounts for the often infantile nature of his relationships with white women. This quasi-incestuous love affair with nature was further troubled because the newcomers could not ignore the peoples already settled in the West who enjoyed a bond with the land that the immigrants could not share. So the white man found a dark-skinned rival whose presence intruded on his jealous love for the wilderness. That rivalry troubled the psycho-sexuality both of the whites themselves and their conception of Native Americans' nature. Since the new arrivals meant to possess the land by seizing it from its original inhabitants, they soon demonized the latter by intuitively making them the object of their collective shadow projection, as all peoples do with their enemies when they prepare to go to war. These racist shadow projections endured long after the end of the Indian wars and tainted the Western genre, where they remained a staple feature through much of the twentieth century. Furthermore, the impact of woman as anima was marginalized. She seldom functions as an archetypal image whose power can give a man insight into the contents of his unconscious and enrich his personality.

The psychosexual relationship between the frontiersman and the landscape is captured in this bit of dialogue from *The Indian Fighter* (1955): "To me, the West is like a beautiful woman, *my* woman. I like her the way she is. I don't want her changed. I'm jealous. I don't want to share her with anybody. I'd hate to see her civilized!" The character who speaks these lines, Johnny (Kirk Douglas), does find female companionship by the end of the film. As Izod stated, this is somewhat uncharacteristic for the archetypal frontier hero. But in the film, Johnny's choice of love interest is an Indian girl (Elsa Martinelli), who is portrayed as a wild child of nature. Though he is clearly offered the companionship of a beautiful and willing white woman (Diana Douglas), this frontier hero chooses the native, as she is linked with the Western landscape in a way that a white woman could never be.

In Izod's Jungian interpretation, the landscape itself is the "anima" archetype — the feminine side of the hero's personality — and the object of his love and affection. This is why, in the typical representation of the frontiersman, the hero is never quite comfortable in a romantic relationship with a woman, because his heart will always remain with the land itself, his first and only true love. Hence, the Western hero often does not get the girl in the end; he is left alone to "ride off into the sunset," returning to the wilderness as a solitary animal, a lone uncivilized wanderer, a "lonesome cowboy," at home only with the land. The endings of John Ford's *The Searchers* (1956) and *My Darling Clementine* (1946) provide excellent examples of this theme. Though the hero (John Wayne and Henry Fonda, respectively) could certainly stay within the fold of women and domestic society at the end of their stories, they choose to return to the wilderness, turning their backs on the women and townspeople that they so valiantly protected. And while the role of the female character is typically underplayed in the Western, the role of the landscape is typically accentuated, making the scenery in the Western as equally important a character as the hero or villain. Every fan of the genre knows that a good Western must impart a strong sense of the frontier landscape. A major appeal of the Western is that it gives its viewer a feeling for the outdoors, the vicarious pleasure of riding out on the open range, which is why most almost every camera shot in a typical Western is an external shot. A Western purist would contend that the primary job of a Western film is to depict the glory and majesty of the frontier landscape. Everything else — plot, character development, conflict — is secondary.

While the function of the anima archetype is fulfilled by both the land and the female, the Western hero himself epitomizes the animus archetype. He is a character that is completely and utterly masculine, to the point where he cannot even relate to his own emotions. In turn, the Native American is often portrayed as the shadow archetype, the representative of savage, wild emotions, and the dark adversary for the hero in their oedipal rivalry over the maternal landscape. Though the land itself is a pivotal part of every Western, the landscape of the Western is only ground. Its sole purpose is to function as the birth ground, testing ground, and memorial ground for the mythological cowboy hero. As such, the landscape is populated by a host of symbols that are peculiar to the Western setting and scenario. These symbols are usually related to the closing of the frontier, which represents the death of the land as an Eden-like wilderness, as society, modernization, and population bring with them the evils and corruption of the civilized world.

Barbed wire always represents the end of an era. The modern-day Western, *Lonely Are the Brave* (1962), begins with the cowboy hero, Jack Burns (Kirk Douglas), cutting down barbed wire so he can pass through a field on his horse. The cutting of the wire represents the notion that this character is out of place in his setting (20th-century America) and that he is actively rebelling against his own environment. In King Vidor's *Man Without a Star* (1955), the cowboy hero, Dempsey Rae (Kirk Douglas), says: "I don't like wire! I don't like anyone who uses wire!" As the embodiment of freedom and independence, the cowboy hero's lifestyle is antithetical to the purpose of barbed wire, which is meant to close in open ranges and punish anyone or anything who wishes to ride free over the plains. When Dempsey says, "The wire's catchin' up with me," he means that the end of his kind of lifestyle is coming to an end, as the presence of barbed wire portends the end of the mythical landscape, and therefore represents the end of the mythical denizens of this landscape — the frontier hero and the wild Indian.

The railroad is another technical innovation that represents the progress of modern civilization and the end of old ways. In *How the West Was Won* (1962), Henry Fonda plays an old-time westerner. When he hears the train whistle blow, he remarks: "That blame whistle's like the crack of doom for all that's natural." In the realm of the "iron horse," the flesh-and-blood horse loses its function and is therefore doomed to marginalization and semi-extinction. The horse itself is a primary symbol in the Western. Oftentimes, the hero relates on an emotional level only with his horse. For the hero, other people reflect the corruption and duality that people unlike himself represent, while his horse, like himself, represents freedom, honesty, constancy, and purity. The worst villains in Westerns are those who beat or mistreat horses — it is the vilest crime a man could commit in the Western scenario. As Cawelti notes: "The cowboy's special relationship to his horse suggests that human fantasy of unity with natural creatures seen in the centaurs of Greek mythology, in Siegfried's ability to understand the language of birds, and in a hero whose popularity was contemporaneous with the flourishing of the Western: Tarzan of the Apes."

The killing of horses represents the end of the frontier era. In *The Misfits* (1961), Gay Langland (Clark Gable), the cowboy hero, is reduced to wrangling wild mustangs to be sold for dog food. This ignoble vocation represents Gay's state of degradation. In the end, he must set free the mustangs in order to redeem his integrity. In *Lonely Are the Brave*, Dempsey rides a horse while every other character drives a car, jeep, or truck. His outmoded choice of vehicle casts him as an anachronism, but also as a romantic figure, hearkening back to a more glorious time. He meets his end while trying to cross a busy highway on horseback. He and his beloved horse are hit and killed by a truck hauling toilets. In the elegiac Western, all things beautiful and noble are destroyed by the ugly and mundane devices of the modern world.

Often, the landscape itself is depicted as a character that must be saved. Rather than loving, revering, and protecting the land, villains use, abuse, and rape the land. Greedy cattle barons engage in overgrazing (feeding too many cattle on a stretch of open range so that the grass can't re-grow, then abandoning the range), as seen in *Man Without a Star*. Disreputable miners engage in hydraulic mining (using high-powered hoses to level hills, so that the gold can be filtered out, while destroying the landscape), as seen in *Pale Rider*. The animals of the Western landscape are also frequently under attack by the venomous harbingers of civilization. Ruthless buffalo hunters wipe out entire herds at the behest of the railroad. While Indians hunted buffalo in moderation, for sustenance and provisions, the buffalo hunters killed for the distinct purpose of decimating the buffalo population, in order to make way for railroads, settlers, and ranchers. It was also tacitly understood that in destroying the buffalo, the hunters were depriving the Indians of their primary food supply, thus forcing them, via starvation and genocide, to end their traditional ways of life and settle on reservations. The buffalo, in films such as *The Last Hunt* (1956), are perceived not only as a lost element of the frontier landscape, but also as the incarnation of the Indian spirit, as their entire culture and identity was destroyed as a consequence of the semi-extinction of the buffalo on the Western plains. The wolf is another symbol of the Indian spirit. Shepherds, cattle ranchers, and farmers hunted the indigenous wolf populations throughout most of the West into extinction. Like the buffalo, the wiping out of the wolf symbolizes the destruction of the Indian nations. But while the buffalo is a docile, languid animal, the wolf is a fast, dangerous, cunning, and wild beast. So while the buffalo may represent the spirit of the Indians who were simply pushed off their land and coerced into submitting to white mastery, the wolf represents the fierce warrior tribes (typically portrayed in Westerns by the Apache), who fought tooth and nail for their culture and land, but in the end were conquered by superior weapons and numbers. *Dances with Wolves* (1990) is a prime example of a Western in which the Indian spirit is symbolized in the character of a wolf.

Another primary Western symbol is the gun, which represents the masculine identity of the frontiersman, who asserts his dominance though violence. In Freudian terms, the gun may be called a "phallic symbol," as it could be seen as the representation of male aggressiveness, masculine domination, and the sublimation of the psychosexual urge into violent activity. The guns of the Old West were either single-fire weapons (the Springfield rifle and the shotgun or "scatter" gun), or repeating-fire weapons (the six-gun revolver and the Winchester, Henry, or Spencer rifle). Any gun that shoots more rapidly than a revolver or repeating rifle, or any weapon that has more firepower than a shotgun, is anathema to the traditional Western setting. Artillery, when used, is typically employed by the tyrant or wrongful aggressor, and even then is usually ineffective. Violence in the Western is personal: one man taking aim at another, shooting one bullet at a time. Weapons of relatively mass destruction — artillery, bombs, machine guns — are too messy, too imprecise, too mechanized to impart the sense of individual skill and artistry that the Western gunfighter must employ in his violence. The six-gun in the Western is a noble weapon, akin to the medieval knight's sword, as it requires skill and knowledge to be used effectively, and because it is designed for man-to-man combat. The machine gun is always representative of the end of the Western era. It relies on a high volume of fire rather than shooting skill for its effectiveness, and is linked historically to the horror of wholesale slaughter via mechanized weaponry, introduced to humanity in the first world war. Whether employed by the anti-heroes at the end of *The Wild Bunch* (1969), or by the villainous Indian agent in *The Vanishing American* (1925), the use of the machine gun represents the end of the mythological age of Western chivalry and the dawn of the modern age of mechanized, impersonal killing. This type of violence is incapable of manifesting any degree of honor, as it makes death itself meaningless.

Western mythology began with the captivity narrative, which imparted to readers the notion of "a fate worse than death." To be captured by Indians, especially for a woman, meant the inevitable horror of atrocities, torture, and rape. Even though there is little historical evidence that Indians ever engaged in the rape of their female captives, the Western myth assumes that all female captives will be subjected to gang rape until death, or prolonged miscegenation as an Indian's "wife," which inevitably results in insanity. For children, the fate worse than death was more existential in nature. If they were to be raised as Indians, losing their inherent whiteness via the process of psychological and cultural identification with the red man, then what value did their lives have, at least in the eyes of their white compatriots? And even for men, captivity brought the assumption of the many tortures and atrocities recalled in the captivity narratives: being burned alive, being skinned, limbs hacked off, eyes gouged out, etc. All of these notions took part in the genesis of the "last bullet" theme in the Western myth.

In Westerns, the last bullet theme is often raised, never explained explicitly, and seldom employed. In John Ford's *Stagecoach* (1939), when their seems to be no hope that the band of passengers will escape from the attacking Apaches, the Southern gambler (John Carradine), having saved the last bullet in his revolver, puts his gun up to the young mother's (Louise Platt) head. However, before he pulls the trigger, the peal of a cavalry trumpet sounding the charge is heard in the distance, and the last bullet is spared from use. Nearly the exact same episode is depicted in the Indian attack sequence of *Union Pacific* (1939). In Anthony Mann's *Winchester '73* (1950), the hero (James Stewart) gives the pretty girl (Shelley Winters) a loaded revolver, just before the Indians attack their position. She thanks him, then says: "Don't worry, I know all about the last bullet." A rare instance of the last bullet actually being used is depicted in the anti–Western *Ulzana's Raid* (1972). In the film, a cavalryman is overrun by a large band of hostile Indians. Rather than using his gun to engage in futile battle, he immediately kills the woman in his charge and then shoots himself. The viewer is shocked by the cavalryman's apparently impetuous act, until later on in the film, when the film shows us in vivid detail the portrait of a "fate worse than death"— a white woman tortured and raped by Indians to the point of insanity.

The Custer Archetype

Richard Slotkin (1992) referred to Custer's Last Stand as "the central fable" of the myth of the frontier within the Industrial Age. "To contemplate Custer was to turn from the tragedy of fraternal strife to the classic quest of the republic's heroic age, the mission to bring light, law, liberty, Christianity, and commerce to the savage places of the earth." In the mythopoeic stage of the Western genre, depictions of the cavalry officer archetype were tied close to the actual artifact. Custer was portrayed as a hero. His valiant fight at Little Big Horn was a grave defeat, and his death a moral lesson in the cost of overconfidence and conceit. In the romantic stage, Custer's status was raised to the level of a mythical hero. He was a divine king, symbolizing the Old World tradition of chivalry and bravado. In Raoul Walsh's *They Died with Their Boots On* (1941), Errol Flynn portrays Custer as a nobleman warrior, a messianic martyr, whose blood had to be spilled on the frontier in order for the new America to rise from the ruddy dust. In the psychological Westerns of the late 1940s and 1950s, such as *Fort Apache* (1948) and *The Last Frontier* (1955), the character was typically depicted as a controversial figure. The Custer archetype was a rigid martinet, often portrayed as either the antagonist to the hero, or as a conflicted hero. He's torn between his own shortcomings — obsession with personal honor and glory, recklessness, stubbornness, caste-snobbery — and his strengths — bravery, allegiance to the army, and determination. In this sense, Custer represents the Western hero in full, the living embodiment of the central qualities of independence, isolationism, and individualism, depicting both the glory and the folly of these dubious character traits.

In the consummatory anti–Westerns of the postmodern era, such as *Soldier Blue* (1970) and *Little Big Man* (1971), the cavalry officer was depicted as the ultimate American villain, a reckless, foolhardy, narcissistic, bloodthirsty warmonger, interested only in his own honor and glory, and quite willing to exterminate countless innocent Indians to gain his prominence, while being equally indifferent to the lives of his own men. In the age of revisionist and anti–Westerns, Custer's Last Stand becomes allegorical to the war in Vietnam. It represented the demise of the vainglorious classical hero in America. Custer had degenerated in status from hero, to anti-hero, and finally to villain, representing the inability of the European white man to understand and thereby conquer the Native.

Western Myth/American Dream

The Western myth reflects the culture, history, and ideals of an entire people via the narrative of a single identification figure: the frontier hero. For the American people of the 18th and 19th centuries, the frontiersman archetype embodied all of the aspects of the quintessential American. He was a strong, brave, white Christian who was fierce enough to settle on a land that was not his, and through the power of his own will and violent determination, conquer all of his rivals to claim the land for his own. In the 20th century, film took over as the dominant medium for the retelling of the American myth. For a population still largely composed of new immigrants and the children of immigrants, the theme of the intrepid frontiersman claiming and conquering the American West was just as resonant as it was for the 18th-century colonists and the 19th-century homesteaders.

The American Dream is at the heart of the Western myth. The dream of economic independence, cultural self-determination, and freedom of individual expression are what enticed people to come to America, and it is the same dream that lured frontiersman and settlers out west. In myth, the dreams of many become condensed into a single tapestry, a collective dream, in which the hopes, ideals, fears, and prayers of an entire nation are projected onto a shared set of symbols and archetypes. As Joseph Campbell (1948) stated: "Dream is the personalized myth, myth the depersonalized dream." For many Americans, and for most of the 20th century, Western films provided the medium for this national mythology. The genre is both a reflection and a projection of the American collective unconscious, and while it is no longer a dominant force in the popular arena, its effects on the nation's psyche will be long-lasting and substantial.

2

White Knights of the West

The hero is a Galahad with a six-gun, a Perseus of the purple sage.
In his saddlebags he carries a new mythology,
an American Odyssey that is waiting for its Homer.
And the theme of the epic, hidden beneath the circus glitter
of the perennial Wild West show, is the immortal theme of every hero myth:
man's endless search for the meaning of his life.
— Peter Lyon, 1959

The legends of the knights of King Arthur's court and their various quests provided much of the inspiration for the frontier hero of the Western film. Replace the helmet with a Stetson, the sword with a Colt revolver, retain the noble steed, and the medieval knight becomes a cowboy. The knight's joust, which had been transformed into the gentleman's pistol duel by the 18th century, was easily transformed into the quick-draw showdown in the Western. A curious combination of history and humbug, the quick-draw showdown probably never happened once in the Wild West, or anywhere else.

Nevertheless, as a movie interpretation of a pistol duel, the quick-draw showdown was perfectly adapted for the medium of film. Rather than two men methodically taking turns at their shot, the simultaneous quick-draw showdown was suspenseful, then sudden, an exciting explosion of action that was wonderfully cinematic. But more important than the genesis of the showdown is the psychology behind it — namely, the rules of conduct that drove men in Westerns to kill or be killed over the slightest breach of their personal code of honor.

The Code of the West

The Western code of honor also dates back to the age of chivalry, in which knights glorified courage, virtue, and personal honor above all, even above life itself. The Arthurian tales are filled with accounts of knights fighting to the death over seemingly trivial matters of personal honor. According to the code of honor, any disrespect, insult, or challenge to one's name, reputation, or courage demands "satisfaction" in the form of a violent, often deadly conflict. The code can be summed up in two Latin dictums of medieval origin. The first is "*nemo me impugnit,*" which means, "no one impugns me." The second is "*lex talionis,*" the "rule of retaliation." Put together, the two imperatives are a deadly mix. Every insult or challenge is perceived as a direct threat to one's personal sense of honor (often referred to by scholars as "primal honor"). The threat is a "primal" menace, as it targets the core elements of a man's identity: his reputation, his name, his masculinity, and his standing within the community. Therefore, the code requires that umbrage to one's personal sense of honor must be "satisfied" via swift and decisive retaliation. This retaliation must be violent, as another old saying prescribes: "*Words are no satisfaction for words.*"

The Northern and Western European code of honor migrated to America in the 17th and 18th centuries, principally among the Scots-Irish immigrants who settled in the Southern colonies and states, establishing what scholars now refer to as the "Southern culture of honor and violence," which exists as a social phenomenon to this day. This culture is noted for its consistent, swift, and problematic use of violence, especially gun violence, to enact revenge and vigilante justice (shootings and lynchings), whether justified or not. The Southern culture also has a high respect for individualism and independence, as can be seen in the enduring veneration of the Confederate rebellion. This cultural ethos of touchiness about honor, extreme individualism, the social expectation of violent retaliation, a culture of gun adulation dating back to Colonial days, and an equally fervent love for whiskey and hard liquor that was endemic to the Scots-Iris traditions, resulted in a toxic mix of revenge, booze, and handguns that all summed up into lots of shootings. It was these men, the products of the culture of honor and violence in the American South, who would move out west after the Civil War, looking for a new start as ranchers and cowhands on the Western plains. The myth of the frontier hero was based on these real people: mostly Southern young men, often former Confederate soldiers, who drank heavily, gambled, were quick with a gun and knew how to use it, and were prone to deadly demonstrations of their firearms expertise whenever they thought that their honor was besmirched in the slightest way.

Western Escapism

In his seminal 1959 *Time* magazine article, "The Six-Gun Galahad," Peter Lyon claimed that "*...the Western helps people to get away from the complexities of modern life and back to the 'restful absolutes' of the past.*" By this, he was referring to the simple and direct ways that people on the Western frontier resolved their conflicts.

> In the cowboy's world, justice is the result of direct action, not of elaborate legality.... Says sociologist Philip Rieff: "How long since you used your fists? How long since you called the boss an s.o.b.? The Western men do, and they are happy men." Says motivational researcher Ernest Dichter: "America grew too fast, and we have lost something in the process. The Western story offers us a way to return to the soil, a chance to redefine our roots."

The rough-and-tumble characters of the Western film, whether heroes or villains, give their viewers a vicarious sense of release. The average movie-goer could not punch out his obnoxious boss, and in the case of the most typical Western fan, the average young boy or adolescent male could not punch out his father or teacher, but in the Western, no such social restraints seem to exist. Beyond the violence of the obligatory shootouts, the Western fight scene became equally obligatory. They were especially apparent in the John Wayne movies of the late 1950s and 1960s, such as *Rio Bravo* (1959), *The Searchers*, *The Comancheros* (1961), *North to Alaska* (1960), etc. In films such as these, the fight scene became a caricature of itself— a riotous explosion of aggressive energy, made comical by breakaway furniture and candy glass. The raucous Western fight scene found its ultimate tribute in Mel Brooks's Western spoof, *Blazing Saddles* (1973), in which the scene is forced to go ultra-absurd, as the Western genre had already made the fight scene a preposterous mockery of itself. In *Blazing Saddles*, the fight scene takes up the entire third act of the film, bursting out of the Western scenario and emerging into the back lots of the Hollywood studio in which it was filmed. In the Western, anger, aggression, and anxiety were dealt with immediately and with extreme force, providing a primal catharsis for its young male viewers, who identified with their Western heroes not only psychologically, but also in their manner of behavior, dress, and speech. Violence could be fun and amusing, in the case of the fistfight, or it could be lethal, in the case of the gunfight.

As for the film characters, the Southern culture of honor was often embodied in their roles. The heroes of *The Searchers*, *The Texans* (1938), and *Jesse James* (John Wayne, Randolph Scott, and Tyrone Power respectively) were all former Confederate soldiers. Sometimes, as in *Stagecoach* and *Dark Command* (1940), the Southerner was cast as the villain or "heavy" (John Carradine and Walter Pidgeon, respectively). The reason for this trend may have been due to the Northern domination of the film industry and their dim view of the Southern culture of honor, perceiving it as retrograde and anathema to the ideals of modern society, even though the real cowboys from which the Hollywood myth was created were primarily Southern young men. But, as everyone knows, the film industry was never particularly interested in historical accuracy.

The Vengeance Quest

The "Code of the West," according to the Western film, recycled the Southern culture of honor in an adulterated, bastardized manner. The theme of vengeance, which epitomized both "*nemo me impugnit*" and "*lex talionis*," became the central theme, in one way or another, in almost every Western. However, there was a crucial difference between the motive and fulfillment of the hero's revenge and the villain's. The hero's vengeance was always honorable. He was wronged egregiously, typically through the murder of his wife, fiancée, father, or brother. For example, in *My Darling Clementine*, Wyatt Earp's little brother (Don Garner) is murdered by the Clantons. The killers, escaping justice, must now face individual justice at the hand of the hero, Wyatt Earp (Henry Fonda). The hero's justice is an honorable act, a just one, and not only fulfills the hero's personal need for "satisfaction" but also performs a task of social value, in ridding the town of Tombstone of the evil Clantons and restoring order from chaos.

The villain's vengeance, on the other hand, is not just. It is typically a personal vendetta. In *High Noon* (1952), Frank Miller (Ian MacDonald) has sworn to kill Marshal Will Kane (Gary Cooper) because Kane arrested him and put him in jail for his many crimes and murders. The villain is clearly a bad man who was wrong to begin with, and the revenge he seeks is unwarranted and dishonorable. Furthermore, the vengeance serves no moral or social purpose. His only aim is the wrongful killing of a good man. Though both forms of vengeance seek the same end in killing, the psychological reasoning behind the two types of killing are completely opposite. The hero is reluctant to kill. He does so only when he's left with no choice. When he

Vengeance Quest. Henry Fonda (far right) as Wyatt Earp faces Walter Brennan (far left) as Old Man Clanton and his sons (from left to right), Ike Clanton (Grant Withers), Phin Clanton (Fred Libby), Sam Clanton (Mickey Simpson), and Billy Clanton (John Ireland), in John Ford's *My Darling Clementine* (1946, 20th Century–Fox).

finally does kill, the hero finds no joy in it. Rather, he experiences it as a distasteful and ugly task that nevertheless has to be done. In contrast, the villain relishes the act of killing. He finds a primal release in the blood-flow and seems to desire it above all else. There is a sadistic and psychosexual aspect to the villain's desire for blood, which relates well to Freud's concept of the "Thanatos." Referring to the Greek god of death, the Thanatos is the destructive drive, the opposing counterpart to Eros, which is the constructive drive. The Thanatos represents the primal will to destroy rather than to create, to hate rather than love, and to kill rather than heal. The villain's insatiable lust for blood is psychopathological, a neurotic obsession in which the libido is directed entirely and obsessively in the direction of the Thanatos. The villain is a victim of the "killing sickness." A bullet from the hero's gun is the only cure.

In the Psychological Western, the hero/villain duality is blurred as each character is made more complex and more real. In the process, each character becomes less polarized and both the hero and villain appear to suffer from the same conflicts. The hero, no longer a pure white knight, is also afflicted, in varying degrees, with the killing sickness. In films like *The Searchers* and *Winchester '73,* both heroes (John Wayne, James Stewart) and villains (Henry Brandon, Stephen McNally) are psychopathological. They are driven to death and destruction like homicidal maniacs. Peter Lyon wrote: "*Often in the modern Western a sudden sympathy flashes between hero and villain, as though somehow they feel themselves to be secret sharers in a larger identity. Often the hero cannot bring himself to kill the villain until fate forces his hand, and then he performs the act almost like a religious sacrifice (Shane).*" In the film Lyon refers to, *Shane,* the title character (Alan Ladd) is painfully self-conscious of his ignominious past as a gunfighter. When, in the climactic shootout, he confronts the villainous gunfighter (Jack Palance), he kills him as if he were killing a part of himself, wiping out his own shadow, all the time knowing that the stain of blood will never go away. Wherever he goes, whatever he does, the shadow of killing (the mark of Cain) will always follow him. In the memorable final scene, rather than staying with the good folks he saved, he must ride off alone into the wilderness.

The hero's quest in the psychological Western is driven by obsessive revenge. Existential psychoanalyst Rollo May referred to these types of obsessions as "daemonic"—dark, fixated compulsions which, if fulfilled, are ultimately self-destructive. Nevertheless, since the Code of the West is firmly grounded in the vengeance quest, the Western hero has no choice but to follow his destiny. Much like the protagonists in Film Noir, the Western hero is doomed to a tragic fate of loneliness and wandering. His quest often makes him a social exile. And—like in Film Noir—this sense of tragedy and doom is often a pervasive feeling in the Western film.

Revenge is the defining element of all four of the Western hero personas: the cowboy knight, the honorable marshal, the lone crusader, and the rebel outlaw. All of these characters are different versions of the same man, driven by the same quest. *My Darling Clementine* provides the perfect example, as Wyatt Earp fills the role of all four of these personas. At the beginning of the film, Earp is a cowboy, moving his herd along with his three brothers. When the Clantons rustle his herd and kill his youngest brother, Earp swears vengeance at his brother's grave—taking on the persona and quest of the cowboy knight. In the following sequence, he agrees to become the marshal of Tombstone, taking on this second persona in order to further his quest of finding his brother's killers, but also because of his instinctual desire to bring order to the lawless frontier town. As the town marshal, he becomes a lone crusader, the only man willing to stand up to the brutal

Clantons. In the end, Earp must abandon the law in order to defeat the Clantons and fulfill his quest for vengeance. As he exits the jailhouse to meet the Clantons at the infamous "shootout at the O.K. Corral," he leaves his badge behind, choosing not to arrest the Clantons, but to deliver his own individual brand of justice. As the rebel outlaw, he chooses to kill them.

The Frontier Hero as Role Model

The frontier hero was too much of an individualist to be a religious man. He was a man of action, not of words or prayers, and certainly too proud to bow in genuflection or beg forgiveness. The walls of the church were too narrow to accommodate him. When the scornful widow (Lauren Bacall) in *The Shootist* (1976) tries to shame the legendary hero (John Wayne) into going to church, she says: "The doors of the church are open to everyone." He replies: "My church is the outdoors — no doors out there!"

As an archetype, the Western hero was a figure to be worshipped, custom-made for a hero-worshipping society like America. It would have been below his station to worship another, even a god, for he was a god — or at least a demigod — in the fashion of classical demigod heroes such as Hercules or Perseus. The frontier hero was a man born of the pure earth of the Western plains, but he was also a god, an American god, who was worshipped and adored by numerous generations of devout moviegoers (mostly young males). His temple was the cinema. His flock sacrificed only the ticket price to see a vision of the heavenly father of the lost frontier. And now, this god is all but dead, but he lives on in the memories of those who loved him (mostly older males) and can still be seen on the classic movie channels of cable television.

More significant than the cowboy's heavenly status was his function as a role model for the millions of boys and male adolescents who grew up watching his many films and television shows. When the Western genre reached its peak of popularity in 1950, Hollywood released fifty-eight Western features, over a third of all feature films released that year. In 1959, with only three channels available, there were forty-eight Western series on television, and of the top ten shows at that time, eight were Westerns. The target demographic for many of these films and TV shows were boys and male adolescents. Indeed, the environment portrayed in the Western was a sort of wonderland for the young male. Characters in Westerns were not "men," they were "boys." They called themselves "boys" ("Let's head 'em off at the pass, boys!"). They acted like boys — fighting, playing cards, sleeping in bunks, never bathing, swearing, doing whatever they wanted whenever they felt like it. They referred to each other with nicknames rather than proper names ("Bat" Masterson, "Doc" Holliday, "Buffalo Bill"). Many of these nicknames utilized the word "Kid"—e.g., "Sundance Kid," "Billy the Kid," "the Waco Kid"—indicating that the outlaw was really just a big child with a gun. When not carousing in town, they lived a robust and exciting outdoor life on horseback that would seem blissful to the average young male. And even their official title was that of boys—they were "cowboys," not "cowmen" or "cowpersons." The Western was a glorification of arrested male development, in which physical prowess and aggression displayed though fist fighting and gun violence determined one's social status in the peer group. In the Western, total emersion in vice, immediate gratification, and personal liberty were not curtailed by nagging mothers or disapproving fathers.

The boys who grew up in the era in which Westerns saturated the airwaves and cinemas emulated their frontier heroes in every way. They spoke like them, dressed like them, walked like them, fired cap guns like them, pretended their apple juice was whiskey, imagined their crayons were cigarettes, and rode their dogs as if they were horses. It also just so happened that the "Golden Age of Westerns" coincided with the childhood of the "Baby Boomers," born in the late 1940s and early 1950s, who would become the first generation of Americans to grow up watching television. The Baby Boomers, now in their fifties and sixties, rule this country, controlling the majority of its wealth, power, legislative bodies, and diplomatic policies. Most of the "power brokers" in 21st-century America are middle-aged white men who can still remember spending many a childhood afternoon lying on the living room floor in front of the television, or else sitting in the theater at the Saturday afternoon matinee, wearing a plastic cowboy hat and holding a plastic cap gun, watching their favorite frontier heroes save the day. What lessons did these boys learn from the role models they were inculcated with on both the big and small screens? Are these lessons still significant in the 21st century, forty years since the beginning of the Western's decline?

In his book, *The Cry for Myth* (1991), Rollo May analyzed the "Myth of the Frontier," pointing to the Western ethos of isolationism, independence, and individualism as the principal influence on the modern age of America, an age that May labeled the "Age of Narcissism." This modern age, May contended, was stricken with loneliness, violence, drug and alcohol abuse, a narcissistic sense of entitlement, and a neurotic need to assert power over others. According to May, the American idealization of the "lonesome cowboy" archetype and the mythical "Code of the West" are direct precipitants of some of the defining characteristics of our nation: violence, firearm fixation, alcoholism and rampant drug use, anti-authoritarianism, xenophobia, racism, and a general sense of moral and global superiority, backed up with massive military force.

On September 17, 2001, less than a week after the terrorist attacks on New York City and Washington, D.C., George W. Bush gave a nationally broadcast press conference, in which he delivered the famous line: "*I want justice. And there's an old poster out West, I recall, that says, 'Wanted: Dead or Alive.'*" He went on to explain that he wanted Osama Bin Laden — "*dead or alive.*" Eighteen months later, George W. Bush led America into war with Iraq. One of the ostensible reasons was to capture one of America's most hated enemies, Saddam Hussein, and to bring him to justice ... *dead or alive*. One could say with a high degree of certainty that George W. Bush never actually saw a real poster that read "Wanted: Dead or Alive." But we could readily assume that he saw depictions of this poster, probably many times over, in Western movies and TV shows.

The influence of the frontier myth, the cowboy hero, and his Western code of honor as a role model for the male youth of America was undoubtedly broad and significant during the heyday of the Western. Whether this influence is still apparent today is a matter of conjecture. However, we must not forget that the essence of the Western is an idealism no longer found today in movies or television. Regardless of modern revisionism and reinterpretations, the Western was unabashedly patriotic, unapologetically individualistic, and single-minded in its idealization of the rugged, self-sufficient frontiersman. The Western provided the male youth of America with a singular father figure, a role model with a thousand faces, but only one message. As Peter Lyon so eloquently stated: "*In the freedom of the great plains the story of the West had its beginnings; in the freedom of the heart it seems to seek its end. In its finest expressions, it is an allegory of freedom, a memory and a vision of the deepest meaning of America.*"

In perhaps the most mythical of the classic Westerns, *Shane*, we encounter a hero who sums up the American dream in a poignant fashion. Like the immigrants flocking to America's shores, Shane is a man seeking to make a new start. He wants to leave behind the shadow of his past and begin again, a promise that the "land of opportunity" historically offered to everyone. Shane is the embodiment of the independent spirit, unafraid to travel alone in search of his heart's desire. The latent psychological power behind the film is the fact that the entire story is seen through the eyes of a young boy, little Joey (Brandon de Wilde). This impressionable young boy is the identification figure, the character that the audience — especially the young

Mythical Hero. Alan Ladd (left) as Shane and Brandon De Wilde as Joey in George Stevens's *Shane* (1952, Paramount).

males — relate to. They experience Shane as Joey does: a romantic, chival-rous champion, who enters his world like a dream, solves all of his problems through great bravery and at enormous personal risk, and then rides off alone into the wilderness, a haunted figure who no longer fits in his time, as he belongs to a long lost era, a mythical period of American history that existed mainly in our own imaginations. When Joey calls out to him — "*Shane, come back!*" — in the famous closing scene, he's experiencing a longing and nostalgia that can probably only be properly understood by the generation of Americans who grew up during the Golden Age of Westerns, when the frontier hero was king, and when the golden-haired frontiersman represented hero, father, America, and everything a young man should aspire to. But Shane is gone, and he will never return.

3

The Civilized and the Savage

"I've killed women and children. I've killed just about everything that walks or crawled at one time or another. And I'm here to kill you, Little Bill, for what you did to Ned."

— William Munny (Clint Eastwood) in
Unforgiven (1992).

In his "frontier thesis," Frederick Jackson Turner described the frontier as "the meeting point between savagery and civilization." The Western is the setting where these primal forces clash. The meeting of the savage and the civilized takes on various forms in the Western: cowboys versus Indians, cavalry versus Indians, marshal versus outlaws, etc. As the genre progressed and grew in sophistication, the definitions of savagery and civilization were called into play. Often, characters that had typically been depicted as savage — Indians and outlaws — began to be portrayed more sympathetically, while characters that had always been painted as representatives of civilized society — lawmen and cavalry officers — were revealed as savage and barbaric. At times, it became difficult to differentiate between the heroes and the villains. The Western anti-hero was born. And as the psychological Western reached its peak, we began to see characters whose natures were a complex and conflicting mixture of both savage and civilized elements.

In his book, *The Six-Gun Mystique Sequel,* John Cawelti develops a tripartite distinction of Western characters, based on Turner's notion of the savage and the civilized. On the civilized side are the settlers and townspeople. On the savage side are the villains, traditionally played by outlaws or corrupt officials, and occasionally by hostile Indians. And in the middle, functioning as a mediating force, is the hero, whose character is an amalgamation of both savage and civilized elements.

Unlike the hero and outlaw, the homesteaders and townspeople are immobile, tied down to their land or town, and incapable of movement. They're often depicted as cowardly, because they have families and property to worry about as well as their own lives. They need to be inspired or provoked into violence, even in their own defense. These harbingers of civilization are interested in taming the west, establishing civilized society, creating law and order, and modernizing the environment. They are generally motivated by the needs of the community, as represented by the institutions of the church and state, and they openly deride individualism and independence, whether it is depicted in the hero or the outlaw. In fact, the townspeople often mistrust or fear the hero almost as much as the outlaw, not only because he is a stranger, but because, like the outlaw, he is unsettled. The hero isn't constricted by the borders of the town or to the ancient rituals and principles of civilization as they are. He represents freedom, which is associated with both wildness and violence. Hence, the hero is both a savior and an outcast within civilized society.

Examples of this conflicted relationship between the townspeople and their hero can be seen in two classic films that were both released in 1952, *Shane* and *High Noon*. In *Shane*, the homesteaders mistrust Shane because of his past as a gunfighter. Though he is an honorable man, they fear his knowledge and mastery of violence. When he is able to identify the villain's hired gunman, Wilson (Jack Palance), the homesteaders confirm their mistrust of Shane, as his knowledge of the killer gunfighter establishes his own relationship with the savage. At the end of the film, even though he saved the town from the evil cattle baron in a cathartic shootout, Shane must leave the town. "There's no living with a killing," he tells Little Joey. "There's no going back from one. Right or wrong, it's a brand ... a brand sticks. There's no going back." A similar denouement is depicted in *High Noon*. Throughout the film, the marshal, Will Kane (Gary Cooper), tries to rouse the townspeople to help him fight a band of outlaws who are coming to town to kill him. Each of the representatives of civilization — the priest and churchgoers, the judge, his own deputy, and even his mentor, the former sheriff— refuse to help him. In the end, he kills the outlaws himself. But he won't stay in the town that he risked his life to defend. He throws his badge into the dirt, preferring exile to the company of civilized cowards.

The classic Western villain is a ruthless outlaw. Not tied down by wife, business, or home, he's mobile, able to move in and out of town at will. He's wild and uncontrollable, like the wilderness itself. In certain ways, he's more

Searching for Honor. Gary Cooper (right) as Marshal Will Kane, being disappointed by his embittered mentor, Lon Chaney, Jr., as former marshal Martin Howe, in Fred Zinnemann's *High Noon* (1952, Stanley Kramer Productions/ United Artists).

like the hero than the townspeople, especially in his response to danger. He's no coward. If anything, he's too easily moved to brazen displays of bravery and violence. Like the hero, he usually has a sense of honor, but the honor is misdirected or mistaken. The outlaw seeks out violence, rather than avoiding it, which is the critical difference between the gunfighter hero and the outlaw villain. While the hero is reluctant to kill, the villain relishes the act, and provokes it.

The hero, as Joseph Campbell wrote, has a "thousand faces." In the Western, the hero is usually a cowboy or lawman, occasionally he is a cavalryman or homesteader, and sometimes he is a "good badman," an outlaw or gunfighter who is nevertheless a decent and honorable man. Like the villain, he has the power of movement, but he can also settle down, though he usually chooses not to. In order to stay true to his wild, restless nature, the classic Western hero turns his back on civilization after the hostile forces of the wilderness have been subdued. He rides off into the sunset, more comfortable in the wild open plains than in the confines of the inert town.

With his combination of civilized and savage elements, the hero represents a mediating force between the passive stillness of civilization and the violent wildness of the frontier. Though he's motivated primarily by individual honor, he typically chooses to be on the side of law and order. Nevertheless, when the chips are down, he often has to go outside the law to find justice on his own terms. And though he defends the townspeople, his heart is set against the destruction of the wild frontier via the establishment of towns and railroads. Like the savage, he mourns the death of the open range and fears the loss of freedom and independence that will come as the result of the fencing in of the frontier. In the end, the hero and the townspeople, including his love interest, are often incompatible. He plays a sacrificial role, risking his life to save a town that he cannot stay in. Instead, he ascends from town to wilderness, vanishing into the setting sun, like a savior of Biblical or mythical proportions.

John Ford's *Wagon Master* (1950) offers an excellent example of Cawelti's tripartite distinction. The film is a nation-building picture, glorifying the pioneers who trail-blazed the first paths into the wilderness and opened up the frontier. In nation-building films, while the homesteaders in the wagon trains are seen as the heralds of civilization — the people who will eventually inherit the West — it is their frontiersmen guides who take on the role of the hero. The frontiersman hero belongs to the wilderness, and it is his task to lead the emissaries of civilization past the dangerous elements within the frontier and deliver them to the chosen land. Hence we see the frontiersman hero in the nation-building picture stuck in the middle of Cawelti's tripartite distinction. In *Wagon Master*, Travis (Ben Johnson) and his faithful sidekick Sandy (Harry Carey, Jr.) are horse traders hired as wagon masters by a wagon train of Mormons seeking passage across the wilderness to their new homesteads. On the way, they must encounter both Indians and outlaws. The Mormons are Christian fundamentalists. They are extremely conservative. The outlaws are sinners and the Indians are heathens in the eyes of the Mormons. The frontiersmen are in the middle. While the frontiersmen respect the Mormons and doubtless have Christian backgrounds, they also have respect for the Indians, as they are more akin to the Indians in their reverence of nature. Also, in their freewheeling attitude towards life, the frontiersmen are also more akin to the outlaws, as opposed to the rigid, austerely pious Mormons. As the wagon train makes its away across the wilderness, the wagon masters play the role of mediators between the civilized Mormons and the wild inhabitants of the frontier.

Their first act of mediation occurs when the wagon train comes upon a broken-down wagon full of dance-hall girls and a patent medicine salesman who's addicted to his own product. These two archetypes of the West, the golden-hearted whore and the disgraced drunken doctor, are rejected by the uptight Mormons. The irony is that the Mormons themselves were just exiled from town by the leery Protestant townspeople, who mistrust the strict practices of the Mormons. The Mormons, for their part, fail to see this irony. In the first act, the frontiersmen helped the Mormons by agreeing to become their wagon masters, despite the prejudices of the Protestants. Once again, in the second act, they play the role of cultural mediators by letting the ailing whores and drunken doctor join the wagon train, despite the objections of the stuck-up Mormons. As representations of the middle ground, the frontiersmen were able to bridge the gaps between the prejudiced, the pious, and the promiscuous.

Later on in the second act, the wagon masters help the wagon train avoid conflict with a tribe of Indians by mediating a parley, which allows for safe passage through Indian territory. And finally, in the end, the frontiersman heroes save the Mormons from the dangerous outlaws who have hijacked the wagon train, in the only way that outlaws can be dealt with. The fatal climactic shootout could not have been performed by the Mormons, whose religion forbids violent acts. Only the frontiersmen had the essential balance of violence and honor that allowed them to live with one foot in the civilized world and the other in the wild. Hence, in the Western genre, it is the frontiersman hero who serves as both gatekeeper and guide for any Easterners venturing out west.

The Outlaw Hero

The outlaw brand of Western hero traces his heritage back to the Robin Hood legend of medieval England. Though he is a thief and a wanted criminal, the Western Robin Hood is a hero because his criminal acts are directed against a greater evil, which invariably takes the form of a greedy and autocratic tyrant. While the outlaw hero has been portrayed countless times in Western films, the most romantic and lionized version is Henry King's 1939 classic, *Jesse James*, starring matinee idol Tyrone Power in the title role, with Henry Fonda as his equally heroic brother Frank and Jane Darwell as their mother. The villainous tyrants are the railroad barons, portrayed as scalawags and carpetbaggers, who send their ruffian goons out to the small farmers on the Missouri frontier, forcing them to sell their land to the railroad for a pittance. Though his backstory is not mentioned in this film, the real Jesse James was a Southern boy who, at the tender age of sixteen, fought with William

Quantrill's band of Confederate raiders. This troop of guerrilla fighters was infamous for their terrorist tactics and their vicious, bloodthirsty attacks. Many of the later versions of the Jesse James legend focus on these early days, understanding Jesse's outlaw career as a product of a traumatic and violent youth, rather than as a heroic vengeance quest.

In the 1939 film, Jesse's motivations towards crime are mainly personal but also political. After Jesse and Frank fight the railroad goons in defense of their home, Barshee (Brian Donlevy), the head railroad goon, returns to their farm with the law, in an attempt to "arrest" them. However, Jesse and Frank are not there, and Barshee winds up killing their mother by mistake. Jesse, of course, must defend the family honor by killing Barshee, but even though he does so in an honorable showdown, he is now wanted by the law. He and Frank decide to make a living as outlaws and choose to rob trains, as they blame the railroad as the root of their problems. In seeking vengeance against the railroad, the James brothers become folk heroes, as they represent a front of individualistic defiance against the tyranny of the railroads. This type of movie outlaw was particularly resonant in the 1930s, during the Great Depression, when the average American felt cheated by the foreclosing banks and Wall Street fat cats. Audiences could experience catharsis vicariously through the violent thievery of the outlaw. The Depression-era gangster hero, epitomized by Hollywood actors such as Humphrey Bogart, George Raft, and James Cagney, was easily transferable to the Western scenario.

As subtext, we also understand that Jesse represents the South, defeated in the Civil War but still clinging to its honor, while the railroad represents the North, the ruthless, greedy, industrialist power that wants to rob the poor Southerners of the only thing they have left: their land. In this film, the outlaw-versus-railroad theme is symbolic of the continuing conflict between North and South throughout the Reconstruction Era. Though Power and Fonda forgo the Southern accent, their obsession with personal honor certainly has a Southern feel to it, and the James family still has a "slave"—a black servant they call Pinky (Ernest Whitman)—who clearly represents an artifact of the old glory days of the South. (In real life, the James family owned a small tobacco plantation and seven slaves, before the turmoil of the Civil War drove the family to ruin.) The James gang even perform their robberies with a flair of Southern gentility and charm, saying "Thank you, Sir," and "Much obliged, Ma'am," as they rob the train passengers. They refuse to take the women's jewelry. When they're done, they remind the passengers to "sue the railroad" for their losses, thus ridding themselves of the guilt of robbing innocent people and shifting the blame squarely onto the head of the Northern railroad barons.

The South vs. North subtext is even more explicit in the sequel to *Jesse James*, Fritz Lang's *The Return of Frank James* (1940). In the film, Frank embarks on a vengeance quest to kill his brother's murderer, while being pursued by the Railroad. Unable to track him down honestly, the Railroad soups up a phony charge against Pinky, the Jameses' faithful servant/slave, and threaten to hang him unless Frank turns himself in. Frank surrenders to the law. The court scene is a public spectacle, but to the Railroad's dismay, the tide turns in favor of the James boy. His lawyer is a newspaper editor and also his deceased brother's father-in-law (Henry Hull). He paints Frank as a hero for sacrificing himself to save Pinky: "...you'd risk your own neck to save the life of a poor, innocent old darky." The case becomes increasingly more about lingering political difficulties, as the Southern jury and judge become more and more resentful of the Northern prosecuting attorney, who is clearly representing the Railroad's interests. When the "Yankee" lawyer refers to the Civil War as the "rebellion," the judge takes grave offense and sternly corrects him: "Rebellion, did you say, sir! If you are, by any chance, referring to the late unpleasantness between the States, that, sir, was a war for the Southern Confederacy!" Frank's lawyer has little difficulty convincing the jury of ex–Confederate soldiers that Frank's service with Quantrill's Raiders merits him the status of war hero and that his subsequent battle against the Railroad is but a continuance of his brave actions against the pillaging Northern invaders. He is found "not guilty of anything," even to the charge of robbing a railroad office, which Frank openly confessed in court that he committed. When the verdict comes in, his lawyer shouts out: "We licked 'em! The dad-blasted Yankees! We licked 'em!"

The traditional aspects of the outlaw struggle are also clearly laid out in *Jesse James*. Besides the struggle for personal honor and vengeance and the subtext of North versus South, there is the typical conflict between imperialist tyrants and individual men, most often portrayed as the cattle baron versus independent ranchers or homesteaders, or in other cases, the banks and/or railroads versus the homesteaders. In the latter case, we see a representation of East versus West, as the banks and railroads are based in the Eastern metropolises. They see the frontier as a storehouse of unlimited resources, a means of increasing their own wealth. They want to rape the land, fence off the frontier, and claim everything within it for their own. They will not stop until the entire nation, from sea to sea, is nothing but a sprawling metropolis, with no natural beauty and no peaceful stretches of open plains, and all of it owned by a few greedy tycoons. In opposition to the Eastern city folk stand the noble Westerners, the independent ranchers and homesteaders, as well as the outlaw gunfighters.

In the final act of the film, it becomes clear that the outlaw life of constant running, killing, and robbing, is fast turning Jesse from a country gentleman into a man who is "crazy wild." (In other renditions, it is Jesse's formative youth as a guerrilla warrior with Quantrill's Raiders that turns him wild.) In any case, we do get the sense that the life of the outlaw always foments deep conflict within the individual. One cannot kill continually and retain one's sanity. Eventually, the killing becomes a pattern of behavior that the killer needs and craves, a killing sickness that consumes the soul, and can only be cured by death. This awareness of how an ordinary man can turn into a psychopathic murderer seems implicit in Westerns and is almost always delivered as a plea for reformation to the outlaw hero, made by his female love interest. As the figure representing the hero's anima — the feminine qualities of tenderness and love — only she can persuade the savage beast to tame himself. She does this by convincing the outlaw to turn himself in (allowing the beast to have himself caged), so he can redeem himself for his sins and rejoin society as a normal man, healed of the killing sickness. This plot twist, which could also be seen in some of the various "biopics" of Billy the Kid, never comes to fruition. As the outlaw hero is in essence a tragic hero, his story invariably ends in tragedy. In *Jesse James*, Jesse tries to turn himself in, accepting a plea bargain, but is betrayed by the railroad baron (Donald Meek), who goes back on his word and tries to hang him. Jesse escapes, but eventually is convinced again by his love interest (Nancy Kelly) to give up his violent ways. Jesse goes into hiding, but is quickly betrayed by a member of his own gang (John Carradine), who shoots Jesse in the back for the reward money. The fact that Jesse is done in by a traitor within his own gang, rather than a lawman or railroad goon, draws a parallel between the Jesse James legend and the Jesus myth. Like Jesus, Jesse was a hero to the oppressed, a folk hero. He was hated by tyrants but loved by the poor. He rebelled against imperialism, and although he was betrayed by a Judas figure, his legend lives on till this day.

The Curse of the Gunfighter

Eleven years after he directed *Jesses James*, Henry King made *The Gunfighter* (1950). Thematically, the film starts off in the third act of the Jesse James story. Ringo (Gregory Peck), an infamous gunfighter, comes to town to see his wife (Helen Westcott), the village schoolmarm, and their son. He wants them to escape with him to California, but he is haunted by the sins of his past. No matter where he goes, some young hotshot with a pistol

Curse of the Gunfighter. Gregory Peck (left) as Jimmy Ringo, faces Skip Homeier as Hunt Bromley, the reckless youth looking to make a name for himself by tangling with the infamous "Ringo Kid," while Karl Malden, as Mac the bartender, looks on impassively from the background in Henry King's *The Gunfighter* (1950, 20th Century–Fox).

wants to challenge him to a gunfight, merely to make a big name for himself. He is also hunted by the brothers of men that he killed, caught in the incessant cycle of retributive violence, which ends only in death. This is the curse of the gunfighter, which has become part of the mythos of the Western genre, and could be attributed in large part to Nunnally Johnson, who penned the script for *Jesse James* and co-wrote *The Gunfighter*. The curse is the fate of doom that befalls anyone who chooses the shadowy path of gunfighting. The outlaw cursed with this fate is a combination of archetypes. He is both hero and shadow. He is also known as the anti-hero.

California is often represented as the outlaw's fantasyland. It is the farthest west you can get, a place where a man can escape his past identity. In this sense, it is the frontier of the frontier, the west of the west. Other outlaws, such as Jesse in *Jesse James* and Will (Clint Eastwood) in *Unforgiven* (1992), saw in California the same dream of redemption and new beginnings. The dream of California in the minds of movie outlaws set in the 19th century was doubtlessly relevant to the fantasies of 20th-century moviegoers, who saw in California the place where dreams could come true, whether it was the Depression-era farmer's dream of economic salvation or the young actor's dream of Hollywood stardom.

In *The Gunfighter,* the housewives in the town condemn Ringo and join together as a unified voice against him, forcing him to leave. This familiar theme of town banishment represents the feminization of the frontier. Once the West has been settled and civilized, there is no more room for the type of men who fought to conquer and tame it. As Slotkin (1985) noted: "...in the backwash of a closing Frontier, traits that had been productive and heroic might become antisocial and dangerous." The gunfighter, once a hero, is now perceived as an element of the savage, rather than a protector from it. Within this zone of the feminine, the outlaw — who represents the undomesticated (or un-emasculated) male — is no longer welcome. Like the whore and drunken doctor who are banished from society in films like *Stagecoach* and *Wagon Master*, it is the collective moral voice of female society that builds the final fence along the frontier. It is the influence of domesticity that exiles the feral relics of the frontier era from civilization. The outlaw cannot exist in a place where the domestic needs of the feminine predominate over the freedom and independence of the masculine. For a while, Ringo holes up in the saloon (the last bastion and refuge of masculine territory in the town), but in due time, he must go.

After meeting his son for the first time, Ringo leaves with the vague promise from his wife that she'll see him in a year and possibly go with him to California, if he's truly reformed. But before he can ride away, he's shot and killed by Hunt (Skip Homeier), a young hotshot trying to prove his mettle. Ringo lies to the sheriff (Millard Mitchell), telling him that he drew first, so that Hunt may avoid being hanged. In this way, he passes the curse of the gunfighter on to the man who killed him. This is a much more fitting revenge, as the curse, in Ringo's experience, is a fate far worse than death. In the final shot of the film, we see Ringo's ghost riding off alone into the sunset. Similarly, at the end of *Jesse James*, we see Jesse's father-in-law, a newspaper editor, eulogizing Jesse at his funeral, praising him as a folk hero: "He was one of the doggone-est, gawldingest, dadblam-est buckaroos that ever rode across these United States of America!" The implication is that he will use the power of the press to redeem Jesse's name. As the outlaw hero is cast in a sympathetic role, even his death cannot impede the sentiment of potential redemption, which is at the heart of his character.

The Marshal Hero

There is a fluidity in which the gunfighter makes the transition from outlaw to lawman and vice versa. Of the many examples, it can be seen in the marshal/sheriff characters in *The Gunfighter, One Eyed Jacks* (1961), *Pat Garrett and Billy the Kid* (1973), *Unforgiven,* and *Wyatt Earp* (1994). This easy shift is facilitated by the fact that the two archetypal characters require the same skills of violence, domination, and gunmanship. The only difference is that they practice these skills on opposite sides of the societal fence. In essence, the outlaw and lawman represent two sides of the same coin. Whether the critical roles of persona and shadow are depicted as a conflict between two characters (lawman vs. outlaw), or as one character conflicted within himself (the good badman, the anti-hero), it is the struggle between the civilized and savage elements of human nature that is at play.

In most of the film versions of the Billy the Kid legend, we see two characters that are equally conflicted. Billy (Jack Buetel in *The Outlaw* (1943), Paul Newman in *The Left Handed Gun* (1958), Kris Kristofferson in *Pat Garrett and Billy the Kid* (1973), is a good badman, an essentially decent kid with a wild streak who takes the code of the West to its logical extreme. He kills to avenge the death of his father figure and then kills anyone who threatens his freedom or his honor. He is a savage young man with a good heart. His pursuer and antagonist, Pat Garrett (Thomas Mitchell in *The Outlaw,* John Dehner in *The Left Handed Gun,* James Coburn in *Pat Garrett and Billy the Kid*), is a former outlaw turned lawman. He has taken on the persona of a civilized man, but his duty as a sheriff requires a savage act — the killing of his good friend, Billy. In completing this dark task, Pat Garrett encounters the savage element within his own psyche and destroys a part of himself that is both wicked and pure.

Cowboys and Cattlemen

The cowboy character, in all his variations, represents an interesting mix of the civilized and savage. Like the townspeople, homesteaders, and settlers, he is engaged in honest work. He makes his living by the sweat of his brow, providing a useful product for a developing nation. But unlike the more civilized types, the cowboy is not tied down to a specific spot. He is always riding the open range, engaged in herding or on long, extended cattle drives. Out in the wilderness, he has no recourse to the law and is at all times beset by the dangers of the wilderness: Indians, rustlers, wild animals, rival cattlemen, outlaws, and even the hazardous elements of nature itself. He must defend himself and his stock with violence; therefore he must retain an element of savagery within himself. Justice on the range involves either a bullet or a rope, with few alternatives. When he comes to town, it is not to act civilized, but to act wild, in a juvenile spree of drunkenness, promiscuity, gambling, and fighting. The cowboy is just as likely to be a hero as a villain. He treads the line between the different sides of frontier society.

A staple of the Western genre is the aged cattle baron and his feral cowboys. The cowboys who do his evil bidding are typically his sons, or young men who play the role of adoptive sons. The cattle baron is interested in power, which to him is represented by massive tracts of land on which to graze his limitless herds of cattle. From a mythical perspective, the cattle baron is derived from the primordial dragon of medieval legends. The dragon is emblematic of greed. He terrorizes the villagers, demanding regular tributes of gold and virgins, which he hordes in his lair. This act is the essence of greed, because the dragon has no use for either gold or virgins, yet he demands much of both and hordes them to himself, where they can do no good. Similarly, the cattle baron has more land and stock than any one man can use, yet he constantly yearns for more and uses vicious, ruthless, and dishonorable tactics to attain them.

Walter Brennan played the cattle baron most memorably in *My Darling Clementine* as Old Man Clanton. In a telling scene, he flogs his sons with a bullwhip when they have an interchange with Wyatt Earp and Doc Holliday that doesn't end in violence, even though guns are drawn. "When ya pull a gun," he shouts at them, "kill a man!" Clearly, the wild barbaric sons learned their manners from their father, who always prods them towards violence rather than teaching them diplomacy or restraint. In a similar scene in *The Big Country* (1958), the cattle baron (Burl Ives) is sorely disappointed when his sons tell him that a rival cattle company drove his herd away from water and no blood was shed. "Why ain't you dead?" he asks them, without a hint of irony in his voice. "You let 'em run my cows off, and you come back standing up!"

The notion that a group of men, isolated in the wilderness and devoid of the civilizing influences of women, religion, and town life, would regress into a clan of savage barbarians is evocative of the belief that the wilderness itself has the effect of turning human beings into savage beasts. As proof of this belief, the clan of barbaric brothers will frequently rape any woman who crosses their path. Their quickness to rape is indicative of their lack of connection with a feminine figure (typically there is a conspicuously absent mother figure in the clan), resulting in a maximization of masculine aggression, unchecked by feminine empathy or sensitivity. In Ford's *Wagon Master*, the Clegg clan are a band of wild outlaws. Even though they are trying to lay low as they hide out within the Mormon wagon train, one of the barbaric brothers can't help himself. He rapes an Indian girl at a powwow with the local tribe. In Sam Peckinpah's *Ride the High Country* (1962), the Hammond clan live in a remote mining camp. When one of the brothers takes a wife, the others all assume that it will be share and share alike. The poor girl (Mariette Hartley) is still in her wedding dress when the brothers try to rape her. Similar themes of barbarity and rape at the hands of a band of feral brothers can be seen in *Will Penny* (1968) and Anthony Mann's *Man of the West* (1958).

The Killing Sickness

The theme of regression to savagery is perhaps the signature motif in the Psychological Western, which tends to focus on the internal struggle between violence and restraint within the conflicted hero's psyche. The character driven to psychopathological madness by a killing sickness — a Thanatos obsession or a daemonic compulsion to kill — is qualitatively different from the hero seeking honor through revenge. The vengeance quest is specific, directed at the particular man or men who killed the hero's loved one(s). In contrast, the object of the psychopath's killing sickness is vague, generally directed at entire categories of people, for instance Indians, whites, Mexicans, or anyone who pushes his buttons, like father figures, authority figures, demurring women, and other threats to his masculinity or dominance. Also, the hero's vengeance quest has a definite beginning and end. After the hero finds and destroys his quarry, he will presumably resume a normal life, his thirst for blood quenched forever. The psychopath's killing sickness, on the other hand, is incurable. His bloodlust will only continue to intensify with each man that he kills, and his thirst for death will only be quenched when he himself dies.

There are a limited number of character types who are afflicted with the killing sickness. The sickness can come about as a result of witnessing and engaging in the horrors of war — the "psychologically wounded" type. Frequently, the killing sickness is seen as the driving force behind outlaws and juvenile delinquents who kill for the thrill, or to prove their manhood by destroying other men — the "psychopathic killer" type. Another character commonly afflicted with the sickness is the persecuted Indian who wants to wipe out all white people and, his counterpart, the prejudiced or traumatized white man who wants to wipe out all Indians — the "genocidal" type. Each of these psychopathological character types will be explored within the context of a few representative films in which they are depicted. Examples of the psychologically wounded type are Lt. Crofton (Addison Richards) in *Northwest Passage* (1940) and Col. Owen Devereaux (Glenn Ford) in *The Man from Colorado* (1948). Examples of the psychopathic killer type are William Munny (Clint Eastwood) and The Schofield Kid (Jaimz Woolvett) in *Unforgiven* (1992). And examples of the genocidal type are Major Rogers (Spencer Tracy) in *Northwest Passage,* Ed Bannon (Charlton Heston) and Toriano (Jack Palance) in *Arrowhead* (1953), and Ulzana (Joaquin Martinez) in *Ulzana's Raid* (1972).

The Psychologically Wounded Type

The elaboration or fabrication of Indian atrocities against white people as a justification for war was a political tactic that hearkened back to the original captivity narratives of the 17th and 18th centuries. Ironically, far more atrocities were committed by whites than by Indians. Even the trademark atrocity of scalping, universally associated with Indians, was a European invention, introduced by French and Belgian fur traders, who would pay hired killers for the scalps of enemy Indian tribesman. The barbaric practice was later adopted by the territorial governments of the southwest, as depicted most vividly in Sydney Pollack's *The Scalphunters* (1968). Slotkin (1992) noted that the intensification of fighting in any war is fueled by reports of atrocities committed by the enemy. The witnessing of war atrocities and acts of savagery increase the hatred and aggression already felt towards the enemy to a state of frenzied hostility. It literally drives soldiers to madness, inspiring reciprocal acts of psychopathic savagery and leading to an escalating cycle of brutality, in which atrocities on one side lead to atrocities on the other, and so on. At an early point in this cycle, distinctions are drawn along racial lines, dehumanizing the entire enemy race, in part because of the inhuman atrocities they commit. Paradoxically, the rationale behind a stance of dehumanization (atrocities committed by the enemy) also becomes a rationalization for committing atrocities (genocide of the subhuman savage race).

Slotkin referred to the primal aggressive drive to meet savagery in one's enemy with equal amounts of savagery as "genocidal rage" — a hatred so intense that a soldier wants not only to kill his enemy, but to wipe his kind off the face of the earth. He will kill women and children, decimate entire civilian villages, and commit the most repugnant acts of savagery in order to satiate this genocidal rage. In Slotkin's view, it is this state of psychopathic madness that leads to "the horror"—the stark realization of the bestial depths that human beings can sink to. The horror is at its most profound when a soldier not only witnesses the atrocities of others, but partakes of them himself, committing acts so foul and degraded that he cannot believe what he himself is capable of doing. In this sense, Slotkin's use of the word "horror" is a reference to the age-old expression, "the horrors of war." It may also be a literary reference to Kurtz's famous final words—"The horror! The horror!"—in Joseph Conrad's novella *Heart of Darkness*. In Conrad's work, the horror revealed within the heart of darkness is the "darkness of barbarism" in the heart of every man, which is only slightly covered by a veneer of social order, the "light of civilization." Francis Ford Coppola adapted Conrad's novella to the screen in *Apocalypse Now* (1979) by transferring the scenario to Vietnam. But the theme of Conrad's novella—civilized man encountering and integrating atrocities, barbarism, and "the horror" in the land of the savage—is a dominant theme in the Western.

Soldier Blue (1970), a revisionist anti–Western made during the Vietnam War era, revisits the issue of atrocities in the Western scenario in light of the contemporary revelations of war atrocities committed by U.S. soldiers in Vietnam, specifically the massacre at My Lai in 1968, in which hundreds of peaceful Vietnamese villagers were slaughtered, mostly women and children. There were numerous reports of rapes, dismemberments, mutilations, torture, and other acts of barbarism committed by U.S. soldiers. In the first act of the film, a Cheyenne attack on a U.S. Cavalry payroll dispatch results in the death, dismemberment, and mutilation of 21 cavalrymen. The cavalry's punitive action against the Cheyenne, depicted in the third act of the film, is taken despite the call of surrender made by the Cheyenne chief, who rides out before the cavalry attack carrying a white flag of surrender and an American flag of truce. The cavalry troop decimates the tribe, killing hundreds of women and children. The vivid depictions of gang rapes, dismemberments, mutilations, torture, and the ruthless slaughter of helpless innocents and little babies, are shocking and revolting. The viewer's horror is amplified when the film's epilogue reveals that the cavalry attack in the movie was based on a true event, the 1864 massacre of a Cheyenne village in Sand Creek, Colorado. The unavoidable associations with the My Lai massacre that viewers must have made at the time of the film's release were doubtlessly exacerbated by the fact that the court-martial proceedings for the army soldiers indicted for war crimes in Vietnam were being held at the same time that the film was out in theaters.

Soldier Blue's revisionism also extends to the most ancient artifact of the Western myth, the figure of the white woman captive. Candice Bergen plays the young woman who was taken captive by the Cheyenne. Rather than losing her mind, she gains an appreciation for the Indian way of life and sympathizes with their plight. Though she's "gone native," her state of mind is not depicted as the psychopathological consequence of repeated rape and torture. Rather, after living amongst both whites and Indians, she has realized that while both cultures partake in atrocities and massacres, it is the white man who is exponentially more brutal and savage.

Northwest Passage

King Vidor's *Northwest Passage* is a Colonial-era Western that tells the tale of Rogers' Rangers, a troop of American soldiers who battle hostile Indians on the wild frontier of upstate New York. Robert Young plays Langdon Towne, a civilized young man (a Harvard educated artist), who will encounter and integrate the horrors of savagery while serving with the Rangers. Spencer Tracy plays Major Rogers, the leader of the troop who uses tall tales of Indian atrocities to spur both his British commanders and his American soldiers to war. He tells a British officer: "Those red hellions up there have come down and hacked and murdered us, burned our homes, stolen our women, brained babies, scalped stragglers, and roasted officers over slow fires for five years!" This is enough to convince the officer to commission a preemptive attack on an Indian village. Later on, Rogers calls on a comrade to remind his soldiers why they're fighting. Lt. Avery (Douglas Walton) recounts a past experience with Indians to his men: "Philips had a piece of skin torn upwards from his stomach. They hung him from a tree by it while he was still alive. They chopped his men up with hatchets and threw the pieces into the pines so there wasn't any way to put 'em back together again. They tore my brother's arms out of him! They chopped the ends of his ribs away from his backbone, and pried them through his skin one by one...."

The sequence in which the Rangers massacre an Indian village, literally slaughtering hundreds of men, women, and children, is unique in its era for its stark depiction of brutality and unflinching ferocity. Some of the Rangers revel in the horror, their genocidal rage revealing itself as psychopathic, ghoulish bloodlust as the white man regresses to savage, engaging in mutilation and atrocities and turning their hatchets on women and children. To provide retroactive justification for the massacre, Rogers interviews a female white captive, who says: "They took me seven years ago, killed my husband and knocked my baby's head against a tree. My husband's scalp is over there with seven hundred others." She refers to a drapery of scalps adorning a side of the village. The other white captive woman has seemed to suffer an even worse fate. She's gone native. She curses the major, calling him a "white devil," but the major is unfazed. "She's white," he says, "so she goes back!" The Rangers take her with them against her will. She is a victim of so much savagery that her mind has accepted what the white man perceives as the ultimate madness — the rejection of her own whiteness and the subsequent identification of herself as an Indian. This is the ultimate horror.

On the return journey, the major makes a gruesome joke to his men who complain of having nothing to eat but dried corn. While they at least have the corn they pillaged from the French/Indian village, their French pursuers will have to resort to cannibalism if they want to survive. He tells his Rangers: "What'ya think the French are gonna find when they get to St. Francis? Nothing but roast Indian!" Later on, Langdon Towne witnesses the essence of "the horror" firsthand — Indians engaging in a retributive action against some white captives. He reports what he saw to the major: "When they cut up Dunbar, he was still alive and screaming... They killed them all! They were playing *ball* with their heads!"

The most fascinating character in the film is Lt. Crofton (Addison Richards), a soldier who has not only seen and engaged in the horror, but relished it and completely identified himself with it. He has crossed over the line into psychopathology, his ego so intertwined with the savage that he derives a primal, psychosexual thrill from the atrocities of war. He carries with him a garish "souvenir," a decapitated Indian head, which he's saving to eat once the troop's supply of corn runs out. The difference between this type of ghoulish degenerate and the macabre, disturbed serial killers of modern horror movies is that the former is an American soldier fighting for his country. His cause justifies his actions, though the film stops short of praising his excesses. The lesson is that one must become a savage to defeat the savage, but after the battle, one must return to normalcy. For those who cannot make the psychological return trip, they are the "walking wounded," the psychologically traumatized victims of war. In modern parlance, we call this illness post-traumatic stress disorder (PTSD). When Crofton literally goes over the edge, jumping off a cliff in a psychotic frenzy, Rogers stands on the edge and offers a solemn salute to the soldier's memory, signifying that the wounds of war are psychological as well as physical. Shortly after this scene, another soldier manically takes off into the woods, "running home."

He is the victim of a psychotic break, another member of the walking wounded.

The Man from Colorado

In the opening scene of *The Man from Colorado*, we find Colonel Devereaux (Glenn Ford) commanding a regiment in the Union army. He has a defeated troop of Confederates pinned down in a gorge. Though they raise the white flag, he orders his artillerymen to wipe them out. The use of artillery, as opposed to rifles, represents dishonorable killing in the West — a slaughter rather than a fight. Upon viewing the consequences of his orders, the carcasses of dead rebels strewn over the rocks, a trace of guilt gleams in Devereaux's eyes. He returns his regiment to its fort, only to learn that Lee had surrendered at Appomattox while he was away. The war was over, making the massacre doubly pointless. That night, he writes in his journal: "I killed a hundred men today. I didn't want to. I couldn't help myself. What's wrong with me? I'm afraid. Afraid I'm going crazy!"

Devereaux returns to his hometown of Yellow Mountain, Colorado, fearing for his own sanity and haunted by the atrocities he witnessed and committed during the war. On his first night home, he's confronted by a ghost of his past, a rebel soldier who survived the massacre. The man accuses him at gunpoint of butchery: "...you killed them under a flag of surrender. You killed a hundred decent men. What for, Colonel? For a morning's entertainment? For pure, crazy love of killing? You're no hero. You're an insane murderer." The word "insane" is an emotional trigger for the self-doubting Devereaux. He disarms the rebel with a sucker punch and shoots him twice with his own gun, once again engaging in unnecessary killing, proving the dead rebel's point that he is an "insane murderer."

Devereaux's psychopathy is referred to as a "sickness" by his wife and friends. The film, made directly after World War II, is clearly an attempt to deal with the many veterans returning home with "combat fatigue," a psychological illness now referred to as post-traumatic stress disorder. The film also deals with other social problems relating to veterans, as the plot revolves around a group of disenfranchised miners whose claims were taken over by a gold baron while they were serving in the army. The theme is representative of the plight of contemporary veterans, who lost their jobs while fighting on the European and the Pacific fronts and returned home to face unemployment and poverty. Devereaux in particular represents the plight of the walking wounded, men who turned savage while engaging in the horrors of war, and then had trouble with the transition back to normalcy after returning home to civilization.

The consequences of Devereaux's killing sickness rises in intensity through the course of the film. Because he was appointed a federal judge of the territory, he literally has the power of life and death over the men in his jurisdiction. He wields this power with little restraint. His first violent act is to have a highwayman hanged, though the process seems more like a lynching than a legal execution. Then he has an innocent young man hung. His attempt to hang six more innocent men is thwarted. He goes to the mining town where the men are hiding out, but when the townspeople refuse to surrender the men, Devereaux burns down the town. This act of urban terrorism is clearly an allusion to the infamous atrocities of another Union commander, General William Tecumseh Sherman, who was also called "crazy" by many of his contemporaries. Sherman's strategy was called "total warfare." He burned down entire towns and plantations, displacing and killing many civilians on his "scorched earth" campaign through Georgia and South Carolina, leaving much of the South in ruins and cinders in his wake. In contemporary terms, Devereaux's torching of the town may have been a reference to the "war crimes" and atrocities committed against civilians during World War II. Certainly, the horrors of the Holocaust committed by the Germans and their collaborators is brought to mind, but other savage attacks against civilians — the attack of Pearl Harbor by the Japanese, the air bombardment of Stalingrad by the Germans, the firebombing of Dresden and Tokyo by allied forces, the atomic bombing of Hiroshima and Nagasaki by the Americans — were all recent enough to be associated with Devereaux's criminal act of arson. The point made by the film is that war is Hell, as it makes devils out of men.

The Psychopathic Killer Type

In Clint Eastwood's last Western to this date, *Unforgiven*, Eastwood plays an elderly outlaw, Will Munny, who is looking back at his life in retrospect. Though he has reformed his ways, he is still trying to come to terms with the flaws of his own character, as well as the guilty conscience that results from a life of killing. Will's antagonist is a brutal and corrupt sheriff named Little Bill (Gene Hackman). As indicated by their sharing of the same name, Will and Bill represent different sides of the same coin. Both men are former outlaws trying to become settled men of property. Will is struggling to start a pig farm. Little Bill has a steady job as a lawman and is building his own house. Will, however, is a horrible pig farmer, and Little Bill is a total failure as a carpenter. They both have trouble breaking the mold. In fact, Little Bill's dying statement — "I don't deserve this.... I was building a house!" — testifies to his belief that he was somehow redeeming his life of violence by settling down and upholding the law. Just like his counterpart, Will, Little Bill remains unforgiven for his past sins.

But while Little Bill finds death at the end of Will's shotgun barrel, Will does seem to find some kind of redemption, as the closing epilogue states that he ventured to California with his children, and prospered in dry goods. As California represents the land of redemption for ex-outlaws, we wonder if Will actually does find forgiveness within himself in the far western frontier. Perhaps it is his self-knowledge that merits his redemption. While Bill was fooling himself as town marshal, promoting himself as a man of law and order, while he was actually a tyrant, a brutal bully, and a sadist, Will was torturing himself over his deep conflicts regarding his violent past. When he replies to Bill's last words, "Deserves ain't got nothing to do with it," he drives home the fact that Bill has been denying his sins, while Will has been revisiting his crimes and repenting for them. However, following the bloodbath of the final scene, in which Will single-handedly kills a half-dozen men in

Western Anti-Heroes. Clint Eastwood (right) as William Munny and Morgan Freeman as his friend Ned Logan in Clint Eastwood's *Unforgiven* **(1992, Malpaso Productions/Warner Bros.).**

cold blood, it remains doubtful that he will ever escape the demons of his own savage acts.

Even before the many killings in the latter half of the film, we see that Will is tormented by the horrors of his own misdeeds. In a telling scene, we see Will confessing to his friend Ned (Morgan Freeman) that he is still haunted by his past: "Ned, you remember that drover I shot through the mouth and his teeth came out the back of his head? I think about him now and again. He didn't do anything to deserve to get shot, at least nothin' I could remember when I sobered up." For Will, killing is always associated with drinking. He has to be drunk in order for his civilized inhibitions to be let down, allowing his savage aggressive instincts to take over. When he was reformed by his wife, he gave up both drinking and killing. But with his wife long dead and his pig farm failing, Will takes on a job as a hired killer, in order to make enough money to start fresh and support his two kids. As he descends into the moral abyss of killing, he begins drinking again. He uses the whiskey as both a facilitator and an anesthetic. The liquor allows him to access the dark area of his soul where Will the Killer resides, and afterwards, it relieves the pain and guilt that arises as a result of what Will the Killer does. Prior to the final showdown, he drinks an entire bottle of whiskey before riding down to the saloon to kill Little Bill, in revenge for torturing his friend Ned to death. Upon entering the saloon, Little Bill confronts Will with his sordid past. "That's right," Will admits. "I've killed women and children. I've killed just about everything that walks or crawled at one time or another. And I'm here to kill you, Little Bill, for what you did to Ned." When drunk, Will becomes a stone-cold killer, free of all the self-doubt and empathy that hampers him in his sober state.

The role of the innocent young man who encounters the savage is played by The Schofield Kid (Jaimz Woolvett), a partially blind adolescent who wants to become a vicious gunfighter like Will once was. The Kid's blindness is symbolic of his lack of understanding of what it means to be a killer. He is nearsighted, unable to see things for what they are, and unable to see what lies in front of him if he continues on his reckless path. The Kid entices Will to join him on his mission as a hired killer. He pretends to be an experienced gunfighter ("I'm a damn killer myself, 'cept I ain't killed as many as you because of my youth"), but he is really a novice, a virgin in the sphere of killing. He thinks that killing is exciting and glorious. Instead, he learns that killing is neither noble nor gallant, it is ugly and sickening. After he kills his first man, he admits to Will: "I ain't never killed no one before." The reluctant mentor to the youngster in the field of savagery, Will stoically replies: "Well, you sure killed the hell outta that guy." The Kid continues with his confession: "That was the first one ... first one I ever killed. You know how I said I shot five men? It weren't true. That Mexican that come at me with a knife, I just busted his leg with a shovel. I didn't kill him or nothing, neither." In pity, Will finally gives forth the only wisdom he has about the act of killing: "It's a hell of a thing, killing a man. Ya take away all he's got, and all he's ever gonna have." Following this bit of existential insight, The Kid gives up his dream of becoming a gunfighter. "I ain't like you, Will," he says. Having had his first taste of the horror, as well as the guilt and pain that ensues from it, The Kid chooses a lighter path, a path which will one day lead to the forgiveness of his sins. As for Will, he will probably always remain unforgiven for what he has done. But at least he provided the opportunity for a new beginning for his own kids in California, while also fostering a new beginning for the kid who mistakenly wanted to be like him, The Schofield Kid.

The Genocidal Type

In *Arrowhead*, Ed Bannon (Charlton Heston) is a cavalry scout who has an extremely conflicted attitude towards the Apache Indians. His father was killed by the Apaches. He was taken captive as a young boy and raised as "the adopted son of an Apache medicine man." As an adult, he hates the Apaches to the last drop of his blood and wants nothing more than to see their kind wiped off the map of America. His position as a cavalry scout allows him to use his knowledge of Apache traditions and tactics against them. In Bannon's own words: "Ya gotta think like 'em to lick 'em!" However, because he was raised among Indians, and because he is a civilian scout rather than a soldier, the cavalrymen distrust him, referring to him as "the white Apache." He is a man torn between two worlds. He is white and hates Indians, but he's not accepted among his white brethren. And while he directs all of his energies into the fighting of the Apaches, he has a profound and abiding respect for their culture and ways — a much deeper respect than any of his white compatriots.

Bannon's identity conflict is represented in his divergent romantic interests: a genteel white lady (Mary Sinclair) and an Apache half-breed (Katy Jurado). The external love conflict symbolizes the internal conflict between his preferred persona of a purebloooded white man and the haunting shadow of his Apache upbringing. In the end, he must integrate both sides of his torn identity in order to defeat Toriano (Jack Palance), the Apache leader who represents the physical incarnation of Bannon's shadow, his dark-skinned "blood brother." Like Bannon, Toriano hates his enemy with every ounce of his being. He lives only to see the day in which his enemy is driven off Apache land forever. Realizing the futility of this dream, he will settle for spilling the blood of as many treacherous "white devils" as possible

Bannon's attitude towards the Apache, while reverential, is also hateful. He wants nothing more than to destroy them, to wipe them off the land completely, using any means necessary. The hunger to avenge the death of his father, his need to wipe out the psychological stain of his own captivity, and the disgrace of having to come of age among the savages, provide more than enough motivation to justify his thirst for Apache blood. As with the settlers and soldiers of the 18th and 19th centuries, it is not the ethnocentric philosophies of white supremacy or "Manifest Destiny," nor is it the practical rationalizations of expansionism and imperial domination that provide the justification for the genocidal policies of Native American relocation and elimination on the Western frontier. It is the motivations of vengeance, hatred, and anger—aroused by the captivity narratives and tales of atrocities—that fuel the fires of U.S. aggression and hostility against the Indian peoples.

It is significant to note that in the final battle between Bannon and Toriano, Bannon does not confront and kill his shadow in the white way (he doesn't shoot him). Rather, they fight in the traditional Apache way—no weapons—in a hand-to-hand wrestling match, in which Bannon breaks Toriano's back. Even when ridding himself of his shadow, Bannon shows more respect for the Apache tradition than for the white tradition, which would have involved the use of heavy guns and artillery, and which would have resulted in the needless destruction of hundreds of soldiers and warriors of low rank, rather than just the death of one leader. The Apache style of battle between two men of high rank stands in stark contrast to the European style of battle between numerous men of low rank. While the Apache method of warfare, though brutal and bloody, resulted in the survival and coexistence of both warring tribes, the white European method resulted in the wholesale slaughter and virtual extermination of the entirety of the weaker people. Which method of warfare is more savage?

Ulzana's Raid

Western film directors before the late 1960s had to be very careful in their references to atrocities. In the days before film ratings for adult content, it was understood that children would be viewing any movie released by a studio, so themes such as rape, torture, and mutilation had to be approached with much tact. In essence, the method was to show the disgusted and appalled faces of the people witnessing the horror, rather than the actual horror itself. This method began to change in the 1960s, when film violence and sexual themes started to become more graphic. *Ulzana's Raid*, released in 1972, depicts explicitly the horror and savagery that was only alluded to in earlier Westerns.

The tagline for the film expressed the notion that both Indians and Whites on the Western frontier were guilty of acts that could be called savage: "*To Defeat the Apaches, They Had to Be Just as Savage*." In one of the first scenes of the film, a cavalryman outnumbered by Apaches shoots the white woman he is escorting and then himself. The act at first seems overplayed, even with the tacit understanding of the "last bullet" theme, but his fateful decision is quickly understood when we see the Apaches, led by their chief, Ulzana (Joaquin Martinez), mutilating the cavalryman's body by cutting out his liver and playing catch with it, while nearby, the sole survivor of the attack, a little boy, is left weeping by the side of his dead mother. Later on in the film, the Apaches flay and burn a settler alive, shoving his dog's tail in his mouth to stifle his screams, and gang-raping his wife to the brink of death. When we see this poor woman beaten and ravaged and driven to madness by the horror of her attack, we understand both the rationale for the last bullet and how the aura of savagery and horror created by this method of terrorism can be used as an efficient means of gaining psychological power over an enemy with superior numbers and arms.

But the Apache rationale for savagery is mystical rather than practical. In the film, the role of the young civilized man who encounters the savage is played by an idealistic cavalry lieutenant, DeBuin (Bruce Davison). When he asks his Apache scout, Ke-Ni-tay (Jorge Luke), why Ulzana and his warriors torture and mutilate their victims for hours on end, the scout replies: "To take the power. Each man that die, the man that kill him take his power. Man give up his power when he dies. Like fire give heat. Fire that burn long time, many can have heat.... Here in this land, man must have power."

As a prelude to Ulzana's genocidal raid, he was stripped of his ego identity by the white man who robbed his land, destroyed his people's traditional way of life, and forced him and his tribe to live in poverty and disgrace on the reservation. His raid was a means of redeeming his own sense of psychological power, a way to die with honor. Each white that he killed and tortured added an ounce of self-respect to his fractured identity. In contrast, the cavalrymen who engaged in the mutilation and scalping of Apache corpses did so for the more ignoble purposes of vengeance, intimidation, and spite.

Upon witnessing his own cavalrymen mutilating the body of Ulzana's young son, DeBuin is shocked and dismayed. His white scout, McIntosh (Burt Lancaster), remarks: "You don't like to think of white men behaving like Indians. It kind of confuses the issue, doesn't it?"

The Terminal Environment

A common element in all of the Western character types is the fact that they exist in what Slotkin referred to as "a terminal environment," a place in time that is fleeting. The Wild West was only wild for a brief period in history, a few decades between the end of the Civil War and the closing of the frontier at the end of the 19th century. The men who became heroes in that environment either died young or lived to see the end of their own era, when civilization closed the mythological frontier in a cloud of railroad smoke and auto engine exhaust. The cowboy hero was no longer able to move his cattle freely along the prairie, as the closing of the frontier heralded the end of open range "free grazing," an issue dealt with in *Shane, The Man Who Shot Liberty Valance* (1962), and most recently, *Open Range* (2003). In the modern era, the marshal hero's brand of individual justice would become anachronistic. When the towns they protect become civilized, the townspeople demand a style of justice that is less violent and more bureaucratic. The demise of the marshal hero as the lone crusader of justice is represented in the theme in which the marshal must leave the town that he has just saved, as he is no longer needed or wanted (for instance, *High Noon, My Darling Clementine, Invitation to a Gunfighter...*).

In the case of the gunfighters and outlaws, because they fight against their destiny, trying desperately to change themselves in the last act of their stories, their fate is typically death or disintegration into the vast emptiness of the frontier, as symbolized in the traditional ending in which the hero rides off into the sunset. As Slotkin noted: "Their story will have to reach its climax in a fast-draw shoot-out, in which their calling will reach its pinnacle of achievement — followed by its exhaustion. And they will become critically conscious, before the end, of just what has gone wrong with them and their world." Death meets the title characters of *Jesse James* and *The Gunfighter*, as well as most of the Billy the Kids and other outlaw characters in numerous film depictions. Riding off into the sunset, as in the endings of *Shane, Rancho Notorious* (1952), and countless others, is only a more glamorous and romantic depiction of death, as we can only assume that the gunfighter/outlaw will continue to ride on his path of violence, which can only end in his own demise. However, it is this critical awareness of their own imminent doom which makes all of the Western hero types so romantic and so intriguing. In living and triumphing within the terminal or "fatal" environment, the Western heroes teach us how to live with honor and how to face death with courage and integrity.

4

Western Women

"There are only two things more beautiful than a gun: a Swiss watch or a woman from anywhere."

— Cherry Valance (John Ireland), in *Red River* (1948)

The traditional Western is about honor and redemption. The hero embarks on a quest for honor. This quest, however, is a dark one, as it almost invariably involves both vengeance and violence. The quest, therefore, is a descent. Like Orpheus's journey, it is a dark passage into the netherworld, an encounter with the primal wilderness and its savage inhabitants: the shadow. Though honor through vengeance and violence is sought and achieved, the hero now finds himself tarnished with the mark of Cain — his hands stained with the sin of blood. He must now find redemption for his dark deeds through integration with a symbol of light and peace: the goddess figure. In short, the hero finds honor by encountering his own shadow (killing a man), then redeems his soul by integrating the goddess figure (loving a woman).

According to Cawelti: "Women pose a basic threat ... because they are the harbingers of law and order enforced by police and courts, and of the whole machinery of schools and peaceful town life. These institutions make masculine courage and strength a much less important social factor." As women, in most cases, represent aspects of the family that come into fruition with the development of civilization and society, they naturally play an antithetical role in relation to the Western hero, who epitomizes freedom, independence, and individualism. In a similar vein, French notes: "...while not necessarily a latent homosexual, the hero secretly fears women and the civ-

60

ilization, compromise and settled life they represent; he sees them as sources of corruption and betrayal, luring him away from independence and a sure sense of himself as well as from the more comforting company of men."

Nevertheless, there are few Westerns without women, though their roles may be small. Oftentimes there are only one or two women in the entire cast, and their parts are relegated to a couple of functional scenes. However, the roles that women play in Westerns are integral to the development of the hero's character. To a certain extent, it could be said that a Western is not a Western unless there is a female character for the hero to interact with, as it is the hero's treatment of this woman, even more so than his actions in violent conflict, that define his character.

It has often been said that there are only two types of women in Westerns: the schoolmarm and the whore. This was never true. Many of the Westerns in the silent era were Indian subjects, in which the women were neither schoolmarms nor whores, as these roles were relegated strictly to white women. The dichotomy of Western types for Indian women were the half-breed and the full-breed Indian (the latter typically represented as the "red bride" archetype). Apart from these four types of female lead roles, there were a variety of supporting roles for women: cranky old grandmothers, tough old squaws, and moralistic middle-aged housewives. And, as the genre developed, a new kind of Western woman developed, as a separate-but-equal counterpart to the frontiersman hero archetype. This woman, "the frontierswoman," embodied the spirit of the West in terms of the female role in conquering the frontier. She was as hardworking as a cowboy, as brave as a marshal, and tougher than the meanest outlaw. In short, she was the mother of the Wild West, who gave birth to a new generation of Americans on the new frontier.

The Schoolmarm

The traditional role for the young unmarried white woman in the Western is that of the schoolmarm. She's a good girl: modestly dressed, polite, virginal, prudish, stuck-up, upper class, and usually a brunette (whores tend to be blonde). She is invariably of 100 percent white blood, while the whore is often of mixed breeding. She usually rides in a stage, on a train, or on the passenger side of a cart. When she does ride horseback, she rides sidesaddle, whereas women of lesser breeding straddle the horse in an unladylike manner. Often she is a Southern belle, representing an aura of gentility that the hero is only vaguely familiar with. She is also from the East. The schoolmarm is civilized, and she brings civilization with her in the form of education. She stands in stark contrast to the dance-hall girl (whore), who caters to the wild, undomesticated urges of frontier men. If the typical dramatic roles for women are said to represent the Madonna/Whore dichotomy, than the schoolmarm certainly embodies the Madonna side of this division. The schoolmarm is pure and virginal. To the hero, who is unpure by nature of his violent acts, her pureness represents spiritual redemption. If, by the end, she accepts his love and returns it, his soul is redeemed.

The Whore with the Heart of Gold

Going back to the Bible and the earliest myths and legends, whores have always been popular characters in literature and drama. They have a natural place in Westerns, as any dangerous frontier setting will be populated mainly by men, establishing a need for sexual recreation provided by the female flesh trade. For most of the history of Westerns, up until the 1960s, the censors required that the subject of prostitution be dealt with tact, in order to spare young viewers the corruption of their souls. Usually, the whore's occupation is either never directly mentioned, or it is obscured by calling the character a "showgirl" or "dance-hall girl." For example, in *Destry Rides Again* (1939) and *My Darling Clementine* (1945), Frenchy (Marlene Dietrich) and Chihuahua (Linda Darnell) are "showgirls," an occupation which is clearly indicative of promiscuity and debasement. Showgirls are promiscuous by reputation, while whores are promiscuous by profession. In any case, the title "showgirl" in old Westerns is simply a euphemism for the word "whore," with the fringe benefit of offering a musical number in the middle of the film to lighten the picture up. In *Stagecoach* (1939), Dallas (Claire Trevor) is exiled from town by a troupe of middle-aged housewives because of her dubious occupation. We don't know whether she is to be considered a showgirl or a whore, and it doesn't matter, because it is tacitly understood that the former term is clearly a euphemism for the latter.

In contrast, modern Westerns not only treat the subject of prostitution without euphemism, they tend to dwell on the sordidness of these women's lives to the point of morbidity. In the contemporary cable television series *Deadwood* (2004–2006), the old way of dealing with prostitution is turned on its head, as the whore's situation is not only depicted realistically, but in such a graphic way as to repulse and shock the viewing audience. Whores are disease-ridden sex slaves controlled by brutal and greedy pimps. The Chinese whores are kept in cages, rarely fed, and never cleaned. When they die, their bodies are quickly burned in clear view of all the other whores, or else chopped up and fed to the pigs. Their cages are immediately refilled with new immigrant girls, sold into bondage by their impoverished fathers back in China. A similar but less gaudy depiction can be seen in the cable television miniseries *Broken Trail* (2006).

Nevertheless, like Frenchy, Chihuahua, and Dallas, the showgirl/whore is always seen as a redeemable character, a woman who could eventually re-enter society, if not as a respectable lady, then at least as a reformed woman with a shadowy past. Unlike her male counterpart, the outlaw gunslinger, the whore is not necessarily doomed to a life outside of civilized society ending in a violent death — though that is often her fate. The whore at least has a chance of redeeming herself, as long as her golden heart remains true. This potential for redemption is a key element of the frontier story, as the West represents a land of new beginnings, an opportunity to leave the past behind and become reborn.

In *Deadwood*, we are introduced to Trixie (Paula Malcomson) as a drug-addicted, disease-ridden whore, who is frequently beaten by both sadistic johns and her brutal pimp. Her redemptive transformation is depicted as a gradual process, in which Trixie's confidence in herself is slowly built up through her evolving relationships with Alma (Molly Parker), the rich widow from the East, Swearingen (Ian McShane), the greedy pimp who nevertheless cares enough about her to encourage her first few tentative ventures into respectability, and Sol (John Hawkes), a Jewish businessman, who falls in love with Trixie and offers her a quasi-respectable alternative to prostitution, as his woman.

In traditional Westerns, whores and showgirls have a variety of fates. If she is lucky, she plays a complementary role to the hero. She redeems him with love, and he redeems her with the respectability and social acceptance that comes with marriage. This is the consummation that occurs in *Stagecoach* and *Winchester '73*. If this character type is unlucky, she dies for her sins. In *Destry Rides Again* and *My Darling Clementine*, the showgirl/whore loves the good badman, but he does not accept her because of her promiscuous occupation. In their final act, Frenchy and Chihuahua save the men they love from a bullet, but at the price of their own lives. Their characters are ultimately redeemed, yet they do not live to reap the benefit. In *My Darling Clementine*, the man whom Chihuahua loves, Doc Holliday (Victor Mature), uses her death as a motivation towards vengeance, which culminates in his own violent death. In *Destry Rides Again*, the man whom Frenchy loves, Destry (James Stewart), also uses her death as a motivation towards vengeance. However, he survives the shootout, allowing him to pursue romance with the virginal schoolmarm.

The Halfbreed

Chihuahua, the showgirl with a heart of gold in *My Darling Clementine*, is of ambiguous racial stock. Her mixed ethnicity is only dealt with in subtext, i.e. when Wyatt Earp (Henry Fonda) tells her: "I should take you back to the Apache reservation where you belong!" Apparently, she is part Apache, though her name, "Chihuahua," infers Mexican heritage, while her skin color is clearly white. Chihuahua's feelings of racial inferiority are drawn out in her rivalry with the schoolmarm, Clementine (Cathy Downs), for the love of Doc Holliday. Not only is she a lowly showgirl/whore, she is also not a pure white. Clementine, on the other hand, epitomizes the Madonna archetype. She is virginal, educated, high class, Eastern and Southern, and of course, lily-white. An interesting love triangle is formed, in which the sinful Doc Holliday feels inferior and unworthy of Clementine's love, while Chihuahua, dealing with her own inferiority complex, is constantly trying to prove herself worthy of Holliday's love.

Chihuahua's self-consciousness about her low social status is exacerbated by her intense reaction to Holliday's cruel jibe, when he tells her: "Go sing your silly songs somewhere else!" She finds comfort in the arms of Billy Clanton (John Ireland). Though she is justified, her inconstancy is seen as a corollary to her promiscuous nature. But Chihuahua's character finds redemption when she reveals that Billy was the owner of a piece of evidence that proves that the Clantons killed James Earp. Billy shoots Chihuahua for her betrayal. Her confession and punishment are perceived as a selfless sacrifice that she makes in order to help Doc. In her subsequent ordeal, Doc operates on her without anesthesia, purging her soul of all sin and finally earning her what she desires the most — Holliday's love and respect. When she eventually dies of her injuries, her death inspires Holliday to assist Earp and his brothers in their final showdown at the O.K. Corral. Holliday's courageous performance at the shootout and his heroic death redeem his soul, leaving the only two major characters left alive — Earp and Clementine — to find love with each other. Earp's sin, his bloody vengeance quest, is wiped clean by Clementine's pure, redemptive love. Earp rides off into the sunset, vowing that he'll return. Clementine remains behind in Tombstone, making it clear that she will be staying on as "the town schoolmarm," just in case anyone was worried that she would take up Chihuahua's recently vacated position as the town slut.

In general, the female halfbreed is a conflicted character. Usually in love with a white man, she feels racially inferior to him and must prove herself worthy of his love. Probably the most famous female halfbreed in the Western genre is the character of Pearl Chavez (Jennifer Jones) in King Vidor's sprawling epic, *Duel in the Sun* (1945). By her name, she is clearly part Mexican, but she is also part white and part Indian as well. In the film, she is drawn to both brothers in a powerful and rich Texan family. The good son, Jesse (Joseph Cotton), loves her and wants to marry her, despite her mixed heritage. The bad son, Newt (Gregory Peck), feels only lust towards her. He uses her sexually, abuses her physically, verbally, and psychologically, and refuses to marry her. Though she feels for both men, her passion, associated with her dark blood, overcomes her reason. She falls in love with the wrong brother, a mistake which dooms her to dishonor and death.

The Red Bride

The full-blooded Indian maiden who falls in love with a white man is one of the oldest archetypes in frontier literature. Slotkin (1985) referred to this character type as "the red bride," and described her as follows:

> ... the Indian princess who sexually tempts either the hero or some subordinate white character. Pocahontas is of course the first such figure, and there are others.... The red bride offers sensual pleasure, and with it the key to an intimate possession of the wilderness-as-wilderness. Her passionate nature awakes forbidden sexual impulses in a form that is at once attractive and repulsive: attractive in that she is a woman outside the taboo structure; repulsive in that the idea of going beyond the taboo brings guilt and certain renegadery.

When there is a love interest between an Indian maiden and a white leading man, the Indian is almost always the chief's daughter. As in the Pocahontas legend, this casting plays a functional role in the story. Her ability to sway her father, the chief, at the crucial moment, allows the hero to save himself and his own people from certain death at the hands of the Indians. This theme could be seen in films such as *Broken Arrow* (1950), *The Big Sky* (1952), and *The Indian Fighter* (1955). The interracial relationship between these star-crossed lovers represents the never-realized dream of a peaceful and equitable coexistence of both races in the Western territories. But while the love between the classic white lovers, Romeo and Juliet, is depicted as pure and virtuous, there is usually a wild, violent element in the love scenes between the white man and his red bride. In *The Big Sky* and *The Indian Fighter*, the white man doesn't seduce the Indian, he chases her through the woods, captures her, and forces himself upon her. This act of aggressive lovemaking may be symbolic of the white man taking and raping the Indian land.

The irony is that the Indian girl falls in love with her rapist during or directly after the act itself. This nonsensical twist absolves the white male audience of any sense of guilt and seems to tie in directly with the wilderness-as-woman theme.

The archetype of the wild woman, Nature's child, is evoked by the image of the nubile Indian maiden frolicking in the virgin woods. She is wild and free, like a beast of prey. She cannot be wooed and seduced like a civilized woman. She must be hunted, pursued, captured, and overpowered like a wild animal. Like the wilderness itself, she must be tamed and subdued via physical strength and stamina. In keeping with the structure of the hunter-hero archetype from which the frontiersman hero is derived, since the hunter has captured and subdued its prey, she rightfully belongs to him. Because he has the ability to tame the wild, whether it is represented as Indian land or Indian woman, he deserves to have it. Furthermore, though he is typically tempted to marry a white woman and join a white community, he refuses this temptation, choosing instead to remain in the wilderness and to marry his red bride.

The Woman as Anima

For the ultra-masculine Western hero, the female character often plays a complementary role to the male persona. Whereas he represents all of the aspects of the animus: strength, courage, aggression, and will, she represents all of the aspects of the anima: sensitivity, compassion, nurturance, and compromise. Together, they compose a psychologically balanced and androgynous entity — a couple who complete each other. When this corresponding feminine presence is not there, the hero character is left unbalanced and incomplete. There is a restlessness and uneasiness about this character, who is bereft of the normal scale of human emotions. His insensitivity, over-aggressiveness, brashness, and inability to compromise make him a danger to himself and others. This type of character, marked by his disconnection from the feminine and his inability to relate on an emotional level with anybody, is the basic building block of the Western anti-hero.

The "dead wife theme" is a common element in most of the great Western anti-hero characters. This character is a wild man who was once tamed by a woman. When this woman died, he suffered the loss of his own anima, forcing him to regress to his former state of ultra-masculine wildness. He must return to the wilderness as a solitary animal, a lone, uncivilized wanderer. Ethan Edwards (John Wayne) in *The Searchers* epitomizes this type of character. In the first scene, Ethan returns to the home of his brother. He has led a wild life as a Confederate Raider and outlaw, but the love and respect that he feels for his sister-in-law (Dorothy Jordan) softens him. He gives his saber to his nephew, his medal of honor to his niece, and settles down to live peacefully on the homestead. Though his love is directed towards his sister-in-law and not a wife, it has the same domesticating effect on him. But when hostile Commanches raid the home, raping, mutilating, and killing the woman he loves, the newly born sensitive side of Ethan's personality is destroyed. His life is now dedicated to vengeance and death.

The dead wife theme provides similar motivation for the vengeful hero in *The Bravados* (1958) and several of director Budd Boetticher's "Lone Pine Westerns," in which Randolph Scott plays essentially the same character in all of the films. His motivation is revenge for the killing of his wife in *Seven Men From Now* (1956) and *Decision at Sundown* (1957). In *Comanche Station* (1960), his motivation is a desperate quest to find his abducted wife. In all of these films, Scott's character is the epitome of constancy. He searches for his lost wife, or for the men who killed her, year after year after year, facing danger and death time and time again, allowing nothing to stop him. In essence, the dead wife theme is a reversal of values from feminine to masculine. While the feminine integrates life and love (Eros) into the hero's character, represented as settling down, raising cattle or produce, and starting a family; the absence of the feminine leads to a morbid obsession with death and destruction (Thanatos).

Will Munny (Clint Eastwood) in *Unforgiven* represents another example of the dead wife theme. Before he met his wife, Will was a cold-blooded killer. His wife made him focus on life. He settled down, started a pig farm, and fathered two children. When his wife died, Will returned to killing. However, his relationship with his wife changed him forever. Though it is awkward, he develops a platonic relationship with a whore named Delilah (Anna Thomson), who was "cut up" by a brutal cowboy in the first act. The whores banded together to put a price on the head of the cowboys who mutilated Delilah. Since Will returned to killing in order to collect this reward, it could be said that he was on a vengeance quest for the sake of Delilah. In any case, his two scenes with Delilah are gentle and quiet, indicating that he can be sensitive with others, and that he has a deep and abiding respect for women. It is this lingering feminine aspect to his personality that leads him away from killing in the final part of the film, in which he travels to California with his children to start a new life.

The Woman as Temptress

Occasionally, women are portrayed in a negative light in Westerns. When this occurs, they almost invariably take on the mythical persona of the temptress. According to Saunders: "Women seem to expose men at their most vulnerable, and sexual encounters are often succeeded by self-disgust. One hesitates to write this off as simple misogyny; the flaws are part of the hero's own make-up." Saunders references two Sam Peckinpah Westerns, *Major Dundee* (1965) and *The Wild Bunch* (1969), as examples of films in which the hero's demise is precipitated by a sexual encounter. In the latter film, women are depicted as being particularly vile, slutty, and two-faced. The purest character in the film is an idealistic young Mexican with the extremely apt name of Angel (Jaime Sanchez). Though he is an outlaw, he steals only to raise money and arms for his suffering people, who are raising a grassroots rebellion against the oppressive federal government. Upon returning from a dangerous mission, Angel finds that his beloved woman has left him to become the concubine of General Mapache (Emilio Fernandez), the embodiment of the dictatorial regime. As she sits on Mapache's lap, licking his ear and tormenting the cuckolded Angel, who observes from a distance, Angel can stand no more. He draws his gun and shouts out "Punta!" before shooting her through the chest. This act leads to Angel's demise and, in a roundabout way, the demise of all of his comrades as well.

The leader of the bunch of outlaws, Pike Bishop (William Holden), is similarly betrayed by a woman of low morals. After recreating with a whore, Pike decides to lead his band of outlaws in a suicidal gunfight with Mapache's men. During the climactic showdown, Pike is shot in the back by a concubine of one of the general's men. He turns, and before blowing her away with his shotgun, shouts out: "Bitch!" *The Wild Bunch* was considered iconoclastic in its day for both its negative depiction of women and its depiction of graphic violence against women, and even for its explicit use of obscene language directed towards women.

The Frontierswoman

Just as the hero represents a mediating force between the civilized homesteaders and the savage outlaws, the frontierswoman represents a mediating force between the schoolmarm and the whore. Unlike the other two types, which are essentially stereotypes, the frontierswoman is a real woman. Neither as debased as the whore nor as hopelessly virginal and pure as the schoolmarm, the frontierswoman is gritty but wholesome, honest but also sexual, and earthy yet still refined. As an endpoint for female characters in transition, she represents redemption for the whore (Dallas in *Stagecoach*) and sacrifice for the schoolmarm (Clementine in *My Darling Clementine*). For Dallas, marrying the hero means escaping from the tragic fate of prostitution and accepting the hard but honest work of frontier life on a ranch. For Clementine, marrying the hero means forsaking her life of luxury and privilege back East for a life of danger and struggle in the frontier town of Tombstone.

Jean Arthur played the rugged frontierswoman type in several movies: first as Calamity Jane in Cecil B. DeMille's *The Plainsman* (1936), then as Phoebe Titus in *Arizona* (1940), and then again, most memorably, in George Stevens's *Shane* (1952), which was her last film role. In *Arizona,* Arthur played the "only American woman in Tuscon," a tough but pretty gal who goes from holding a shotgun to baking a pie in about one minute. In *Shane,* Arthur embodied the sacrifice inherent to the frontierswoman's life, giving up the comforts of civilization and city life in order to share in her husband's dream of a new life of freedom and limitless possibilities amidst the beauty and majesty of the Western frontier. However, legendary actress Barbara Stanwyck is most associated with the frontierswoman archetype, having played the role in many Westerns, such as George Stevens's *Annie Oakley* (1935), Cecil B. De Mille's *Union Pacific* (1939), John Farrow's *California* (1946), Anthony Mann's *The Furies* (1950), Allan Dwan's *The Cattle Queen of Montana* (1954), Rudolph Maté's *The Violent Men* (1955), Sam Fuller's *Forty Guns* (1957), and most memorably, as Victoria Barkley in over 100 episodes of the extremely popular Western television series *The Big Valley* (1965–1969).

More recently, women in Westerns have been cast in the role of "medicine woman." Jane Seymour played the tile role in the popular TV series, *Dr. Quinn, Medicine Woman* (1993–1998), and Cate Blanchett played a frontier medicine woman in *The Missing* (2003). The healer is a natural role for women, as the healer archetype in ancient myths and legends was typically a goddess or sorceress. Elderly women in Westerns often take on the role of mentorship for younger women in transition. They are the ones who teach the young schoolmarm how to live out west. In *The Virginian* (1929), Ma Taylor (Helen Ware) is an old frontierswoman who gives the schoolmarm (Mary Brian) a rude awakening about the realities of life out west, after the girl has trouble dealing with the fact that her love interest (Gary Cooper) was forced to lynch his best friend. "This is a new country we're building," she tells her, "and there ain't no room for weaklings — men or women!" In order to accept the Western hero for who he is, the schoolmarm must learn the harsh realities of the West. The elderly frontierswoman is often the one who takes the schoolmarm to school for this lesson.

Nearly a quarter of a century later, in *High Noon* (1952), Gary Cooper's love interest, Amy (Grace Kelly), faces the same conflict. Cooper plays the town marshal, Will Kane. His young bride, Amy, is struggling to transform herself from a schoolmarm type (a pacifistic Quaker) into a true frontierswoman who is willing to accept her husband's use of deadly force when necessary. Amy's mentor is not an elderly frontierswoman; she is a significantly older but still vital woman of dubious repute named Helen Ramírez (Katy Jurado). Helen has much more experience than the innocent young Quaker girl, and is therefore able to give Amy the proper guidance that will prepare her for a life in the Wild West. Amy walks out on her husband when he tells her that, rather than running, he's staying in town to fight the outlaws who are coming in after him. Amy cannot understand why her husband would face violence and death rather than running from it. She seeks out Helen, who was once romantically linked with her husband, and asks her: "Why is he staying?" "If you don't know," Helen replies, "I cannot explain it to you." As Amy turns to leave, Helen asks her: "What kind of woman are you? How can you leave him like this? Does the sound of guns frighten you that much?" Later on, Helen explains her own position a bit more: "I hate this town. I always hated it! To be a Mexican woman in this town...." Amy says "I understand," but she probably doesn't. Will loved Helen once, but he never married her. Instead, he married a virginal white girl from back East who is half his age. The importance of both race and age is quietly understated in this film. It is always implied rather than explained directly. Nevertheless, Helen tries to help the naïve young girl by giving her the direction she needs: "I don't understand you. No matter what you say. If Kane was my man, I'd never leave him like this. I'd get a gun. I'd fight!" "Why don't you?" Amy asks her. "He is not my man," Helen replies bitterly. "He's yours!" In the end, Amy rises to the occasion, shooting an outlaw in the back to save her husband. The key element in the frontierswoman's personality is her ability to understand both her husband's persona as well as the harsh realities of frontier life and to accept the inevitable violence that results from this combination.

Other memorable depictions of the elderly frontierswoman include Miss Canaday (Aline MacMahon) in *The Man from Laramie* (1955), Jane Darwell as Jenny Grier in *The Ox-Bow Incident* (1943) and as Sister Ledeyard in *Wagon Master* (1950), and Olive Carey as Mrs. Jorgensen in *The Searchers*. Olive was the wife of Western screen legend Harry Carey and the mother of Harry Carey, Jr., who would also become a staple of Western films. Director John Ford worked with all three Careys, so it was only natural that he would cast Olive as the quintessential frontierswoman in his magnum opus of the Western genre. In *The Searchers*, Mrs. Jorgensen delivers what is possibly the key line in the film, as the men discuss the trials and tribulations of living in hostile Indian territory: "It just so happens that we be Texicans! A Texican is nothin' but a human man way out on a limb, this year and next — maybe for a hundred more. But I don't think it'll be forever. Some day, this country's gonna be a fine, good place to be. Maybe it needs our bones in the ground before that time can come."

The Western Heroine

There is a long tradition of Western heroines: female characters that play the heroic role of savior/fighter, as opposed to the supporting role of love interest. Calamity Jane, Belle Starr, and Annie Oakley were all real historical characters who became famous in their day, more because of the novelty of women engaging in the traditional male pursuits of Indian fighting, gunfighting, and sharp-shooting than for their actual accomplishments. In movies fictionalizing their exploits, the Western heroine typically plays a "mannish" woman, a female character in a male's costume and persona, who eventually integrates her feminine side by falling in love with a real man who is her equal. In purely fictional depictions of the Western heroine, the female character usually follows the same road to redemption as her male counterpart.

Cat Ballou (1965) is by all accounts the best Western heroine movie, mainly because it doesn't take itself too seriously. As a musical comedy, the film pokes fun at the Western genre and offers a heroine (Jane Fonda) who is somewhat believable as both a sensuous young woman and as a violent outlaw. Other films that try to take a quasi-serious approach to the female gunslinger character, such as *Bad Girls* (1994) and *The Quick and the Dead* (1995), fail miserably. The female outlaw in the Western scenario is an oddity — she never truly existed — so it's nearly impossible to take this character seriously. That is not to say that there is no place for women as lead characters in Westerns, though it will always be a male-oriented genre. *The Missing* is a good example of a Western with a female lead that works, mainly because the heroine is not a woman in man's clothing (a gunslinger or lone crusader), but rather, she embodies the established Western archetype of the frontierswoman, playing a true woman of the West, rather than a screenwriter's conceptualization of what a male Western hero would be, if he were a pretty woman.

There is also room for female characters in Westerns who defy the traditional roles provided for them. By far the most frequent female character in Westerns, the whore, is traditionally redeemed either by death and/or by the love of the hero. Modern Westerns have shown an interest in depicting the whore as a potentially proactive and self-redeeming character. This theme was played out poorly in *Bad Girls*, but in a much more thought provoking way in *The Ballad of Little Jo* (1993), in which the heroine (Suzy Amis) disguises herself as a man in order to survive in the West with her dignity intact. As the genre itself slowly fades into obscurity and obsolescence, there is little hope that the Western will experience another grand revival. However, it is likely that new and unique perspectives on the Western scenario will appear from time to time, sustaining interest in the genre for a long time to come. Contemporary Westerns that explore issues of sexual orientation (*Brokeback Mountain*), race (*Dances with Wolves*), and female perspectives (*The Missing, The Ballad of Little Jo*) offer hope that the genre may endure as an existent and vital part of American culture.

5

Atonement with the Indian

"I don't go so far as to think that the only good Indians are the dead Indians, but I believe that nine out of ten are, and I shouldn't inquire too closely into the case of the tenth."

— Theodore Roosevelt, 1886

Starting with the original settlement of the American colonies, there were two contrasting views of the natives. The prevailing view of the Puritan colonists was that the natives were savages, pure and simple, whose degraded state of living and complete lack of inhibition and sexual restraint put them in league with the Devil. To the Puritans, undomesticated nature was impure. Sex was sinful. Anything wild and untamed was deemed to be evil. Some of the Puritans actually believed that the Indian tribes were the lost tribes of Israel; modern-day Mormons still believe this to be true. The lost tribes, having been isolated in a debased state of uncivilized nature, without the guiding light of Christianity to lead them, became corrupted and degraded. They were fallen men, wild men, to be feared and loathed. The captivity narratives, used by Puritan ministers to scare and edify the settlers, warned their parishioners that to consort with the natives was to consort with the Devil himself.

The contrasting view came from the non–Puritanical philosophies of the European Enlightenment. The humanists, romanticists, and primitivists tended to espouse the notion of "the noble savage"— the idea that human beings are essentially good, but they are corrupted by society and civilization, which tend to engender corrupting influences such as private property, political power, and so on. Rather than nature and sex being evil, debased, and chock full of original sin, the enlightened view saw nature and sex as inherently good things that are corrupted by the deeds and ideas of men. Therefore, the Native American, as a product of uncivilized nature, is a noble savage and emblematic of all that is inherently good about the human race.

The noble savage view of the Indian was not popular among the mainly Puritan settlers of the 18th century, but the notion caught on in the 19th century, as non–Puritanical influences began to take hold in American culture. The works of James Fenimore Cooper were particularly influential in portraying the Indian as a noble savage. Cooper's "Leatherstocking" cycle of novels, which featured the character of Natty Bumpo (more commonly known by his Indian name, Hawkeye), was a perfect example of the "White Indian"—the white man who lived in nature among the natives—in order to live a purer, less corrupted lifestyle. The 19th century saw a highly romanticized view of the noble Indian savage take hold in the literary circles of the Northeast, as can be seen in such works as Henry Longfellow's epic poem "The Song of Hiawatha" and the various "biographies" of Daniel Boone. Ironically, this positive view of the Indian only took hold after the native tribes of the Eastern states had already been completely vanquished and marginalized.

For most of the 20th century, Western films handled the Indians in three ways. The most typical depiction is that of the "force of nature." In these films, generally set on the Great Plains, the plot deals mainly with white people conflicting amongst each other, with the threat of an Indian attack always looming menacingly in the background. There are no particular Indian antagonists; they are neither heroes nor villains, just forces of nature, like the wilderness itself, that pose an environmental threat to the white protagonists. From a mythological perspective, these Indian characters may be seen as "threshold guardians"—powerful figures that guard the entryway into the divine realm (the Western frontier), whom the hero must overcome in order to continue on his journey. Their role is functional, without any moral quality, and they could just as easily be replaced with a swarm of locusts, a tornado, or a stampeding herd.

Occasionally in these films, one Indian character, typically the chief, will actually be given a few lines. Here, the noble savage is often depicted. He is a brave warrior, willing to fight tremendous odds against a better-equipped army in order to defend his people and his way of life. The third type of depiction, which is by far the least common, is when the Indians are the actual antagonists, drawing first blood against the white people and provoking violence amongst peaceful settlers. The prejudice that many modern audiences have against the genre, the belief that all Westerns are just about cowboys versus Indians, is just plain wrong. Most Westerns are not about

Indians at all. When Indians do appear, they are more likely to be depicted as either victims of white aggression, or simple forces of nature, that are neither good nor bad.

The history of the treatment of the Indian in Westerns is complex. Many of the early silent-era Westerns were Indian subjects, in which Indians played central roles and were often well developed characters. When the genre faced its first major decline in the Depression era, the Western became almost exclusively a B-picture genre, resulting in much more simple scenarios in which the Indian was typecast primarily into the "force of nature" role. This was a diminution for the Indian character, as he was rarely seen as a real person, just as a character who in numbers was a natural threat and in solitude was a figure of disdain. This simplistic and negative depiction of the Indian continued through the grand revival of the genre in 1939 and through the 1940s. Then, in 1950, two films were released that depicted the Indian not only in a positive light, but as the tragic victim of the white man's corruption and greed. *Broken Arrow* (1950) and *Devil's Doorway* (1950) were seminal films that pioneered what was later to be referred to as the "civil rights Western."

The evolution of respect for the Indian in Westerns could be traced by looking at some key films. The first feature-length version of James Fenimore Cooper's most famous novel, *The Last of the Mohicans* (1920), depicts a variety of Indian characters, from the villainous savage, Uncas (Albert Roscoe), to the noble and gentle Chingachgook (Theodore Lerch) and the solemnly tragic Tamenund (Jack McDonald). In this film, Indians play major roles and are more or less depicted as real men. A few years later, in the film adaptation of Zane Grey's famous novel *The Vanishing American* (1925), we see the Indian as a tragic hero who is ultimately betrayed and destroyed by the villainous white men around him. A few years later, *The Big Trail* (1930), which featured John Wayne in his first starring role, depicted Indians as faceless forces of nature amidst the other natural dangers of the Great Plains. The film's treatment of the Indian was emblematic of the way they would be treated throughout Depression-era Hollywood, when Westerns were relegated to B-movie status and the Indian limited to the role of anonymous natural threat. After nine years of sticking it out in serial Westerns, Wayne was given his second opportunity to star in an A-picture, in John Ford's *Stagecoach* (1939). As for the Indian, his treatment in this film, and in most films of that time, was virtually the same as in *The Big Trail*.

A brief but telling scene in John Ford's *My Darling Clementine* (1945) illustrates a general prejudice felt towards Indians in pre–1950s Westerns. In the first act of the film, Wyatt Earp (Henry Fonda) is trying to get a shave, but is continually interrupted by bullets flying into the barber shop. It appears that Injun Joe is in the saloon, drunk, and shooting aimlessly in all directions. Earp sneaks into the saloon and disarms the disorderly savage with a blow to the head, then drags him outside. "What kinda town is this?" Earp exclaims reproachfully. "Sellin' liquor to Indians!" In the West, it is common knowledge that all Indians are drunks if given alcohol. Hence, liquor should be withheld from the ignorant savages, just as candy should be withheld from little children. Earp tells the drunkard, "Indian, get outta town and stay out!" He punctuates his statement by kicking Injun Joe in the rump. Though the treatment of the Indian is retrograde, it does depict him as a tragic, pitiful figure, as opposed to a savage force of nature. He is humanized a bit in that he is given a face, albeit a pathetic, disparaging face. In the 1940s, the Indian began to be depicted more often as an abject victim of white aggression, rather than the instigator of hostilities, as seen in films such as *They Died with Their Boots On* (1941), *Buffalo Bill* (1944), and *Fort Apache* (1948).

Starting with *Broken Arrow* and *Devil's Doorway*, a much more respectful, remorseful, and even reverential treatment of the Indian took hold in the Westerns of the 1950s, completely reversing the genre's projection of the Indian archetype. In 1946, Wyatt Earp established himself as a heroic man of action by degrading and exiling an Indian. By 1960, the principle heroes of *The Magnificent Seven*, Chris (Yul Brynner) and Vin (Steve McQueen), establish their characters in a diametrically opposite way. Old Sam up and died on the street. His coffin is mounted on the hearse and ready to be buried up on Boot Hill, but there's one problem — Sam was an Indian, and the white men in town say he's not fit to be buried in the white man's cemetery. Chris and Vin drive the hearse up to Boot Hill, facing off with a band of bigoted, gun-toting ruffians in the process, just to give a dead Indian a proper burial. Their treatment of Old Sam amounts to a somber reverence for the symbolic corpse of the Indian peoples, whom the white men so callously destroyed in their conquest of the West. The hero is now defined by his abiding respect for the Indian, rather than his loathing of them.

The Vanishing American

"We have unmistakable proof that throughout all past time there has been a ceaseless devouring of the weak by the strong ... a survival of the fittest." This statement, quoted from Herbert Spencer's "First Principles," is the opening title card for *The Vanishing American* (1925). It espouses the philosophy of Social Darwinism, the prevailing rationalization of the conquering European imperialists, who at different intervals either wiped out, disenfranchised, or enslaved all of Africa, most of Asia, and the entire western hemisphere. The message expressed within the statement is that the noble savage must make way for the noble gentleman. Because this doctrine is veiled in the empirical and objective guises of science and history, it is beyond the field of subjective morality, and therefore it is not immoral. This specious reasoning allowed white men to commit genocide and enslave hundred of thousands, while still calling themselves righteous Christians. The rationalizations used by imperialists are political as well as philosophical, as Buscombe (1988) points out:

> From the beginning, Europeans have perceived Native Americans according to their own political and economic needs. Around the year 1000 Vikings from Greenland and Iceland met Native Americans in "Vinland" and described them as "small and treacherous-looking"—and killed them. Five hundred years later Columbus found them gentle and physically strong—and helped enslave them. New England Puritans in the 17th century saw them as devil-worshippers or even children of Satan—and massacred them with the help of divine providence. Throughout Native American-white history, as Francis Jennings puts it, the myth of "an Indian Menace" was "the boomerang effect of the European Menace to the Indians."

The first sequence of *The Vanishing American* depicts the conquest of the indigenous "cliff-dwellers" of the ancient desert lands of the American southwest by the more aggressive warrior tribes. It is set in Monument Valley, the timeless stage of the Western myth, which would later become the signature setting of most of John Ford's Westerns. The explicit message is that the "ceaseless" conquest of the weak by the strong was originally exhibited in the warfare between the native tribes, hence there was no ethical difference between the conquest of one native tribe over another and the conquest of the Europeans over all the natives.

Once again, the reasoning is specious. It is based on the ever popular "Naturalistic Fallacy" (also known as the "is/ought" fallacy), which states that because something seems to happen naturally (e.g., the strong defeating the weak), then it is natural and therefore morally correct. The reasoning is fallacious, because it equates objective observation ("is") with subjective morality ("ought"). Just because something naturally *is* a certain way, it doesn't mean that it *ought* to be that way. Just because history, nature, and evolution have shown the tendency for the strong to wipe out the weak doesn't mean that this *ought* to occur. Furthermore, the logic of legitimizing European imperialism by documenting the fact that native tribes have also conquered each other is also flawed. The logic here would be: Though the wiping out of the cliff-dwellers by the warrior tribes may have been wrong, and the wiping out of the native tribes by the Europeans was also wrong, the coexistence of the two somehow makes everything right. In other words, "*two wrongs make a right*," which is a syllogism that anyone can recognize as faulty. The logical corollary of the "naturalistic" approach to this problem is that some day, a stronger race or creed will appear which will wipe out or imperialize the white peoples of the Earth. By the same reasoning, would the future genocide of white Christians be considered just another appropriate step on the ladder of social evolution?

Despite its philosophically flawed beginning, the film goes on to depict an extremely sympathetic portrait of an Indian hero, the likes of which would not be seen again until Anthony Mann's *Devil's Doorway* (1950). The two films are quite similar, in that they both depict Indians as heroic World War veterans who return to America, only to be further mistreated by the white people they risked their lives to defend. As the hero of *The Vanishing American,* Nophaie (Richard Dix), explains: "Since we are Americans, we go fight. Maybe if we fight ... maybe if we die ... our country will deal more fairly with our people." The tragic theme of the red man fighting a war for the white man who still abuses him is dealt with in parallel symbolism, via Nophaie's desperate but unrequited love for the white schoolmarm on his reservation, Marion (Lois Wilson). Though he deserves to be loved by her in return, we know that this can never be, because his racial iniquity will never earn him the ultimate Westerner's redemption, the hand of a pure white woman in marriage. Miscegenation, especially between a white woman and a man of a darker skin color, was a taboo subject in film for most of the 20th century. In the final sequence, Nophaie dies a martyr's death after quelling a rebellion of the mistreated Indians against their corrupt reservation agent. As a reward, Marion declares her love for him, but he only basks in her affection for a moment before he dies. Marion quickly transfers her affection to a white soldier, as Nophaie vanishes into memory.

The White Indian

To the Christian settlers, God and Nature were separate, and in certain ways — such as in the original sin of sexuality — the two were at odds. To the Indians, God and Nature were one. God was Nature, Nature was God. In conquering the Indians, the whites established their God over the land. However, in conquering over both the Indians and their gods, certain whites assumed the Indians' reverence towards the sanctity of the wilderness. These men, "White Indians," were frontiersmen who, in spirit, were more like Indians than white men. The White Indian came to embody the true spirit of the Western hero. It is this duality, the white Christian with the heart of a red native, which represents the reconciliation between these two conflicting aspects of the American identity. The White Indian is both wild and civilized; he belongs to both the Old World and the New World, and though he is Christian by birth, he is almost pagan in his devout veneration of the land.

In mythological terms, two recurring Western archetypes, the white frontiersman and the Indian brave, can both be linked to the most ancient heroic archetype, the hunter hero, whose foray into the wilderness is symbolic of the descent into the unconscious or the soul. While the physical hunter is seeking his prey, the mythological hunter is seeking the essence of his soul, or in psychological terms, the essence of his identity. Like the hunter, the Western hero must become like the beast he seeks in order to find and conquer him. He must become as violent and aggressive as the man he seeks to vanquish. And when the moment comes for the kill, at the shootout or showdown, there is "atonement" between the hero and his shadow figure (to borrow Joseph Campbell's use of the term). The hunter reveres his prey at the moment he kills it, drinking its blood in a ritual act of worship, in which he sanctifies the animal's act of sacrifice and becomes "at one" with the animal's spirit. So too does the Western hero kill his man, attaining his vengeance with both honor and reverence, and becoming "at one" with his own shadow. The achievement of vengeance is a moment of epiphany for the hero, a realization that the same dark forces at work in the antagonist's soul are also at work within the hero's soul as well.

The integration of the frontiersman and Indian brave archetypes via the common symbol of the hunter hero creates a synergy between the two mythologies that materializes in the figure of the White Indian. On a psychological level, this archetype represents an unconscious need for white Americans to justify the systematic destruction and elimination of the Indian peoples. By assimilating the spirit and ideals of the Indian into the white American ethos, we negate the sense that he is vanquished and destroyed. Yes, the "Vanishing American" is gone, but he lives on as a crucial element within the central heroic figure of American culture. He is an inextricable part of the Western hero's identity and an irreplaceable figure in the American mythology. And on a psychological level, the integration of the Indian spirit into the Western hero's character is an "atonement." By ritually reenacting, via the cultural medium of film, the critical moment in history in which the white hunter killed the Indian, the Indian's spirit is resurrected, and the sin of slaying him is atoned, as the white hunter becomes "at one" with the people he destroyed.

The archetypal Western hero, rather than being an "Indian hater," is typically portrayed as not only a friend to the Indian, but as his only sympathetic ear among the throngs of Indian-hating bigots crowding into the frontier and pushing the red man out. The hero's alliance with the Indian, his intimate knowledge of his customs, language, and landscape, his shared reverence of nature, freedom, and the open plains, his mutual respect for the endangered life of the buffalo, and his sympathy for the Indian's plight, add to the notion that the hero has more in common with the Indian than with the average white man, especially the white Easterner, whose refined manners are typically a thin veneer for the hypocrisy, mendacity, corruption, and greed of civilized society. In Westerns, the White Indian is most often depicted as a cavalry scout, as portrayed by John Wayne in *Fort Apache* and *Hondo* (1953), Ben Johnson in *She Wore a Yellow Ribbon* (1949) and *Rio Grande* (1950), Charlton Heston in *Arrowhead*, and Kirk Douglas in *The Indian Fighter*. Sometimes, the White Indian is a white man who has "gone native" to live among the Indians, either abandoning white society by choice or being taken captive. The former case is depicted in *The Last of the Mohicans* (1920/1992) and *Dances with Wolves* (1990), while the latter case is depicted in *A Man Called Horse* (1970) and *Little Big Man* (1971). Other times, the archetype is portrayed as a mountain man, such as the characters of Uncle Zeb (Arthur Hunnicutt) in Howard Hawks's *The Big Sky* (1952), and the title character (Robert Redford) in Sydney Pollack's *Jeremiah Johnson* (1972).

The Indian Fighter

In André De Toth's *The Indian Fighter* (1955), the White Indian is a cavalry scout, Johnny Hawks (Kirk Douglas), who seems to be the only white man in America who appreciates the naturalist poetics of the Native American. After hearing that there is gold on Chief Red Cloud's territory, Johnny tries to explain the pragmatic but morally bankrupt philosophy of materialism to the Sioux leader: "Gold will buy horses, blankets.... You're very rich!" The chief (Eduard Franz) wisely replies: "Will gold bring back the buffalo your people will kill? Will it clean the streams your people will fill with filth as they search for the yellow iron? Will it bring back the beauty of the land? I'm already rich in the only wealth I want ... that which you see about us." Here, Red Cloud refers to the untainted virgin woods surrounding his camp.

Like all White Indian characters in Westerns, Johnny's story calls into play conflicted allegiances. His independent values guarantee that he will never fit in, either among the whites with whom he shares his racial heritage or among the Indians, with whom he shares a spiritual bond with the land. There will always come a point where someone, typically a white man, will ask him: "What side are you on?" (In this film, the question comes from Captain Trask (Walter Abel), the captain of the cavalry brigade in danger of being massacred by the Sioux.) Invariably, the White Indian does choose a side — the white side, using his knowledge of the Indian to help his white brethren. This help can come in two ways. In the first way, the White Indian, in the tradition of Kit Carson and the loyal cavalry scout, will help the cavalry destroy the Indians in battle. In the second way, he will use his allies among the Indians to broker a last-minute peace deal, thus averting a massacre and the spillage of both red and white blood. The Indian ally is typically a female love interest who is also the chief's daughter — the archetypal "red bride" or "Pocahontas" theme. This is the case in *The Indian Fighter* and *The Big Sky.*

But while the White Indian is the one man able to conjure a temporary peace between these two competing communities, he typically cannot find peace for himself. Unable to settle down in any community, red or white — unable to civilize his own wild nature — the White Indian must reconcile himself to an unsettled existence on the wild frontier. Thus, at the end of *The Indian Fighter*, we leave both the Sioux camp and the cavalry fort, as we see the wagon train of white settlers traveling westwards. In the stream, surrounded by his beloved wilderness, we see Johnny and Onahti (Elsa Martinelli), his untamed red bride, both naked, cavorting like young animals, but clearly unattached to either the white or Indian communities. We leave them in this idealistic state, choosing not to acknowledge the racial conflict that will doubtlessly affect their future lives and the lives of their children.

The Last of the Mohicans

A common leitmotif in James Fenimore Cooper's novels is the white child being raised by Native Americans, e.g. Hawkeye in *The Last of the Mohicans*. In giving the hero Indian surrogate parents and having him raised in "the wild," Cooper's tales seem to key in to a sense of wish fulfillment that is universal to all hero mythologies. In his book *The Myth of the Birth of the Hero* (1914), Otto Rank outlined the basic pattern of psychological themes in the archetypal hero's saga. According to Rank, shortly after the hero's birth, he is separated from his biological parents and "...is saved by animals, or by lowly people." The wish fulfillment experienced vicariously by the young reader is the fantasy of being raised, not by his ordinary, boring, and mundane real parents, but rather by wild animals or by people who are as wild as animals. Hence, the plethora of stories in which a young boy runs off to the circus to work and play among the animals and sideshow freaks, as in James Otis Kaler's seminal novel, *Toby Tyler, or, Ten Weeks with the Circus* (1880); or stories in which a boy is raised by wild animals, as in Rudyard Kipling's *The Jungle Book* (1894) and Edgar Rice Burroughs's *Tarzan of the Apes* (1912); or stories in which a boy sails off with wild pirates, as in Robert Louis Stevenson's *Treasure Island* (1883), and so on. These stories appeal to young boys because they deal with the conflict of wanting to live a wild life of freedom, while simultaneously cherishing their comfortable home and civilized parents. The theme of the boy-hero growing up in the wild was particularly popular in the late 19th and early 20th centuries, which happens to coincide with the closing of the Western frontier and the subsequent emergence of the American frontier myth. In relating to and identifying with the White Indian hero, the boy identifies with a character who — like himself — is part civilized, but also part wild. The primitive, wild side of the Western hero's character stems from his intimate relationship with the Native American. Hence, the Native American in this instance symbolizes an infantile state of freedom and wildness (in Freudian terminology, the "id") that exists before parental forces instill the discipline and domestic restraint required by civilized society (the "superego").

Of the many film depictions of James Fenimore Cooper's *The Last of the Mohicans*, Michael Mann's 1992 version is the most recent, the best produced, and the most accessible to modern audiences. It is an extremely well made and beautiful film, depicting Colonial-era New York State as the natural paradise of virgin woodlands it once was (the movie was actually filmed in the Blue Ridge Mountains of North Carolina). In keeping with the origin of the frontier myth, the captivity narrative, the plot is essentially a series of captivities and rescues. This plot provides a canvass for the true message of the film — the spirit of the Native American and its relation to the White Indian. Cooper's "Leatherstocking" character, known better by his Indian name, Hawkeye (Daniel Day Lewis), is a white man raised by an adoptive Mohican father, Chingachgook (Russel Means). While Cooper gave his White Indian character the more rustic English name of Natty Bumpo, the film gives him the more proper English name of Nathaniel Poe, though it doesn't really matter, for at heart, the character is really Hawkeye, the white man with the Mohican soul, whom Cooper describes as "the man without a cross." Hawkeye is a white man not tied down by the constrictions of Christianity, white civilization, or allegiance to the English crown.

The film begins with a deer hunt. Chingachgook, Hawkeye, and his adoptive brother, Uncas (Eric Schweig), chase down and kill a deer. Chingachgook recites an ancient hunter's prayer of grace: "*We're sorry to kill you, Brother. We do honor to your courage and speed, your strength.*" Though the blood ritual is implied, the filmmakers cut to the next scene rather than show it, perhaps because they did not want to suggest that these men are savages. In truth, the hunter's prayer and blood-drinking ritual are used as a means of exorcising the savage element out of the necessary act of hunting and killing. The true savages, as the film depicts, are the French and English officers, who employ wholesale slaughter of white soldiers and Indian warriors in order to further their kings' imperialistic ambitions. Nevertheless, the most savage character in the film is Magua (Wes Studi), the Huron antagonist who allies his Indian warriors with the French, purely out of a desire to fulfill his vengeance quest against the English officer, Colonel Munro (Maurice Roëves). As Magua states: "*When the Grey Hair* [Munro] *is dead, Magua will eat his heart. Before he dies, Magua will put his children under the knife, so the Grey Hair will know his seed is wiped out forever.*"

Magua is the most savage character, because his blood lust is so great that it is directed not just at the man who wronged him, but also at his innocent young daughters, Cora (Madeline Stowe) and Alice (Jodhi May). In the Western, the killing and/or rape of women is always dishonorable, the true mark of the savage, whether it is performed by a white or an Indian. Incidentally, Magua does eventually kill Munro and cuts out his heart, though the filmmakers cut to the next shot before Magua eats it. Before Munro dies, Magua promises him that he will kill his children. This seems a bit out of character for this savage, who would have been more likely to take Munro captive, so he could show him the actual sight of his daughters being gang-raped and then burned alive. But however savage Magua is, we are not left to think that his savagery is born out of pure malice and spite. His justification is stated plainly: "*Magua's village and lodges were burnt. Magua's children were killed by the English. I was taken as slave by the Mohawk who fought for Grey Hair. Magua's wife believed he was dead and became the wife of another....*"

As with most Westerns, the film deals with the conflict between civilization and savagery and also idealizes the pioneer spirit of those intrepid men and women who chose to live on the frontier. After witnessing the remains of a Huron massacre of a white family's homestead, Cora asks Hawkeye: "Why were those people living in this defenseless place?" He responds, *"...they headed out here 'cause the frontier's the only land available to poor people. Out here they're beholden to none, not livin' by another's leave."* Within this explanation, we see the ideals of independence, individualism, and isolationism, which will became the hallmark values of the frontiersman hero and the pioneer spirit.

As the series of rescues and captivities ensue, romance develops between Hawkeye and Cora, as well as between Uncas, the full-blooded Indian, and Alice. While Hawkeye and Cora seem at first to be mismatched, their pairing is allowed, as they are both white. But Uncas and Alice, like Romeo and Juliet, are truly star-crossed lovers that could never be. Miscegenation, when the female is a pure-blooded white, is still considered risqué, though it is perfectly acceptable when the male is white and the female is Indian. Uncas is killed by Magua in a desperate attempt to rescue Alice. Distraught over the death of Uncas, Alice jumps of a cliff to her death, rather than submitting to lifelong captivity as Magua's unwilling wife. This suicide is tantamount to the archetypal use of "the last bullet," the white woman choosing an honorable death rather than the dishonor that would result from being ravaged by a savage.

In the final scene, the film evolves from a romantic epic into a self-reflective, melancholic elegy. Chingachgook's climactic soliloquy, delivered as the sun sets over the Western frontier, manages to be both mythopoeic and consummatory at the same time: *"The frontier moves with the sun and pushes the red man of these wilderness forests in front of it, until one day there will be nowhere left. Then our race will be no more, or be not us.... The frontier place is for people like my white son and his woman and their children. And one day there will be no more frontier, and men like you will go too, like the Mohicans."* Chingachgook's prophetic vision correctly foresees not only the demise of the frontier and the Indians who inhabit it, but of the white frontiersman as well.

A Man Called Horse

A Man Called Horse (1970) takes the form of a captivity narrative, but it leads its audience in a novel direction. John Morgan (Richard Harris) is an English lord on holiday, hunting on the frontier of the American Northwest territory. A man born into wealth and privilege, he is existentially lost, so he travels to the wilderness in search of himself. His guides are slaughtered by a Sioux war party, but he is taken captive. After enduring many tortures, he proves himself a man (as opposed to a "horse," as he'd been called and treated by his captors). He demonstrates himself worthy of manhood in the tribe through an act of violence, by killing a brave from the enemy tribe, the Shoshone. Tellingly, while the act of killing itself is accomplished efficaciously by John, it is the culmination of the act — the scalping — which seems most difficult for him. While he killed before as a hunter and as a soldier, the act of scalping is perceived by him as a "savage" act. He must overcome this psychological border between the civilized and the savage before he can become an Indian.

John is initiated into the order of Sioux braves via the ordeal of the Sun Vow, in which he is suspended from the roof of the hunting lodge by beaver claws that are cut into his pectoral muscles. In a delirium of unimaginable pain, he sees a vision of the tribe's spirit animal — the white buffalo — which delivers to him a psychological message of humility and inner peace. This ordeal (aka vision quest or initiation rite) completes John's apotheosis, transforming him from Englishman to Sioux. By becoming an Indian, by becoming de-civilized, he symbolically dies and is reborn as a White Indian. He represents the European turned American, the Easterner turned Westerner, the genteel English fop transformed into a rugged, tough, self-made man. In the film's climax, John becomes the war leader of his tribe, using English army maneuvers to defeat a party of raiding Shoshone. Afterwards, John leaves the tribe, but not as an escaping captive. He is escorted by a Sioux war party and takes his leave as a departing hero. Though he did not expect to be taken captive on his American journey, in the end, John's purpose in venturing into the wilderness was successful. He found what he was searching for ... himself.

In becoming a White Indian, John discovers a deeper understanding of the nature of existence. He realizes that the material possessions he owned and sought, such as the prize bearskins he was hunting as a wealthy sportsman, are meaningless. What is actually meaningful is a true appreciation for the beauty and wonder in life. For the White Indian, this appreciation arises as a function of falling in love with his red bride, who represents nature, as well as the corresponding awareness that nature cannot be appreciated as a material possession (as the white Europeans understand it), but rather as a part of oneself. The mountain man, Uncle Zeb (Arthur Hunnicutt), in Howard Hawks's *The Big Sky* (1952) explains this primal connection between nature, woman, and inner self: "By-beaver there's nothin' prettier than the upper Missouri! She's wild and pretty like a virgin woman. But the prettiest part of it all belongs to her people, Blackfeet ... proud Indians. But they ain't gonna let no white men spy their country. The only thing they're a-feared of is the white man's sickness ... grabbin'! White men don't seen nothin' pretty less they want to grab it, and the more they grab, the more they wanna grab. It's like a fever and they can't get cured."

Once John was initiated into the tribe as a warrior, he was allowed to take a wife. His choice was the chief's sister, Running Deer (Corinna Tsopei). But after his red bride is killed in the Shoshone raid, John decides to leave the Sioux and return to his own people. The Indian woman is his personal connection to the true wonders of nature, appreciated not as an external thing to be conquered, but as an internal spirit to be integrated. Without Running Deer, he has no reason to stay among the Indians, but he leaves the Sioux a changed man. No longer a conquering European, he is cured of the "white man's sickness." John can return to the wilderness without the desire to "grab" it, because he no longer sees himself as a man encountering nature. He is now a part of nature itself. It is this integrative relationship with nature espoused by the Indians, as opposed to the exploitative relation-ship espoused by the Europeans, that is at the heart of the Indian character in Westerns. This is the lesson their character has to teach us.

6

Oedipal and Biblical Westerns

"I'll have no female boys bearing my name."
— Major Tetley (Frank Conroy) in *The
Ox-Bow Incident* (1943)

The Western depicts the period of American history in which the lawless wilderness of the frontier was tamed into a modern civilization. From
this struggle arose the iconic figures of the Old West, whose legends and
exploits would become the seed-grain of the figurative book of Genesis for
an American mythology. The Western provides the perfect scenario for the
timeless and archetypal themes that symbolize the most basic conflicts of the
human condition. These themes may be called "Biblical," as they appear in
the Bible, and they may also be called "oedipal," as they represent the basic
conflicts of the family drama, and they may also be called "mythical," in that
both the Biblical and oedipal themes share their origins in the realm of collective unconscious referred to as "myth," which, in a psychoanalytic interpretation, is the collective projection of universal psychological issues. In
short, it doesn't matter if the setting is 19th-century America, medieval
England, ancient Greece, or the Garden of Eden, the most elemental conflicts in the male drama will always be Father vs. Son and Brother vs. Brother.
These psychological conflicts are universal — they will exist wherever there
are parents, children, and siblings, who simultaneously love and hate their
mothers, brothers, sisters and fathers.

The Sibling Rivalry Western

Alfred Adler's theory of psychology posits the rivalry between siblings
as the single most important antecessor to neurotic conflict. The rivalry

begins with tension between the siblings, who both desire the undivided love and attention of their parental figures. Unlike Freud's oedipal rivalry, the desire for parental love can be directed at either or both parents, not just the opposite-sex parent. In Freud's theory, the oedipal complex is resolved via the projection of psychosexual desire away from the mother and onto an appropriate love object, allowing the male child to perceive the father as a role model to identify with, rather than as an antagonistic figure. In Adler's theory, the sibling rivalry is not resolved, per se; rather, the psychic energy generated from the conflict is channeled and sublimated into other activities, especially those activities which are competitive in nature. He refers to this mechanism as "compensation." The siblings may continue to compete for the rest of their lives, though the purpose or goal of their competitive nature, which had its origins in the need for parental attention, is no longer the driving force. The behavior pattern itself is self-perpetuating. The need to compete and achieve above the other sibling continues to exist despite the lack of any specific end or goal.

The archetypal sibling rivalry theme in film has several levels of conflict. The first level is moral. One brother is good, the other is bad, and they will always come into conflict over a moral choice that can result in either a right or wrong outcome. To reference the most influential sibling rivalry story, Cain and Abel, the conflict begins with Abel's morally right decision to give his best lamb as a sacrifice to God, while Cain chooses wrongly, in deciding to sacrifice his worst fruits. This moral issue relates directly to a second level of conflict, the issue of parental favoritism. God, the archetypal father, favored Abel over Cain. This favoritism was the primary impetus towards conflict between Cain and Abel, just as conflict arose later in the Bible as a result of Abraham's favoritism of Isaac over Ishmael, Isaac's favoritism of Jacob over Esau, and Jacob's favoritism of Joseph over his elder sons. When there are two parents present, a third level of conflict is raised, as one son (the gentle one) is loved more by the mother, while the other son (the aggressive one) is loved more by the father. This pattern of favoritism is evocative of Isaac's family drama, in which the gentle son, Jacob, was favored by his mother, Rebecca, and the aggressive son, Esau, was favored by his father, Isaac. And finally, a fourth level of conflict is romantic. There is a rivalry for the love or affection of the same woman. In this sense, the sibling rivalry theme in film recapitulates the oedipal rivalry, in which father and son vie for the attention of the same woman: mother. In the sibling rivalry, it is the two brothers who vie for the attention of the same woman, who typically plays the role of a symbolic mother figure.

Duel in the Sun

King Vidor's epic, *Duel in the Sun* (1946), depicts post–Civil War Texas as an American land of Canaan. The desert landscape is stark, foreboding, and beautiful. There is only one law in the vast territorial ranch owned by Senator Jackson McCanles (Lionel Barrymore), and that law is his own word. Like the kings and pharaohs of the Greek myths and the Bible, the Western cattle baron is the omnipotent ruler of his domain. His sons must bow to his authority, but they also look forward to the day when one of them will be king. The sibling rivalry in *Duel in the Sun* is between the older brother, Jesse (Joseph Cotton), and his younger brother, Lewt (Gregory Peck). The rivalry between brothers exists on all four of the levels listed above. Jesse is the good son: kind, gentle, and civilized. Lewt is the bad son: cruel, violent, and savage. Their moral conflict involves the building of a railroad in their family's territory. Jesse is for the railroad, perceiving it as a good commodity that will help all of Texas. Lewt, however, is against the railroad, as it conflicts with his father's imperialistic need for absolute control over his vast tracts of land. This leads to the issue of favoritism. Lewt is his father's favorite, as he represents the wild, aggressive, reckless kind of man that the senator himself was when he was younger. Jesse, on the other hand, is his mother's (Lillian Gish) favorite, as he represents her ideal type of man, the Southern gentleman. And finally, there is a romantic rivalry over Pearl (Jennifer Jones), the beautiful halfbreed whom both Jesse and Lewt desire. The moral nature of the two brothers is revealed most explicitly in their differential treatment of Pearl. Jesse treats Pearl with honor, kindness and respect, while Lewt brutalizes her, uses her for sex, but refuses to marry her, because of her mixed racial heritage.

Pursued

Raoul Walsh's *Pursued* (1947) is often referred to as the first psychological Western, or alternatively, a "Freudian Western." With its Freudian themes of repressed childhood memories and oedipal overtones, *Pursued* was an early attempt at using the Western scenario as a backdrop for a serious psychological drama, though it was clearly not the first — *The Ox-Bow Incident*, to be discussed later, predates *Pursued* by four years. Despite its reputation as a "Freudian Western," the central conflict in the film is the rivalry between two brothers, but I doubt that anyone will start calling the film an "Adlerian Western." In the film, Jeb Rand's family is killed in front of his eyes when he is just a little boy. He is rescued by Ma Callum (Judith Anderson), who takes him home and raises him as her adoptive son. He grows up living with his adoptive sister Thorley (Theresa Wright) and adoptive brother Adam (John Rodney). His memories of the horrific night of violence become almost completely repressed, existing only as nightmares and sudden flashbacks.

Conflict arises between Jeb (Robert Mitchum) and Adam, who considers Jeb an "outsider" and begrudges him his equal share in the family's property, as well as Jeb's equal share in the affections of both Ma and Thor. As the children grow into adulthood, the fondness between Jeb and Thor goes beyond sister and brotherly love, which causes Adam to become even more resentful. When the war against Spain breaks out, Jeb fulfills the home's quota for draftees by joining the army. Upon returning home, he and Thor make plans to marry, while Jeb explores his mysterious past, which still haunts his dreams. The conflict with Adam comes to a head — "this ranch isn't big enough to hold the two of us!" — so they toss a coin to see who will leave. Jeb loses the toss. After a vicious fistfight with Adam, Jeb leaves the ranch, vowing to return the next day for Thor. The root of Adam's hatred for Jeb, rivalry over Thor's love, is revealed that night, when Thor tells Adam that she will be leaving him and the ranch to live with Jeb. "You hate me then!" Adam tells her, feeling betrayed. "I love you," Thor replies. "I always thought the three of us would never be apart." "Three! Three!" Adam shouts back at her with frustration. "But why does he count? It's you and me!" Sensing the taboo, incestuous nature of Adam's feelings, Thor tells him: "You're crazy!"

As a means of keeping his beloved sister to himself, Adam tries to kill Jeb, but in the process, is killed himself. Believing that Jeb killed Adam for reasons other than self-defense, Ma disowns Jeb, and Thor distances herself from him. Eventually, Jeb and Thor reconcile, leading to the dramatic climax, in which Jeb's mysterious backstory is revealed. As the enigmatic Grant Callum (Dean Jagger) and his men try to kill him, Jeb remembers in detail the night in which his father, sister, and two brothers were killed. It was Grant Callum, Ma Callum's brother-in-law, who killed Jeb's family, in retribution for the illicit love affair between Ma Callum and Jeb's father. The film ends with Ma killing Grant before he can lynch Jeb, followed by Thor and Jeb riding off together into the sunset. The mythical plot, involving two generations of families torn apart by forbidden love, sibling rivalry, family feuding, and unforgiven vendettas, is complemented by the psychological structure, in which repressed memories and recurring dreams symbolize illicit desires, latent aggression, and long festering hostilities.

Shadows of the Past. Robert Mitchum as Jeb Rand and Judith Anderson as his adoptive mother, Medora Callum, in Raoul Walsh's *Pursued* (1947, United States Pictures/Warner Bros.).

Jubal (1956)

In *Jubal*, the sibling rivalry is figurative rather than literal. Jubal (Glenn Ford) is a drifter who is taken in by a fatherly cattle baron, Shep (Ernest Borgnine), who gives Jubal a job as a cowboy. Shep takes an immediate liking to Jubal, making him foreman—a promotion which fuels the envious rage of Pinky (Rod Steiger), who believes that he should be the foreman, rather than the newcomer. In Western parlance, the ranch is symbolic of the family home, in which the cattle baron is the father and the cowboys his sons. The foreman is the favored son, the brother who will inherit absolute power over the ranch when the father dies. When a younger or newer cowboy is given the position of foreman, the elder or more senior cowboy will see this as unfair, as it is the most ancient tradition that the eldest son should inherit his father's position. This theme of the younger son supplanting his older brother's position (the theft of the birthright) is a recurring leitmotif in the Bible: Cain and Abel, Ishmael and Isaac, Esau and Jacob, Reuben and Joseph, and others. Pinky's jealousy of Jubal's favored position in Shep's ranch is understandable, as it recalls the same feeling of rivalry felt by all children, who crave to be the favored child of their beloved parents.

An oedipal theme is also apparent in *Jubal*. Just as the cattle baron is the figurative father, his wife is the figurative mother. Shep's wife, the young and alluring Mae (Valerie French), plays the role of temptress to Shep, Jubal, and Pinky. As the boss's wife, Mae is forbidden fruit. Sexual desire for her is figuratively incestuous, as the act of sex would be a betrayal to Jubal's and Pinky's father figure, Shep. Mae is infatuated with Jubal, but since he is the good son, he rebuffs her sexual advances. On the other hand, Pinky, the bad son, is infatuated with Mae, but she is disgusted by him. The simultaneous refutation of both Mae, the rejecting mother, and Shep, the dispossessing father, has a destructive effect on Pinky's fragile ego. He concocts a plan, a'la Shakespeare's *Othello*, to make Shep believe that Jubal and Mae are having an affair. In a scene that is highly evocative of the Oedipus myth, Shep confronts Jubal in a saloon. He tries to shoot Jubal, who winds up killing Shep in self-defense. On a symbolic level, Oedipus slays Laius as a consequence of their rivalry over Jocasta.

Meanwhile, back at the ranch, Pinky rapes and beats Mae to the brink of death. His psychosexual energy is given vent in an explosion of aggression, hatred, and lust. But before he can consummate his diabolical plot by lynching Jubal for his killing of Shep, thus eliminating his rival forever, Mae delivers her dying words to the doctor, exonerating Jubal completely, and inculpating Pinky for the crimes of raping and beating her and conspiring to murder both Shep and Jubal. In the end, Pinky is killed for his many sins, while Jubal lives to run the ranch in his figurative father's stead.

Night Passage (1957)

Night Passage depicts the sibling rivalry between Grant McLaine (James Stewart) and his outlaw little brother, Lee (Audie Murphy). In referencing the names of the two highest-ranking Civil War generals, Grant and Lee, the film characterizes the South as America's wild and wayward little brother, who needs to be disciplined but also embraced, as he is taught how to be a good man by his older, more enlightened brother. The eventual reconciliation between the two brothers represents the reconciliation between the North and South during the Reconstruction, which is a recurring theme in the Western genre. The tragic war that pitted brother against brother is frequently cast as a tall shadow in the Western scenario, a recent trauma that needs to be treated and healed.

In the last act of the film, young Lee changes sides and fights with his brother against his former allies, a band of ruthless outlaws. His valor redeems him. Lee dies in the end, in penance for his many sins, just as the Old South had to die in the war in order for a new nation to be born. This death and rebirth is significantly set on the frontier, where the nation itself was reborn through perpetual struggle and bloodshed, from the pre–Colonial era through the 19th century.

The Oedipal Western

Beyond the rivalry for Mother's affections, which in the strict Freudian reading seems vastly overstated, there is another level to the dramatic theme of oedipal rivalry, involving the natural trait for a son to feel that he must equal or surpass his father in the realm of worldly success — whatever this success might entail. Likewise, there is an opposing drive within the father to remain superior to his son, to forever loom over him like a godly master who will always remain more powerful, leaving the son to linger deferentially in his father's shadow. The Western hero, after all, is a man of endless strength, power, and virility. Hence, if the Westerner is a father, then the emergence of a rival who will one day be stronger and more powerful is a direct threat to the Westerner's masculine ego. And if the Westerner is a son, there is an impetus to encounter this dominating figure and challenge his masculinity, in order to prove his own.

Another variation on the oedipal rivalry theme is seen in the father's desire to force his son to follow in his footsteps, to insist that his son love what he loves, hate what he hates, act as he acts, and carry on his father's work regardless of his son's own hopes and dreams. The conflict between the father's domineering control and his son's budding autonomy and individuality is an archetypal stage setter for a violent showdown. In Westerns, the father is frequently cast as the character at fault, as it is his duty to step aside for his son and help him make his way in the world. By reacting to his son's desire for achievement and individuality with jealousy and pettiness arising from his own ego concerns, the oedipal father takes on the persona of tyrant and bully. Perhaps, as in Adler's theory, the oedipal rivalry over success is like the sibling rivalry. It originates in competition over Mother's affections, but eventually is transferred onto other pursuits that are less libidinal. In the Western, this transference is psychosexually charged, because the conflict that originated in the sex/love drive is transformed into a conflict that channels the aggression/hate drive. Thus, Eros becomes Thanatos, sex becomes violence, as the drive towards killing, death, and destruction is fueled by latent sexual desires and internal conflicts. The climactic shootout is the supreme symbol of this transference. As a phallic symbol, the gun simultaneously represents both sexuality and violence. Whereas the gun is a symbol of love and intimacy within the father son relationship (the father teaches his son how to shoot), it is with this same object that father and son will face each other, each one bent on the other's destruction.

In essence, it is the father's role to act as a mentor to his son. He must teach the budding hero what it means to be a man of the West and how to act in accordance with the Code of the West. The father is an identification figure for the son, modeling by way of example the style in which a Westerner epitomizes the essential character elements of masculinity, honor, and aggression. In this function, the father is cast as either a negative role model or as a positive role model. In the Western, the dilemma of defending one's honor and masculinity through violence is almost inevitable. The question is, has the father shown his son that violence must be used only in self-defense, or has he set an example of using violence recklessly, as a means to a selfish and destructive end?

The Ox-Bow Incident (1943)

In what is perhaps the first true "psychological Western," *The Ox-Bow Incident* depicts the various levels of involvement and conflict that a group of Western characters engage in during a lynching of three innocent men. The driving force behind the lynching is Major Tetley (Frank Conroy), a former Confederate officer who takes command of a posse searching for the rustlers who killed a local cattleman. He is obsessed with honor and driven to kill, not just to prove his own dominance, but also because he is intent on "making a man" of his son, Gerald (William Eythe). The universal error of the negative father figure in Westerns is the belief that manhood is achieved through violence. He forces his son to commit acts of violence in order to prove he is not a coward. In *Ox-Box Incident*, Tetley fears that his own son is a coward, though it is indicated in the film that his negative attitude towards his son is clearly a projection — Tetley actually fears that he himself is a coward, possibly as a corollary to a shameful incident he experienced in the war, though the details of his backstory are never revealed.

Tetley forces Gerald against his will to join the posse, then forces him at each step to engage in the actual lynching, though it is far from clear that the men they've captured are actually the guilty party. Gerald does display moral courage by standing up with the minority of men who oppose the lynching, which entails defying his own father, but Tetley doesn't understand this kind of courage. For Tetley, courage is only proven through the spilling of another man's blood. When the time comes for the lynching to begin, Tetley forces Gerald to act as one of the executioners. He orders his son to whip one of the horses while the doomed man mounted on it hangs from a noose. When Gerald tries to abstain from the grisly act, his father scolds him: "I'll have no female boys bearing my name!" But when the gun signals for the horses to be whipped, Gerald fails to whip his horse. Tetley approaches Gerald and viciously beats him with the butt of his revolver.

On the way back to town, the posse discovers that they lynched the wrong men. Upon returning home, Tetley locks his son out of his house, dispossessing Gerald for what Tetley perceived as cowardly behavior at the lynching. Gerald, empowered by a sense of moral superiority mixed with a newfound hatred for his father, finally stands up to the major, bringing him down to size with these words, spoken through the closed front door of their home:

> You loved it! That's why you kept them waiting so long. I saw your face — it was the face of a depraved, murderous beast! There are only two things that have ever meant anything to you: power and cruelty. You can't feel pity, you can't even feel guilt. In your heart you knew those men were innocent, yet you were cold crazy to see them hang ... to make me watch it! I could've stopped you with a gun just as any other animal could be stopped from

killing, but I couldn't do it because I'm a coward.... How does it feel to have begot a weakling, Major Tetley? Does it make you afraid that there may be some weakness in you too, that other men might discover and whisper about?

Though the assault was verbal rather than physical, it shot right through the heart of the major, just as if the words were bullets, and with the same effect. Tetley immediately escapes into a back room. A single gunshot is heard off-screen, signifying suicide. After coming out on top of this figurative showdown, slaying his father with his words of truth, Gerald's expression is that of relief. He has resolved the "castration anxiety" within his oedipal complex by overcoming his fear of his father and standing up to him. In doing so, he released his ego from the awful burden of the major's domineering and corrupt tyranny and, ironically, achieved what his father wanted him to do in the first place. Gerald became a man as a function of destroying the life of another man.

Red River

Howard Hawks's first epic Western begins with a wagon train heading west. Tom Dunston (John Wayne) cuts out of the wagon train along with his trusted sidekick, Groot (Walter Brennan), to claim land for his future cattle ranch. As they are in dangerous "Indian country," he leaves his fiancée, Fen (Colleen Gray), behind in the wagon train, giving her his mother's gold bracelet as a token of their future reunion. Ironically, she is killed when the wagon train is attacked by hostile Comanche. Thus, we see the initial development of Dunston as the independent, isolated hero, who is racked with guilt over his decision to leave Fen behind. After Dunston and Groot fight off an attack by a small party of Comanche, Dunston finds the bracelet on a dead brave. The bracelet symbolizes his lost anima — his emotional, sensitive side, which is wrapped up in his feelings for the two goddesses in his life: his deceased mother, as well as his recently defiled and destroyed fiancée. Without an anima to temper his personality, Dunston's character becomes too masculine, resulting in a persona that is over-aggressive, insensitive, stubborn, and tyrannical.

Just before crossing the Red River into Texas, Dunston and Groot are joined by the sole survivor of the massacred wagon train, a young boy named Matt Garth. He has a cow with him, and Dunston has a bull. Together, they have the beginnings of a herd, and the respective sexes of their animals are clearly significant. Matt's female animal represents his own unblemished soul. Unlike Dunston, he can still relate to other people on a human level.

In contrast, Dunston's male animal embodies his psychological defects, represented in his bull-headed solipsism, his lack of empathy for others, and his insensitivity to the needs and ideas of other men, which will be his downfall.

Dunston accepts Matt as his adoptive son, with the elderly Groot playing the part of adoptive grandfather — a wily old coot beloved by both Dunston and Matt. We see the first signs of Dunston's despotism when he brands the cattle with a "D" for his own name. When Matt asks why his mark isn't on the cattle as well, Dunston replies: "I'll put an M on it when you earn it." Matt has no recourse but to accept Dunston's offer. Moments later, two vaqueros approach, telling Dunston that he is on "Don Diego's land." Dunston refuses to acknowledge the Spanish landlord's right to ownership. When the first vaquero tells him that Don Diego earned the land as a grant from the king of Spain, Dunston says: "You mean he took it away from whoever was here before, Indians maybe.... Well, I'm taking it away from him." To punctuate his assertion, Dunston challenges the vaquero to a draw and kills him. He allows the other vaquero to return alone, to tell his Don that there is a new owner to all of the land between the Rio Grande and the Red River. Though Dunston is clearly the hero, he is just as clearly afflicted with the "white man's sickness," his belief in a brand of Social Darwinism (tacitly racial), which justifies his need to grab whatever he wants and by means of force declare that it is rightfully his.

Fourteen years later, Matt (Montgomery Clift) returns from the war to find a ranch full of cattle, but no market for beef in Texas. Dunston's solution is a long and arduous cattle drive to Missouri, an intrepid journey which would initiate the infamous "Chisolm Trail." The cattle drive will resemble the plot of *Mutiny on the Bounty*. Dunston will grow more and more tyrannical as the journey proceeds, until his brutality and single-mindedness reach the level of psychopathology, at which point Matt is obliged to overthrow his despotic father and take command over the drive himself. Before the drive begins, we see that Matt is wearing Dunston's gold bracelet, indicating that all of Dunston's love and emotion is invested in his adoptive son. Therefore, when Matt leads the mutiny against his adoptive father, all of Dunston's emotional energy is darkened, turning into hate and aggression. After the mutiny, Dunston vows to Matt that he will kill him.

Towards the end of the trail, the saga of Matt's life comes full circle. The cattle drive meets up with a wagon train about to be massacred by hostile Comanche. Matt makes the courageous decision to save the wagon train. In this way, Matt revisits the formative trauma of his youth, but now he is a man instead of a boy, and he is able to save the innocent pioneers, while as a boy he could only hide and observe the massacre. Matt falls in love with Tess (Joanne Dru), a girl from the wagon train, who is only vaguely identified as a prostitute. Matt makes the same mistake that Dunston made: He leaves Tess behind with the wagon train, believing that the road ahead is too dangerous for a woman. Like his adoptive father, he gives Tess the golden bracelet as a token of their mutual affection and future reunion. Tess represents the anima figure, filling the role of mother archetype and romantic love interest for both heroes. She is linked to Matt's mother, who died in the first massacre, and also to Dunston's mother, via the bracelet. Figuratively, she represents Dunston's long lost fiancée, resurrected by Matt's heroic rescue of the wagon train.

Hot on Matt's trail, Dunston comes upon the wagon train and encounters Tess. He immediately notices the bracelet and surmises that she and Matt are in love. Now it's Dunston's turn to relive the trauma of an earlier life, as he hears Tess speak of how she begged Matt not to leave her behind, and he remembers the tragic mistake he made fourteen years before. He immediately equates Tess with Fen and imagines that he could go back in time and start anew. He offers Tess a proposition. If she becomes his woman and bears him a son, he'll give her half of everything he owns. Dunston believes that he can use Tess to replace the adoptive son who betrayed him with a biological son who would remain true. As a bonus, in stealing Matt's woman, he would be repaying Matt in kind for stealing his herd. Tess tells Dunston that she will bear him a son on one condition: that he give up his vendetta against Matt. But Dunston's bloodlust is so great that he cannot agree. His impetus to kill Matt (Thanatos) is so great that even the love of a woman (Eros) cannot dispel it.

The climax of *Red River* is one of the most infamous in film history. According to Hollywood rumor, John Wayne told Howard Hawks that he didn't want to die in the movie, as his fans wouldn't like it, since he was the star. In the story that the script was based on, *The Chisolm Trail* by Borden Chase, Dunston is mortally wounded in the climactic scene, though not by Matt. He is carried back to Texas by Matt and Tess, and in a theme evocative of Biblical patriarchs such as Jacob and Joseph, Dunston dies just after he is carried back across the Red River. This Biblical coda renders the Western frontier, Texas in particular, as the American "promised land" and identifies Dunston as a patriarchal Western hero who delivered this land to his people.

In the film, Dunston approaches Matt with a drawn revolver, demanding a showdown. Even though Matt brought the cattle to market on his own, proving that he was right and that Dunston was wrong, Dunston is still not ready to forgive Matt's insurrection and reclaim him as a son. He tries to provoke Matt into drawing his gun, but Matt won't oblige. Dunston shoots at him, but Matt won't budge, even as a bullet slices him across the cheek. "You're soft!" Dunston growls at him. "Won't anything make a man out of you!" He commences to beat Matt savagely with his fists, but Matt still won't fight. Finally, Matt hits his father back, and a long fistfight ensues, which is eventually broken up by Tess, who in her role as figurative mother to both men, scolds them into boyish submission. The two ultra-masculine heroes, stunned by their own powerlessness when faced by a forceful woman, simply stare at her in shock. Dunston turns and says: "You better marry that girl, Matt." "When are you gonna stop telling people what to do?" Matt replies, tongue in cheek. "Right now," Dunston answers penitently. He tells Matt that they'll be adding an "M" to the Red River brand, thus resolving their conflict and repossessing Matt as a son. "You earned it," Dunston tells him, a gleam of pride in his eyes.

The flawed ending nearly ruins one of the best Westerns ever made. The impetus towards a fatal showdown between father and son is built up throughout the entire film. Ending the story with a Hollywood-style happy ending betrays both the dramatic and psychological structure that the film draws upon. Dunston clearly had to die at the end of *Red River*, preferably at the hands of Matt. By ending the story with reconciliation rather than a fatal confrontation, the underlying feeling is that Matt really is soft, at least according to the philosophy of a man like Dunston, who surely would have killed any man that shot, beat, and degraded him in the way that he did to Matt. Furthermore, we're left with the impression that Dunston has also softened. No longer a tyrant, he will sit back peacefully and retire, allowing Matt to take control of the ranch. This notion of withdrawal from the field of action is completely anathema to Dunston's character. While the classic Western hero epitomizes the stance of uncompromising commitment to his own convictions, typically displayed through violence, *Red River* ends with both heroes compromising and choosing nonviolence over their own convictions. Though it is odd to condemn a film for not being violent enough, in the case of *Red River*, the lack of mortal violence in the final meeting between father and son leaves the film with a psychological conflict that is never completely resolved.

Gunman's Walk (1958)

A forgotten gem, this film has been overlooked by film critics and Western aficionados, perhaps because it is too psychological, even for a psychological Western. The focus of *Gunman's Walk* is on the oedipal relationships between a father and his two sons. With little action and not much plot, *Gunman's Walk* is probably the most transparently oedipal of all the oedipal westerns. Lee (Van Heflin) owns the biggest horse ranch in the territory. He led a rowdy life as a younger man, taming the wild frontier with his guts and his guns and taking many a man's life in defense of his horses, his home, and his honor. But things have changed. The territory is ruled by marshals and judges now, and the wild days are over and done with. Despite all of this, Lee still clings to his waning machismo through acts of recklessness and competitiveness, which can be read as unconscious efforts to remain superior to his sons.

Lee's older son, Ed (Tab Hunter), has grown up under the immense shadow of his father's infamous past. Since he was a boy, he has tried to live up to his father's larger-than-life persona, but always felt inadequate, not quite filling his father's sizable shoes. Aside from the conflict between Ed and his father, there is also a conflict between Ed and his brother, Davey (James Darren). Ed plays the role of Cain in the sibling relationship. Like his father, he is an expert horseman, a skilled shooter, a hard drinker, and wild-natured. He is a racist and sees himself as superior to other men. Davey plays the role of Abel. The younger, more effeminate son, he takes after his deceased mother, and we could assume that he was favored by his mother, while Ed, the aggressive son, is clearly favored by his father. Lee is ashamed of Davey's inability to shoot straight and ride hard and cannot relate to Davey's gentle nature and unprejudiced attitude towards the local Indians. Conversely, Lee is proud of Ed's shooting prowess and bravado. But he is also wary of the fact that his older son has become too wild and conceited and that he can no longer control him. It was Lee's idea to have his sons call him "Lee" instead of "Pa," in order to avoid acknowledging his own advancing age, to help him stay one of the boys and dodge the responsibilities of fatherhood. But now Lee regrets that Ed has no respect for him and sees that his older son is desperate to prove that he is as wild and reckless as Lee himself was in his heyday.

The action begins when Paul (Bert Convy), a local Indian, is hired as a ranch hand. Ed develops a sense of rivalry with Paul, as it is well known that Paul is the best horseman in the territory, a claim that Ed must contend with, as he feels that he must be the best at every manly pursuit. It is also clear that Ed cannot bear to play second fiddle to a common Indian on his own ranch. When a beautiful wild white mare appears in the territory, both men try to capture her. The white mare itself is a potent symbol of natural beauty, and she is also symbolic of the absent feminine figure in the family's life. She represents the space left open by the death of the mother and the lack of some desperately needed feminine gentleness (anima) to curb the rampant aggressiveness, competitiveness, and masculine dominance struggles that are tearing the father and sons apart. To be even more quixotic, we could imagine the white mare as the ghost of the dead mother, haunting the family ranch. Because she is treated brutally — the men seek only to capture and enslave her — the mare's presence becomes a curse. And finally, the whiteness of the mare itself has racial overtones. Ed, in his twisted mentality, cannot allow a red man to capture and thereby taint the purity of the snow-white female. In his obsessive recklessness to capture the mare and prove his superiority, Ed kills Paul by pushing him off a bluff.

While Davey is willing to admit the truth, that his brother is responsible for Paul's death, Lee is not willing to accept this fact. He uses all of his political influence and financial resources to exonerate his son in court, to the extent of allowing a stranger to commit perjury. In the frontier court, the words of a white man — even those of a stranger — outweigh the testimony of the Indians, who claim that another white man killed their friend. But Ed, the prodigal son incarnate, is ungrateful. He continues to flout the law, even after his brush with the gallows pole. Here we see the elder son of the Western ranch king as the arrogant feudal prince, who feels himself superior to other people and above the law. There is also a bit of the juvenile delinquent in Ed's character, the "rebel without a cause," whose anger and resentment at his father seem curiously overblown and unjustified. His motivation is clearly psychological, rooted in deep unconscious conflicts rather than reality, just as his self-destructive actions are unmistakably directed against his father, who is trying desperately to save him. Ed's acts of wanton violence drive him heedlessly towards an inevitable showdown with Lee, in which the better man will have to prove himself through deadly force.

Meanwhile, the good brother, Davey, has fallen in love with Clee (Katherine Grant), the charming halfbreed Sioux, who just happens to be the sister of Paul, the man Ed killed. This interracial romance is unthinkable to Lee, whose attitude towards Indians, as his name portends, is more in line with the racism of the Old South than with his progressive and forward-thinking son. Ed shares his father's prejudices towards Indians. Neither of them are willing to apologize to Clee for the death of her brother, which is all she wants from them. While Lee seems disgusted by the notion of his son consorting with a woman of mixed race, Ed tells Davey that he understands why he would desire a roll in the hay with the beautiful halfbreed, but is flabbergasted by the idea that his brother would actually want to marry her.

Sievert (Ray Teal), the stranger who lied in court to save Ed from a hanging, takes the white mare from Lee as payment for his perjury. Upon discovering this, Ed refuses to let Sievert take the horse. At this instant, we realize that the symbolic significance of the mare is the driving force behind Ed's irrational behavior. In an act of rashness, recklessness, ungratefulness, and psychopathic aggressiveness, he shoots Sievert and is quickly jailed for another shooting. In an ironic moment, Lee goes to his younger son for help, and finds him with Clee. He exclaims: "One son in jail, the other mooning over a halfbreed, I don't know which one shames me more!" He says this after Ed has apparently killed his second man in as many days.

The doctor is miraculously able to bring Sievert back from death's door. Lee goes through desperate measures to get Sievert not to testify against his son. But Ed — always the prodigal — breaks out of jail, killing a deputy in his wake. Unwilling to defend his brother after this third shooting and second murder, Davey refuses to help his father find Ed and hide him away. Lee quickly disowns Davey for his apparent disloyalty, while remaining fiercely loyal to his murderous and, at this point, completely psychopathic elder son. When Lee finally finds Ed holed up on a ridge, ready to shoot the posse coming after him, he realizes that his son has gone over the edge. He sees that he has raised Ed to be a killer, just like himself. "I failed," he admits, "it's not your fault. I was a bad father." Ed replies, "I never had a father!" — indicating that instead of a mentor and appropriate role model, he had only a rival and competitor. Instead of being taught to live in gentle society, he was taught only to kill and to take. In the final showdown between father and son, Lee proves himself the better man by killing Ed.

The last scene assuages the tragic tone of the film. Lee, having learned the error of his ways, reconciles with Davey and even accepts his son's love for Clee, referring to her as a "young lady," before breaking down in tears. The symbolism in the end is that Clee has replaced the lost anima in the family; she has become the new mother figure. Now that the shadow of violence and psychopathic masculine aggression has been purged from the family, gentleness can return. This is what enables Lee to show weakness and emotion, by crying for the son he had to kill. Philip French comments on the film as follows: "...the weak boy who loathes shooting is best equipped for life now that the frontier has closed, and that the apparently strong boy, who revels in guns, has inherited a dangerously outmoded style and outlook. This early realization is amply confirmed by the boy's anti-social conduct, and finally in a climactic gunfight the father is forced to kill his own son — which in symbolic terms involves killing part of himself."

We get the sense that Lee has softened, that his psychology has been dramatically altered, but not through some phony contrivance of plot, as in

Red River, but through the mythical trauma of having to kill his own son. In a Jungian interpretation, by killing Ed, Lee confronts and exorcises his own shadow. The shadow itself can be seen as an unbalanced animus, which is masculine aggression unchecked by any sense of feminine feelings. Eliminating the shadow balances the animus by allowing his persona to integrate the lighter elements of anima, such as sensitivity (represented by Clee) and tolerance (represented by Davey).

The Big Country (1958)

William Wyler's sprawling epic depicts a feud between rival cattle barons that integrates various elements of the Western myth, as well as Biblical and oedipal themes. The film opens with the entrance of the central hero, Jim (Gregory Peck), into the Western landscape. He is from the East, and therefore brings with him the supposedly Eastern qualities of tolerance, liberalism, and diplomacy. Jim is engaged to marry Patricia (Carroll Baker), the daughter of Major Terrill (Charles Bickford), the owner of the biggest cattle ranch in the territory. Jim's stock as a potential Westerner is immediately tested when he is confronted by the Hannassey boys, the sons of Rufus Hannassey, the rival cattle baron in the territory. Led by the eldest son, Buck (Chuck Connors), the wild, drunken cowboys have "fun" with the Eastern dandy by lassoing him. Buck drags him through the dirt from the back of his horse, a typical hazing ritual imposed on newcomers in Westerns. As the quintessential Westerner is always seen riding a mount, forcing a man off his mount is a sign of emasculation. Roping him like a steer and dragging him through the dirt takes the point one step further, dehumanizing the newcomer and treating him like an animal.

Patricia is ashamed that Jim let these rival cowboys degrade him in such a way; she thinks he should have shot them before they could have had a chance to do so. But Jim is opposed to the unnecessary use of deadly force. Upon hearing about the incident, the major is also embarrassed by Jim's nonviolence: "Here in the West, Jim, a man's still expected to defend himself." By "himself," the major is referring to the core of a man's self, which is his honor. A man of the West must be ready to kill or be killed before allowing himself to be disgraced or dishonored in any way. Jim, whose father died in a duel over a matter of honor, sees this type of violence as pointless.

The foreman on the major's ranch, Steve (Charlton Heston), plays the part of the adoptive son, as the major has no biological sons. "I raised him," the major says of Steve, whom he took in as a homeless boy. "I made a man out of him." But despite the father-son relationship between the major and Steve, there is no bond of blood between them. When the major dies, the ranch will go to his daughter, and since she will be married to Jim, the entrance of the future son-in-law indicates to Steve that he is being displaced and disinherited. To add to this figurative sibling rivalry between adoptive son and future son-in-law, Steve is desperately in love with Patricia, but she will have no part of him, as he is just a blue-collar working man with no family to speak of and therefore inexorably below her station. The final level of conflict involves Steve's undying allegiance and loyalty to the major. He believes in the same Western code of honor that the major adheres to, while Jim is faithful only to his own set of individualistic, liberal ideals.

There are oedipal overtones to the respective relationships that Jim and Steve have with the major. Even the relationship between Patricia and the major is evocative of the latter acts of the Oedipus myth, *Oedipus at Colonus*, which focuses on the relationship between the elderly Oedipus and his daughter/half-sister, Antigone. The figuratively incestuous relationship between the major and his daughter is portrayed by their excessive love and idealization of each other, to the exclusion of others. The conspicuous absence of a wife/mother figure in the family accentuates this inappropriate infatuation. The father sees no man as worthy of the love of his daughter, and the daughter can find no man worthy of the love and respect that she has for her father. She desperately wants a man just like the major, in order to satisfy her desire for her father, but is frustrated when the man she finds does not fit the bill. In a telling moment, Patricia tells Jim: "You'll never be half the man that the major is!"

The most striking oedipal theme in *The Big Country* is played out in the Hannassey ranch, between the brutish, despotic cattle baron, Rufus (Burl Ives), and his vulgar, feral sons. The main conflict is between Rufus and his eldest son, Buck. In a short but telling piece of dialogue, Rufus calls for Buck. When his son appears, he asks, "You want me, Pa?" Rufus replies, "Before you was born, I did." In another scene, Rufus's sons return to the ranch to tell him that Terrill's men have run their cows away from water. "Why ain't you dead?" he asks them, quite seriously. "You let 'em run my cows off and you come back standing up!"

The father-son conflict comes to a head when the local schoolmarm, Julie (Jean Simmons), is taken captive in the Hannassey ranch house, as a means of forcing her to sell her piece of valuable property. Buck is infatuated with Julie, but she is revolted by him. Unfortunately, Buck has been lying to his father, telling him that Julie is in love with him and wants to marry him. When Rufus learns the truth, he is once again disappointed with his son, who can apparently do no good in his father's eyes. Julie becomes the object of antagonism in this oedipal relationship. Buck tries to rape her, but is caught in the act by Rufus, who knocks Buck down to the floor and kicks him: "Crawl! You act like a dog, crawl like one! Crawl, I said, crawl!" Buck fights his way off the floor and grabs his father by the throat. Rufus grabs his son by the throat. As they stare each other in the eyes, each wanting to squeeze the life out of the other, Rufus growls prophetically: "One day I might have to kill you!"

The next day, Jim comes to the ranch to rescue Julie. He has fallen in love with her, and he has also bought the land that both cattle barons desperately want. In this way, the conflict over Julie is transferred to Jim and Buck. Rufus stops his son from shooting Jim down with his revolver: "*You don't shoot an unarmed man ... not while I'm around.*" Instead, he forces Buck to face Jim in a proper gentleman's duel, with Colonial-era, cap-lock, one-shot pistols. These dueling pistols have symbolic significance, as they belonged to Jim's father. The viewer is left to assume that these are the same pistols with which Jim's father fought his last duel. Rufus snarls at Buck: "*How would you like to fight fair and square for a change? Lookin' down the barrel of a gun, where your fast draw won't do you any good.... Now gimme' that gunbelt, and for the first time in your life, try to be the man that I'd like you to be!*" Rufus will be sourly disappointed. Buck fires before the signal for both men to fire at once. He misses. Now he must stand ready as Jim takes his shot, but instead of taking it like a man, he runs and hides under a wagon, sniveling. Jim shoots his shot in the air, taking pity on his pusillanimous foe. Rufus spits on his cowardly son with scorn and disdain. In anguish, Buck steals a six-gun and tries to shoot Jim in the back. Before he can do so, Rufus shoots his own son dead.

As in *Gunman's Walk*, the father's killing of his feral son softens him. He has killed the part of himself that is driven to kill. He brings an end to the feud and the imminent bloodbath between the rival clans by calling the major out personally, so the two men can settle the matter between themselves. In classic dramatic fashion, both men kill each other in their final showdown. The ending ties together various loose strands of the Western myth. Buck, the wild cowboy whose violence has no honor, is destroyed by the irresponsible father who reared him. In Freudian terms, for the boy who cannot control his id, castration anxiety is real and terminal, as the castrating father inflicts the ultimate punishment on his wayward son. The two cattle barons, whose greed and personal honor kept the entire territory bound in an endless cycle of violence, put an end to each other and the bloody feud, each dying an honorable death. The Eastern dude, when put to the test, shows that he is worthy to exist in the West, as he finally does defend his honor and the honor of the woman he loves, by abandoning his pacifism and engaging in a duel to the death. The Easterner-turned-Westerner marries the schoolmarm, whose refined looks and manners, as well as her thinly veiled English accent, match her neatly with the gentleman from Virginia. And we are left to assume that Patricia, humbled by the abandonment of her fiancé and the death of her father, will finally accept Steve as her man, especially after he proved himself loyal to the major, even to the point of riding by the major's side at a moment when he knew that they were both more than likely to die. In staying true to the major and marrying his daughter, Steve will inherit the ranch as well as the woman that his adoptive father loved more than anything in the world.

Last Train from Gun Hill (1959)

This oedipal drama, directed by John Sturges, delivers the moral that the apple doesn't fall far from the tree. The father makes the son. The film opens with the vicious rape and killing of an Indian woman (Ziva Rodann) at the hands of a pair of sadistic cowboys. In this somewhat progressive Western, there is a role reversal of sorts, as it is the white men who are the raping savages and the Indian their victim. One of the rapists, Rick Belden (Earl Holliman), is the son of Craig Belden (Anthony Quinn), an archetypal cattle baron. Craig is a tyrannical despot who owns the entire town and everyone in it. He raised his son to be a brutal, vicious womanizer. Craig himself has a lover (Carolyn Jones) whom he beats mercilessly, putting her in the hospital for ten days. Adding insult to injury, he refuses to marry her. He just wants her as a kept woman, rather than making an honest lady of her. We get the sense that Rick's savagery and cruelty to women was both a learned behavior (a result of having his father as a role model) and also a result of childhood trauma and abuse, as we could assume that Craig was abusive to his wife, Rick's mother, and that he was also abusive to Rick himself. Rick's psychopathological sadism may also be a symptom of the antagonistic, conflicted relationship that exists between him and his father.

An element of sibling rivalry is provided by Beero (Brad Dexter), the lead ranch hand, who plays the role of adoptive son. He's as close to Rick as a brother and as loyal to Craig Belden as a son. As usual, the adoptive son is morally better than the biological son, but the father always favors his natural-born son over his adoptive one. Beero's subconscious rivalry with Rick prompts him to point out his figurative brother's faults to Craig. Upon noticing a scar on Rick's face, apparently from a not-so-obliging woman, Beero quips: "You know Rick would do better fighting with men." Craig turns to Rick and says: "Do you hear what Beero said?" Rick replies, "Yes, sir," always sheepish in his father's intimidating presence. "You gonna let him talk like that?" Craig continues, trying to instill his own overblown aggressiveness in his son. "Man, I'd hit him." Rick says, "He's just joking, Pa." Now Craig gets angry, using his rage to fuel the boy's nascent hostility: "What's your name? Come on, boy, what's your name?" "Belden," Rick replies meekly. "What? I can't hear you, boy!" Rick replies a bit louder, as if to a drill sergeant, "Belden." Craig keeps pushing him until he shouts out, "Belden!" "Then be a Belden!" Craig insists. "Hit him!" Rick is incredulous. Craig is forcing him to fight the man who is like a son to his father and a brother to him. "No man jokes like that with a Belden! Now, you hit him!" Still incredulous, Rick asks: "Beero?" Now fuming, Craig persists: "Yes, Beero. If you don't, I'm gonna knock you right through that wall! Now, you hit him!" Craig turns to Beero and tells him, "Don't you pull your punches." Clearly, this is a lesson in male dominance that the father is trying to impart to his son.

Rick takes a swing at Beero, a much bigger and stronger man than he. Beero blocks the punch and then proceeds to knock the living daylights out of Rick, much to Craig's chagrin. Afterwards, Craig takes his humiliated, beaten son aside and reminds him: "Rick, I've told you before. Somebody insults you, you hit him! I don't care if you win or lose, but you fight! Understand?" Rick understands, but he isn't the man that his father is. He cannot succeed in a fair fight against another man. His pent-up aggression is directed towards the weaker sex, women, and even more so towards the weakest of this category, Indian women. On the frontier, the rape and even the killing of an Indian woman is only technically considered a crime. "Hereabouts, we don't arrest a man for killin' an Injun," a local cowboy remarks, "we give him a bounty." However, Rick has made a bad mistake. He raped the wrong Indian woman, the wife of a town marshal, Matt Morgan (Kirk Douglas), who also happens to be a dear old friend of Craig Belden's. Marshal Morgan comes to the Belden ranch in search of the killer/rapist. He quickly discovers that it was Rick Belden and his buddy Lee (Brian Hutton) who perpetrated the dastardly deed.

Eventually, Craig confronts Rick with the truth. Rick tries to excuse himself: "We didn't mean to hurt her, Pa. Honest we didn't ... you said yourself there ain't nothin' prettier than a Cherokee squaw." Craig sees the error of his own ways in his son's reprehensible act and realizes that he shares the guilt. Later, while begging Morgan not to take his son away from him, he admits: "Maybe it was my fault. You know, it ain't easy to raise a boy without a mother." Unsympathetic, Morgan replies, "I know." Rick's murder left Morgan's own son motherless as well. He's resolved to bring Rick to justice no matter what the cost, to see him die slowly, in the "white man's way"— a legal execution. In the final scene, Morgan is bringing Rick at gunpoint to the last train from town. Lee tries to shoot him, but misses, killing Rick, while Morgan's return fire kills Lee. Craig, distraught, challenges Morgan to a draw, and loses. While Craig's death is deserved on the basis of all the violent and despicable things he did to keep Morgan from arresting his son, the underlying sense is that he deserved to die, mainly because Rick's crimes were in large part his own. The father must pay for the deeds of his son, as he made him into the man that he was.

One Eyed Jacks (1961)

In the only film that Marlon Brando directed, the oedipal relationship between the two main characters is quite explicit. Karl Malden plays an outlaw whose actual name is "Dad." Brando plays Rio, his partner, whom Dad refers to as "Kid." Malden is just old enough to be believable as a father figure to Brando, especially since Rio is depicted as a roguish, youthful scamp. The fact that Malden played a father figure to Brando previously in *On the Waterfront* (1954) adds to the father/son association. While escaping a posse, Dad and Rio agree that one man should hold off the posse at the crest of a ridge, while the other fetches fresh mounts. Rio stays behind while Dad goes for the horses, but Dad never returns. He abandons Rio and escapes with all of their gold. Rio is captured and imprisoned. Abandonment by one's father, an ancient mythological theme present in the sagas of many classical heroes, including Oedipus, is a quintessential motivation for revenge in the father/son drama. Rio survives in jail for five years, his hatred for Dad and the need for vengeance being the only things keeping him alive. When he escapes, he tracks Dad down in Monterey.

Dad has gone straight. He's the town marshal (an occupation favored by many ex-outlaws) and a respected family man, with a handsome Mexican wife (Katy Jurado) and a pretty young stepdaughter named Louisa (Pina Pellicer). The father/son metaphor is now complete, as Dad's official status as a lawman places him in an authoritative position over Rio and also because Dad is now a real father. Rio lies to Dad, convincing him that he escaped the posse as well and that he has no ax to grind. In explaining their backstory to Dad's wife, Rio recalls: "I wasn't anything more than a kid when Dad picked me up," establishing completely the fact that Rio looked upon

Dad as a real father. We understand why he considers his abandonment at the ridge a betrayal that goes way beyond one partner simply ditching the other. As the plot progresses, and Rio bides his time in taking his vengeance, Rio seduces Louisa, providing another stitch in the oedipal tapestry. Dad perceives the seduction of his virgin daughter by his figurative son as a terrible betrayal. Dad flogs Rio with a bullwhip in a public act of punishment. He uses Rio's recent killing of a drunk in a fair fight as an excuse for the whipping, but the real motivation is payback for the deflowering of Louisa.

Punishment is a central theme in the Western, as it is linked directly with the themes of father vs. son, civilization vs. savagery, the need to prove or regain masculinity, the vengeance quest, primal honor, and personal justice. Psychologically, whipping is not only incredibly painful, but symbolically emasculating. When a young boy misbehaves, he is "whipped" by his father, typically on the flesh of his rear end, with his pants down. Being whipped by another man represents the notion that your manhood is negated. You are no longer a man, you are a boy. You are publicly "depantsed." And, since the punisher takes the symbolic role of the father, and the victim takes the role of the son, the Freudian issue of "castration anxiety" becomes relevant. The boy's fear of his father is referred to as "castration anxiety," because the boy fears that his father's physical and psychological domination will forever subdue his own need to feel empowered. Castration refers to the loss of the testicles or male genitalia, which in Freudian terminology means the loss of masculine identity and male power. For the Western character, castration anxiety could be interpreted not so much as a fear of punishment, but as a neurotic reaction to it, a desperate sense of inner turmoil, which could only be resolved by avenging the emasculating act of punishment, with an empowering act of violence against the castrating father.

As the condition of being whipped represents the loss of masculinity, the theme of corporeal punishment reappears quite frequently in Westerns. Lynching, hanging, imprisonment, torture, and beatings at the hands of lawmen, posses, trail bosses, and cavalry officers are a ubiquitous subject matter in the genre. In most cases, the character who is punished does not learn anything from his discipline; it merely forces him to seek vengeance in order to regain his honor (masculinity), which was lost to him when he was punished (emasculated). If the victim of punishment is a villain, he will die in his attempt to gain vengeance, typically at the hands of his original punisher. In John Ford's *Wagon Master* (1950), for example, it is the whipped outlaw's desperate need for vengeance that sparks the final showdown between the outlaws and the wagon masters. If the victim is a hero, he will kill his punisher, in this way overcoming his sense of "castration anxiety" and resolving his oedipal complex in the most visceral and satisfactory fashion.

Hang 'Em High (1968) is an example of this sort of vengeance quest. In the first act, the hero (Clint Eastwood) is lynched and left for dead for rustling cattle that he didn't steal. For the rest of the film, he searches for and destroys each of the men who lynched him. In Red River, the first spark of mutiny is flared when Dunston shoots a man because he refuses to be whipped. In The Man Who Shot Liberty Valance, the villain named in the title (Lee Marvin) whips his victims, sadistically taking away their manhood as he tortures them. And in Unforgiven, the villainous marshal (Gene Hackman) mercilessly beats a gunfighter (Richard Harris) for carrying a concealed weapon, in order to make an example out of him. Later on in the film, he whips the hero's partner (Morgan Freeman) to death, providing the motivation for the hero (Clint Eastwood) to wreak vengeance on the wicked marshal.

As with the ubiquitous theme of the rape or murder of a wife, brother, or other loved one, the theme of underserved punishment provides a perfect psychological motivation for a vengeance quest. After the whipping, Dad shatters Rio's right hand. Like a whipping, the breaking or rupturing of the right hand is symbolically emasculating. Without his right hand, the victim cannot shoot and is therefore stripped of the utility of his primary phallic symbol, his handgun, which he uses to assert his masculinity through violence. The theme of the breaking or rupturing of the right hand can be seen in other films, such as Red River, The Man from Laramie (1955), and The Far Country (1954). In these films, the hero must wait for his hand to heal, letting his desire for vengeance simmer and consolidate, before he can confront the man who injured him and reclaim his masculinity by killing him. In keeping with this theme, Rio confronts and kills Dad in the end, a catharsis that quenches his need for vengeance, provides a violent atonement with the father, and leaves him free to pursue love and happiness with his anima figure, Louisa.

The Cowboys (1972)

When Wil Andersen's (John Wayne) hired hands run out on him, his desperation to get his cattle to market forces him to recruit schoolboys as cowboys for his cattle drive. He finds the boys in the schoolhouse, which is portrayed as a stifling environment of female domination. Outnumbered by girls and ruled over by the schoolmarm, the boys are forced to sit still and read aloud female apparel descriptions from a mail-order catalog. This setting is seen as the antithesis of what the Western considers to be the proper male environment — the outdoors, among horses and cattle, engaged in hard labor, and surrounded by harsh, dangerous, and wild elements. Andersen gives them the opportunity to live and work in a venue that will make men out of them. On a psychosexual level, the movement away from the indoor environment, which is dominated by an emasculating matron, into the outdoor environment, in which ego identification is made with the father figure, represents the first step in the resolution of the oedipal complex. On a mythological level, the transition from boyhood to manhood is completed via a rite of passage or initiation into the realm of adult men.

The boys' apprenticeship under Andersen is literally a passage into manhood. They work hard. They steal a bottle of the cook's (Roscoe Lee Brown) whiskey and have their first drinks and their first hangovers. They deal with loss, when one of the boys dies in an accident. And some of them almost lose their virginity when a traveling brothel crosses their path, but the cook insists that the boys are too young for this all-important rite of passage. The madame (Colleen Dewhurst) agrees, spouting a bit of unlikely dialogue that is clearly an attempt to impose 20th-century culture onto a 19th-century scenario: "I guess you're right. The first time should be in the back of a buggy, with a girl that they think they're in love with." However, the true initiation ritual, as is expected of the genre, is achieved through violence.

When Andersen is shot to pieces by a sadistic rustler, Asa Watts (Bruce Dern), the boys prove their masculinity by killing Watts and every one of his rustling partners. The method of killing Watts is somewhat sadistic, pointing out that the initiation is not just about killing, but also about integrating an element of the savage into the young males' identities. The capstone to this rite of passage is the retaking of the herd and the cowboys' completion of the drive on their own, which is equally important as the completion of the vengeance quest. For the Westerner, vengeance should ideally have a purpose, i.e. the saving of a town, the rescuing of a captive, the completion of a mission. By completing the drive, the boys show that they are men. They live up to the expectations set up by their father figure, who had previously told them in his dying words: "I'm proud of ya ... all of ya. Every man wants his children to be better'n he was. You are!"

The representation of Andersen as a father figure to the boys is not subtext. It is explicitly stated throughout the film that the boys see Andersen as a surrogate father, especially to a fatherless and troubled Mexican boy named Cimarron (A. Martinez). When the boys buy a tombstone for Andersen at the end of the drive, Cimarron chooses the epitaph: "Will Andersen —

Beloved Husband and Father." Cimarron had no way of knowing that Andersen actually had two sons who died in late adolescence, so the title "Father" was referring to the way that he and his fellow cowboys felt towards Andersen. It is also clearly established that, through his relationship with the boys, Andersen is redeeming himself as a father. His own two sons "went bad," turning to a life of crime that led to untimely deaths. He blames himself for being too hard on them. This backstory fuels the subtext for the fierce oedipal relationship between Andersen and Watts.

At the beginning of the drive, Watts asks for work for himself and his two sidekicks. He gets caught lying about his references, and then admits that he and his friends just got out of jail. Rather than lending a helping hand to the ex-cons, Andersen turns them away: "Now I don't hold jail against ya, but I hate a liar." "You're a hard man," Watts tell him. "It's a hard life," Andersen curtly replies. We get the sense here that Andersen was too hard on these young men, who were, after all, just looking for honest work. Perhaps he was too hard on his hired hands in the beginning of the film, as per their complaints, which is why they quit on him. And perhaps, in the same vein, he was too hard on his own sons, which is what pushed them away from him and into a life of crime. When Watts faces Andersen next, he has a band of rustlers and an ax to grind. His killing of Andersen is so brutal and sadistic, it is clear that there is some underlying psychological force at play. The subtext is the oedipal conflict. Watts represents a man like Andersen's own sons, a man who hates authority and is driven to psychopathic rage when he feels betrayed by an authority figure. And Andersen represents a man whom we would expect Watts's own father to be like: a "hard," tough, insensitive man, who can be rejecting and cold to a young man in need of warmth and acceptance. As an aside, the conflict between father and son is also played out on a cultural level. Watts's wild and long mane earns him the nickname "Long Hair." In the early 70s, when the film was made, there was still a definite rift in society between the young rebellious hippies with their dirty long hair and the old uptight establishment, whose primary iconic figure was that of the archetypal cowboy himself, John Wayne.

Biblical Westerns

Biblical themes abound in Westerns. The conflict between cattle kingdoms recalls the ancient wars between shepherding tribes in the Middle East, such as the Mideonites, the Canaanites, the Edomites, etc. The scenario of an isolated family in uncivilized territory is the perfect setting for Biblical themes such as sibling rivalry, family feuds, nation building, racial warfare, and man-against-nature stories. To add to this, the Western genre often evokes a distinctly "Biblical feel," stemming from its use of desert settings, the remoteness of its characters from modern society, and the use of lethal violence in the resolution of conflicts. Some Westerns include Biblical allusions as subliminal undertones, hidden in the names of locations and characters.

In *Broken Lance* (1954), for instance, the youngest and most favored son of a patriarchal cattle king (Spencer Tracy) is named Joseph (Robert Wagner). Like the Biblical Joseph, his half-brothers are jealous of his special relationship with their father, especially since he is the youngest and has a different mother. They call him father's "little pet." While the Biblical Joseph's half-brothers sold him into slavery, the half-brothers in *Broken Lance* send Joe up the river to prison to serve time for a crime that his father committed. Similarly, in *Shane*, the names of the homesteaders are Big Joe and Marion, i.e. Joseph and Mary. The character of Shane enters as a savior. Though his first name is never revealed, Shane can be identified as the Jesus figure in this tale of the great American mythological hero. He defeats the evil cattle baron and his accomplices at great personal risk, then ascends to the heavens of the Rocky Mountain peaks astride his horse, figuratively dying for the townspeople, even though they aren't worthy of his sacrifice.

How the West Was Won (1962)

The last grand epic of the genre, directed by three master filmmakers — John Ford, Henry Hathaway, and George Marshall — and produced in the cinematic innovation of "Panorama," is possibly the most self-conscious of the mythmaking Westerns. *How the West Was Won* begins and ends with a long prologue and epilogue, recounting the conquering of the West from "nature" and "primitive peoples," and the taming of the land as a function of the American pioneering spirit. In the final sequence, the camera pulls back from the wild frontier to a series of soaring helicopter shots, depicting massive dams, highway systems, suspension bridges, and metropolises where once lay virgin forests, rolling prairies, and wide open plains. The message, delivered via Spencer Tracy's overbearing voiceover, is that the Western frontier is gone, along with the men and women who conquered it, but the legacy of their accomplishments lives on through the mythology of the West, which the film itself is a part of.

At the core of the film's narrative are the lives of the two daughters of a westward pioneer (Karl Malden). Their names are clear Biblical allusions. The younger daughter, Eve (Carroll Baker), is the ancestral mother of the West. She is a stoic frontierswoman, descended from Quaker parents, but infatuated with Linus (James Stewart), a wild backwoodsman, whom she captures and tames into a loyal husband and settled homesteader. The marriage of these two contrasting American archetypes — the Christian frontierswoman and the nature-worshipping White Indian — results in the birth of the central hero figure in American mythology, the Westerner. Eve and Linus's son, Jeb (George Peppard), is the central hero. The film traces his identity development from homesteader, to cavalryman, to marshal, and finally to cattleman — representing all of the personas of the Western hero archetype, with the exception of the outlaw. It is significant to note, however, that Jeb kills an outlaw in the climactic sequence, representing the final sacrifice required for the conquest of the land and the establishment of civilization: the sacrifice of the wild inner nature of mankind.

A second plot line involves Eve's older sister, Lilith (Debbie Reynolds), whose name is obviously a reference to the mythological character of Lilith, who in the Judeo-Christian tradition was believed to be the first wife of Adam, but due to her carnality and individuality chose to leave Eden. Like her mythological namesake, Lilith chooses to abandon the Eden of the Western frontier in favor of the creature comforts of civilized society found to the east of Eden. While Eve stays out West to marry Linus, the figurative Adam of the frontier Eden, Lilith goes to the city, where she becomes a dance-hall girl. In this way, two of the principal female archetypes — the frontierswoman and the whore with the heart of gold — are established, respectively, in the characters of Eve and Lily. (There are no schoolmarms or halfbreeds in the film.) Lilith eventually settles down in San Francisco, the Western metropolis, with a reformed tinhorn gambler (Gregory Peck). At the end of the film, she redeems herself by becoming a true frontierswoman, moving out to a ranch in Arizona, where she'll raise cattle with the help of her nephew, Jeb, and his family.

The sentiment of white superiority in the film is clearly portrayed through the recurrent voiceovers and soundtrack lyrics, reminding the viewer that the American West is the "promised land" and that the right for the white man to take it from "primitive man" was manifest and in keeping with the laws of nature, or at least with the philosophy of Social Darwinism. Nevertheless, the treatment of the Native American in the film is more or less sympathetic. We see the railroads cutting through their land via broken treaties and double-crossings. We see white settlers and hunters establishing towns and ranches, killing off the buffalo, and disenfranchising the Indian peoples. Though there is a sense of moral ambivalence about this treatment of the Native American, it is still seen as an inevitable consequence of manifest destiny and divine providence, a fatalistic tragedy of natural history, in which the white man was ordained by God to conquer the West, and the red man was ordained to be conquered. A sequel to this film, depicted from the Indian's perspective, with the title *How the West Was Lost* has yet to be produced.

7

Anthony Mann's
Psychological Westerns

"The essential American soul is hard, isolate, stoic, and a killer."
— D.H. Lawrence (1961)

Anthony Mann graduated from directing B-pictures in the early 1940s and excellent low-budget noir films in the late 1940s to becoming one of the most significant and influential director of Westerns in the 1950s. His contributions to the genre, which were called "western noir," "psychological westerns," and "adult westerns" by critics, represent the essence of what is now referred to as the psychological Western subgenre. Drawing much from the archetypal characters and themes of film noir, Mann's Westerns feature villains who are frequently psychopathic, heroes who are socially marginalized and intensely neurotic, and scenarios which call into question the genre's typical motifs of violence, masculinity, and honor. Mann's first two Westerns, *The Furies* and *Devil's Doorway*, both released in 1950, were commercial failures. Nevertheless, each picture represented an interesting approach to the genre. *The Furies* was adapted from a novel by Niven Busch, the writer who penned the novel upon which *Duel in the Sun* was based and who also wrote the screenplay for *Pursued*. In the same vein as these other two Westerns, *The Furies* is an oedipal drama set on an isolated ranch. The plot revolves around a daughter (Barbara Stanwyck) who feels disinherited when her elderly father (Walter Huston) begins to court a potential new bride (Judith Anderson). *Devil's Doorway* revisits the basic theme of *The Vanishing American* (1925), in which an Indian veteran who fought for the American army returns home to find that his people are being oppressed by the same government he risked his life to defend. Delmer Daves's *Broken Arrow*, released the same year, dealt with the same subject matter of Indian disenfranchisement. Daves's film was a huge success, leaving *Devil's Doorway* lying in its wake, relegating Mann's first Western to the status of a lost gem. Together, both *Broken Arrow* and *Devil's Doorway* represent the "new" and revised treatment of the Native American in Westerns, which would portray them primarily as victims of white greed and aggression, rather than fierce savages or wild beasts. This trend began in 1950 and continues to the present day. In later years, *Broken Arrow, Devil's Doorway,* and the many films that adopted the same sympathetic stance towards Indians, were categorized by critics and authors as "civil rights" and/or "revisionist Westerns."

Ironically, the star of *Broken Arrow*, James Stewart, was the actor with whom Mann would establish his most successful collaboration. The director and actor would make eight films together, five of them Westerns. *Winchester '73*, also released in 1950, marked the first pairing of the Mann/Stewart team. Of the four films Mann made that year, including the low-budget film noir *Sidestreet*, *Winchester '73* was the only success. In fact, *Winchester '73* was so successful that it single-handedly promoted Mann to the level of A-picture Hollywood director, while also helping to re-launch Stewart's postwar career as one of the biggest stars in the industry. The success of *Winchester '73* also established a template for the kind of noir-influenced Westerns that would characterize Mann's "psychological Westerns" of the 1950s. In addition to being the first director/actor pairing of Mann and Stewart, *Winchester* was also the first collaboration between Mann and writer Borden Chase. As a writer of psychologically driven Western characters and plots, Chase is one of the most significant behind-the-scenes players in the creation of the psychological Western subgenre. He wrote the story and/or screenplay for some of the most significant films in the subgenre, such as *Red River, The Man from Colorado, Lone Star* (1952), *Vera Cruz* (1954), *Man Without a Star, Backlash* (1956), and *Night Passage*. For Anthony Mann, Chase wrote the screenplays for *Winchester '73, Bend of the River,* and *The Far Country*—three of the five Mann/Stewart films featuring Stewart as a psychologically tormented, vengeance-driven hero. *Night Passage* was apparently slotted by the studio to be another Western directed by Mann, starring Stewart, and written by Chase, but according to Hollywood legend, Mann was frustrated by the studio's insistence on casting war hero Audie Murphy in the co-starring role. He walked out on the production, expecting his longtime partner and friend to follow him, but Stewart chose to stay on, supposedly because he saw the film as a chance to show off his accordion-playing abilities. (Stewart's accordion-playing scenes were later dubbed over by a professional accordion player.) Whatever the cause, Stewart and Mann would never work together again, and neither would Chase and Mann, though it is not clear whether these two men had a similar falling-out.

The five Mann/Stewart Westerns, which were by far Mann's most popular and successful contributions to the genre, were *Winchester '73, Bend of the River* (1952), *The Naked Spur* (1953), *The Far Country* (1954), and *The Man from Laramie* (1955). After his falling-out with Stewart, Mann cast leading men in his Westerns who were tantamount to Stewart in their level of stardom, film persona, association with the Western genre, and Hollywood seniority. In retrospect, it was probably a good thing that Mann stopped using Stewart in all of his Westerns, because although it was a classic pairing, the use of other actors gives variety and texture to the central hero character of Mann's canon. In his later Westerns, Mann's heroes included Victor Mature in *The Last Frontier* (1955), Henry Fonda in *The Tin Star* (1957), Gary Cooper in *Man of the West* (1958), and Glenn Ford in *Cimarron* (1960). Considered as a whole, Mann's Westerns, eleven in total, represent a canon of films that would become among the most revered and influential in the genre, second only (arguably), to the work of John Ford.

Winchester '73

When asked about the prototypical hero character that he creates in his films, Mann replied: "He's a man who could kill his own brother." In no film is this more true than in *Winchester '73*, but in a sense, Mann's Western hero almost always kills his brother — if not literally, then figuratively. The essence of Mann's films is a protagonist/antagonist duality, in which each opposing character is the mirror image of the other. There is always the sense that, if not for a single grain of decency residing deep within the hero's psyche, he could just as easily be the villain. In fact, most of Mann's heroes are in the act of overcoming ignominious pasts as former gunfighters or outlaws, or else they are currently engaged in a morally conflicted occupation — bounty hunting or on a vengeance quest. The line between the hero and the villain he must kill is tenuous at best. Treading this line makes the hero increasingly neurotic, fearful of his own descent into darkness, literally "on edge."

In each of his films, Mann's hero experiences a self-reflective moment. He comes to a point at which his violence can easily cross the line from justifiable to excessive. At this moment, the hero realizes the precipitous state of his own ego, the ease with which he is able to summon the dark energy to kill, and even worse, the primal satisfaction he gains from punishing and destroying the men that he hates. At this moment, he pulls himself back from the brink of psychopathic aggression. This one moment, this epiphany, in which the hero encounters the dark nature of his inner self, and retreats from it, is at the core of each of Mann's Westerns. The story of how the hero reaches that moment (all of the plot, action and dialogue) is merely functional. That singular self-reflective moment is the transcending element within all of Mann's Western films.

Jim Kitses notes: "Mann's response to the Western was not a response to history, as with Ford and Peckinpah, but to its archetypal form, the mythic patterns deeply embedded in the plots and characters of the genre that can shape and structure the action." Unlike Ford, who had a large part in inventing them, or Peckinpah, who had a large part in dissolving them, Mann used the already established conventions of the Western genre to make his point about the dualistic nature of the hero, which is experienced by the audience as a state of constant neurotic conflict. *Winchester '73* is an especially cogent example of the use of a variety of pre-established conventions to create a completely original take on the genre. Scene by scene, the film follows the travels of the gun named in the title, a prized "one-in-a-thousand" rifle, which is unique because of its perfection. At each phase of its journey, the gun is held and taken forward by a representative Western archetype. It begins in the hands of Wyatt Earp (Will Geer), the patriarchal embodiment of frontier justice and the most persistently revived artifact of the Old West. He is the point where myth and history meet. Earp is presiding over a shooting contest. The winner is awarded the prized gun. The top two competitors are men who shoot exactly in the same way, with almost the exact same level of supernatural marksmanship. We don't learn until the end that these men are brothers. The shooting contest reenacts their sibling rivalry, a primal need within each brother to defeat the other. Shooting is particularly significant, as their father — the man whose affection was their original object of rivalry — taught them to shoot. Earp, as the town and genre patriarch and the man judging the contest, fits in symbolically as the father figure to the rival brothers. Eventually, we learn that the hero, Lin (James Stewart), is on a traditional vengeance quest to kill the man who killed his father. The villain, Lin's quarry, is his own brother, Dutch Henry (Stephen McNally). Lin wins the contest by shooting through a postage stamp stuck onto a ring thrown fifty feet into the air. Directly afterwards, his brother ambushes him and steals the Winchester, but has to run before he can kill him.

The story follows the gun. We leave town with Dutch, the archetypal outlaw villain, and his band of gunmen. On his trail is the archetypal hero and his trusted sidekick High-Spade (Millard Mitchell). Various representations of Western archetypes take temporary possession of the gun: a tinhorn gambler/gun dealer (John McIntire), a "noble savage" Indian (Rock Hudson), and a dignified cavalryman (Jay C. Flippen). The gun winds up in the hands of a coward, Steve (Charles Drake), who is traveling with his fiancé, Lola (Shelley Winters), a whore with a heart of gold, who is seeking redemption. At each stage, traditional thematic elements of the genre arise: Dutch having the bartender send a glass of milk to Lin standing at the bar (in the Western scenario, offering a man anything other than coffee or whiskey to drink is an insult to his masculinity), the whore being run out of town by the decency brigade, the doomed gambler revealing the "death card" (the ace of spades), an equally doomed Dutch holding the "dead man's hand" (aces and eights), Lola telling Lin that she knows all about "the last bullet" before they are attacked by Indians, various references to scalping, Indian birdcalls, etc. The film up until this point is taut and entertaining. Despite all of the hackneyed conventions, the original device of the episodic structure centered on the gun itself, as well as Borden Chase's excellent dialogue and Mann's masterful direction, make *Winchester* a fun romp through Western legend and lore. But now the film goes beyond convention, descending into the darker elements of human interaction, in scenes that would come to epitomize Mann's psychological approach to the Western.

Steve and Lola are staying in the house that they plan to move into once they are married. In the house are its current residents, a mother and her two children. In Mann's Westerns, the family is always representative of purity and innocence, the natural state of man uncorrupted by the darkness and violence existing in both the villain and the hero. Into this serene setting invades Waco Johnnie Dean (Dan Duryea) and his band of outlaws. At this stage in the genre, 1950, Duryea's Waco is a character we haven't seen yet. Disarmingly witty and charismatic, his humor and charm are a thin veil over his psychopathic and sadistic aggressiveness. He is a man who gains disturbing pleasure out of seeing weaker men squirm in his presence. He is a bully, a "sicko," a degenerate madman. Sensing Steve's cowardly nature, Waco amuses himself by emasculating him bit by bit, curious to see how far he can push the weakling before he finally stands up for himself. First, Waco forces Steve to make coffee, woman's work. Lola offers to make the coffee, but Waco insists that Steve do it. Next, Waco makes advances towards Lola, right in front of Steve. To add to his shame, Waco forces Steve to wear an apron while he serves the coffee, calling him "kitchen boy." With hands full of coffee and cups, Steve is tripped by Waco, who laughs and says, "Clean it up!" Steve finally cracks under the overwhelming force of Waco's emasculating taunts. He draws on Waco, but is no match for "the fastest gun in Texas." Waco kills him, taking possession of both the Winchester and Lola.

A common theme in Mann's Westerns is the existence of a psychopathic badman, who is usually not the villain, but in league with the villain. The psychopath's violence is erratic and out of control, seemingly unstoppable. At one point, the psychopath confronts the hero, and we are surprised when the hero's nature changes abruptly. Up till this point, the hero's actions are controlled and rational, even when violence is called for. But now, when facing the psychopath, the hero's violence is overwhelming and unstoppable. Perhaps the hero recognizes a bit of himself in the psycho's depraved eyes, and he doesn't like it. He kills the psycho, showing that libidinal energy, when controlled and repressed, is more powerful when it is released all at once, as compared to the energy of the degenerate, who is unable to repress his aggression at all. It is this latent power of repressed hate, aggression, and rage that drives the hero throughout the film and fuels the conflict within him.

The self-reflective moment for the hero in this initial version of Mann's Western formula is quiet, pensive, underplayed, and undefined. High-Spade asks Lin: "Do you ever wonder what *he'd* think about you hunting down Dutch Henry?" By "he," High-Spade is obviously referring to Lin and Dutch's father. "He'd understand," Lin replies. "He taught me to hunt." "Not men," High-Spade answers, "hunting for food, that's all right, but hunting a man to kill him? You're beginning to like it." Lin responds sharply, betraying a slight sense of self-doubt: "That's where you're wrong. I don't like it! Some things a man has to do, so he does 'em." Here, Lin considers the morality of his vengeance quest and accepts it. Killing in the name of honor and justice is acceptable, in contrast to his brother's killing for profit and Waco's killing for the satisfaction of his own perverse drives.

A bit later, Lin and Lola meet again. She tells Lin that Waco killed their mutual friend, Steve. Coincidentally, Lin also knows that Waco is partners with Dutch. Lin approaches Waco and asks him the whereabouts of Dutch. Waco is tight-lipped. Pushed to the edge by his hatred for Waco for killing Steve, and driven to near madness by his obsession to get Dutch, Lin explodes in violence. Without warning, he grabs Waco by the throat and twists his arm behind his back until he howls out in pain. Lin's eyes at this moment betray a glint of madness, the same wild aggression that Waco displayed against Steve. The viewer is led to wonder, was High-Spade right? Is Lin beginning to like it? Waco quickly agrees to take Lin to Dutch. On the way out of the saloon, Waco grabs a gun and draws, but Lin shoots him down before he can fire.

The climactic shootout between brothers is more controlled. It takes place in a remote spot in the desert, on an outcropping of craggy rocks. As they shoot at each other, the brothers exchange quips that revisit their childhood and their primal conflict — "the old man taught you better than that, you're caught beneath another man's gun!" In the end, Lin kills his brother, avenging his father's death and fulfilling his quest for inner peace. His shadow exorcised, he can abandon his destructive quest and begin a life of peace and love with his pretty new girlfriend, Lola, and his faithful friend, High-Spade.

Bend of the River

Mann and Stewart's second collaboration is a nation-building Western, in the tradition of *Red River* and *The Big Sky*. Glyn McLyntock (James Stewart) is a man with a past, currently engaged as a guide for a wagon train of settlers headed for a remote region in the Oregon Territory. Early on, he rescues a horse thief, Emerson Cole (Arthur Kennedy), from being lynched. The two men, designed for the roles of protagonist and antagonist, have much in common. They are Mann's prototypical pairing of persona and shadow — two sides of the same coin. Both Glyn and Cole are former outlaws, Missouri border raiders, running from their pasts. While Glyn is trying to make a fresh start for himself with the settlers in the regenerative environment of the western frontier, Cole is just interested in his next score. "McLyntock of the border, a rancher?" Cole asks Glyn. "I don't get it. Who ya running away from?" Glyn replies, "A man by the name of Glyn McLyntock." Cole is skeptical of Glyn's desire to reform. "Well, what happens when he catches up with you?" Glyn responds earnestly, "I don't think he's gonna catch up with me. I think he died on the Missouri border." Forever the cynic, Cole says, "You're wrong. He'll catch up with you one of these days."

Glyn and Cole reveal their violent natures when the wagon train is ambushed by a small band of Indians. They sneak into the woods and kill each Indian, one at a time, with their knives and revolvers. Killing comes easy to these men, a bit too easy. Upon arriving in Portland, the leader of the wagon train, Jeremy (Jay C. Flippen), learns that Cole was once an outlaw. Unaware of Glyn's sordid past, he confides in him: "I don't like that man Cole.... I heard Grundy say he was a raider on the Missouri border." Glyn replies vaguely, "Well, lots of people used to raid along the border. Some of 'em decided to change." "That kind can't change," Jeremy replies. "When an apple's rotten, there's nothing you can do except throw it away, or it'll spoil the whole barrel." Hopeful for his own redemption, Glyn replies: "Well, there's a difference between men and apples." By the end, both men will be proven right.

Glyn and Cole part ways. Glyn continues on with the wagon train to the remote settlement, while Cole stays in town to seek his fortune. Months later, Glyn returns to town to check on the long overdue supplies that should have been sent upriver to the settlers. If the supplies don't reach them, the settlement will fail, and a hundred people will starve. The supplies are being held hostage by a crooked merchant. Cole helps Glyn escape with the goods, but they come into conflict over their destination. Rather than bringing the supplies to their rightful owners, the needy settlers, Cole wants to sell them to a gold miner's camp for a huge profit. As the story progresses, Glyn becomes more and more violent. Forced to kill when necessary, he sees himself becoming the killer that he once was. The line between justified killing and ruthless murder is logically clear to him, as he explains to a young sidekick, Trey (Rock Hudson), after they fight off an ambush and their attackers retreat. Glyn ceases firing: "All right, they've had it, let 'em go." Cole asks rhetorically, "Why?"—and keeps on firing, clearly enjoying the slaughter. But Trey hesitates and asks Glyn sincerely, "Why?" Glyn replies soberly: "Well, if you don't know, I can't tell you." Trey takes Glyn's moral edification to heart, even as Cole continues shooting at the retreating men's backs, a savage smile on his face.

Though Glyn can see the moral line clearly in his mind, he has trouble staying on the right side of it when he is pushed to the brink. Eventually, Cole turns Glyn's hired hands against him. During a failed first try at mutiny by the hired hands, Glyn wrestles one of the men to the ground and draws his knife. The familiar mad gleam shines in Jimmy Stewart's eyes — this is the self-reflective moment. Before he can plunge his knife into the helpless man's breast, Jeremy's pretty daughter (Julie Adams) shouts out his name in horror. The spell is broken. Glyn comes to his senses. He sheathes the knife, realizing how close he came to reviving the old Glyn McLyntock, the man who Glyn wants to believe died on the Missouri border. Though he retreats from the brink, he will need to recall some part of the old Glyn on the road ahead, in order to survive.

Cole leads the next mutiny, which is successful. The mutineers hijack the supplies. Glyn must wreak vengeance on Cole and his men in order to retake the supplies and save the settlers. The hero's motivation is a classic vengeance quest now. His quarry is his shadowy double, the personification of every one of Glyn's dark emotions: guilt, shame, anger, hatred, greed, savagery, and aggression. In the climactic battle, a band of gold miners trying to steal the supplies, led by Cole, are repelled by Glyn and his partners.

Having learned his lesson well, Trey puts down his gun when the miners retreat. Glyn and Cole fight hand-to-hand in the icy river. Glyn beats Cole senseless, then leaves him to drown in the river, letting the water do his dirty work for him, as they symbolically wash away his sins, and the stains of his past. Only then, after his shadow is exorcised, does Glyn's bandanna come loose from around his neck, revealing the old rope scar. Like Cole, Glyn was once strung at the business end of a lynching rope. As a final reward, Jeremy acknowledges Glyn's disreputable past as an outlaw and concedes that a man can change. "I was wrong," Jeremy admits. "There is a difference between apples and men. Really, there is." The supper bell — supplanting the church bell in the rustic settlement — rings as Glyn brings in the supplies. He saved the community, won the approval of the patriarch as well as the love of his daughter, and can finally close the violent chapter of his life and open a new chapter of peace and serenity.

The Naked Spur

Reprising his role as the angry drifter haunted by a shadowy past, Jimmy Stewart plays Howard Kemp, a bounty hunter on the trail of a ruthless killer named Ben (Robert Ryan). He finds his quarry, but then must get him back to Abilene, a long and arduous journey. By no choice of his own, he must join forces with a wily old prospector named Jesse (Millard Mitchell) and a dishonorably discharged cavalryman named Roy (Ralph Meeker). None of these men are virtuous. Ben is clearly the villain, a ruthless killer interested only in saving his own skin and willing to do anything to do it. Roy isn't much better. He was kicked out of the army for misconduct and is on the run from the local Blackfoot Indians for raping the chief's daughter, an act that he doesn't even consider to be a serious offense. Though Jesse fits well into the role of the amiable old coot, his greed and his gold lust will be his downfall. And while we know that Howard will redeem himself by the end of the picture, he begins his journey as a soulless hunter, posing as a bona fide lawman, interested only in the money he can make from dragging a wanted criminal back to civilization and a waiting gallows pole. All four men are tainted by greed and egocentrism, and there is little distinction between hero and villain.

Ben is accompanied by a girlfriend, Lina (Janet Leigh), a feisty and pretty young tomboy who is fiercely loyal to her man, despite his outlaw status. As typical in the genre, the woman is the only pure character in the film. Lina is a true frontierswoman; neither schoolmarm nor whore, she is as comfortable in the rugged terrain of the Colorado Rocky Mountains as any of the men. Ben uses Lina to breed conflict between his captors, hoping they'll quarrel amongst each other for the bounty, affording him an opportunity to escape. He uses Lina's attractiveness as a lure, frequently asking her to massage his back with the sexually suggestive phrase "Do me." Eventually, Lina discovers that Howard was an honest rancher in his previous life. His ego was shattered by a false woman, who sold off his ranch and then deserted him when he went off to fight in the Civil War. His motive in tracking down and bringing in Ben is to make enough money to start up a new ranch. The attraction between Lina and Howard is more psychological than physical. She's attracted to him because, unlike Ben, Howard is an honest man at heart, who shares her dream of a peaceful life on a frontier spread. And he's attracted to her because, unlike his ex-fiancée, she's constant and loyal to her man. Both characters see possible redemption in each other. As the journey continues, Howard's heroic character is revealed through his honor. Like Lin in *Winchester,* who sought redemption in

Love's Redemption. James Stewart as Howie Kemp, the man with a past, and Janet Leigh as Lina Patch, the girl who stays true to her man, in Anthony Mann's *The Naked Spur* (1953, MGM).

revenge, and Glyn in *Bend of the River*, who sought redemption in saving the community, Howard is seeking redemption as well. But Howard's redemption must come though internal conflict, rather than the achievement of an external goal. Howard must change himself.

After another one of Ben's multiple escape attempts, Howard has reached his limit of patience with his wily hostage. He knows that it would be easier to kill Ben and bring his corpse back for the reward (he's wanted "dead or alive"), and at this point, Howard's hatred for Ben is enough to make him want to kill him. But Howard's basic sense of honor will not allow him to kill Ben in cold blood. This is his weakness, and it is also his virtue. He gives Ben a revolver and challenges him to a quick-draw showdown. Howard's self-reflective moment comes when Ben refuses the duel. Howard commands Ben to draw several times, but Ben refuses to be provoked into action. Roy shouts to Howard, "Kill him!" Howard draws his gun. He aims at Ben, staring at him, the familiar mad gleam in his eye. But the moment passes. Unable to murder Ben, Howard has no choice but to let him live, despite his ongoing attempts at escape and sabotage.

Roy is more than willing to shoot Ben down, execution-style, so Howard is forced to fight him as well. Eventually, Jesse is fooled by Ben's trickery, believing his claim of a nearby gold mine. Jesse leads Ben and Lina on an escape, but is shot down in cold blood by Ben for his trouble. The death of the foolish but kindhearted old man proves to Lina once and for all that Ben is nothing but a degenerate murderer. At this point, Howard's quest becomes more of a traditional hero's trial. He must avenge his partner's death and rescue the beautiful maiden from the ruthless villain. In the climactic sequence, Roy beats Howard to the punch. He shoots Ben in the back. Ben's dead body falls into a whitewater gorge. Ever the greedy materialist, Roy tries to retrieve Ben's corpse from the gorge and drowns in the attempt. Howard fishes Ben's body out of the water and drags it away, setting up another self-reflective and ultimately transformative moment. Lina shouts: "Cut him loose, Howie!" Howard launches into an emotional tirade as he hauls Ben's corpse back to his horse: "I'm takin' him back! This is what I came for and now I got it.... He's gonna pay for my land!" Lena reminds Howie that he's neither a cold blooded killer nor a heartless ghoul. She reminds him that he's burdened by a conscience: "Ben's not dead if you take him back! He'll never be dead for you!" Howie continues dragging the corpse: "I don't care anything about that. The money, that's all I care about, that's all I've ever cared about.... I'm taking him back, I swear it! I'm gonna sell him for money!" Here Howie breaks down in tears, an unusual display of feminine emotion for one of Mann's heroes. He finally realizes who he is. In the end, rather than hauling Ben's remains in for the reward, Howard foregoes the blood money and gives Ben a proper Christian burial. He finds redemption, not through earning the money to buy back his ranch, but by rediscovering his lost honor and winning the love of a fine lady. Howard and Lina ride off together with plans of building a ranch in California, the western frontier of the western frontier, the land of new beginnings.

The Far Country

Mann and Stewart's fourth vehicle is set on the last frontier — the Klondike, Yukon territory. Screenwriter Borden Chase draws from many of the same elements that structured his script for *Red River*. James Stewart plays the role of the rugged, individualistic hero, Jeff Webster, who is traveling as far west as possible to start anew. As Ben, Walter Brennan reprises the role he played in *Red River*, the old coot sidekick, the hero's only friend. Just like Dunston in *Red River*, Jeff is a hard man — stubborn, driven, and not to be trifled with. He is wanted for killing two of his hired hands on the way up north for trying to back out of the drive. Jeff later explains, as an afterthought, that they were also trying to rustle his cattle. Upon arriving on the Canadian border, he realizes that he must steal his own cattle back from the crooked men who run the mining camp town of Scagway.

In the process of evading a dishonest handling fee imposed by the steamboat captain, Jeff and his partners ride their cattle through the town, inadvertently "busting up" a hanging, which was being administered by the town's very Judge-Roy-Bean-like representative of law and order, Mr. Gannon (John McIntire). Ironically, the character that Mr. Gannon is based on, Judge Roy Bean, was played by none other than Walter Brennan in the quintessential depiction of the Judge Roy Bean character, *The Westerner* (1940). Judge Bean was the self-appointed marshal, prosecutor, judge, jury, and executioner for the Texas frontier town he ruled. He was ruthless and corrupt in all of these functions. Like Judge Roy Bean in *The Westerner*, Gannon holds "trial" in the saloon at the poker table, holding a deck of cards in one hand and an open whiskey bottle in the other. He acquits Jeff of the double murder charge (seeing no personal profit in another execution), but then confiscates Jeff's herd of cattle, as a fine for "busting up" his hanging. Jeff makes the facile transition from cowboy to outlaw by stealing back his herd. He then heads northwest, to the edge of the frontier, the icy far country of the Yukon mountains.

The hero role in Mann's Westerns was described by Jeanine Basinger as "the man with a secret." The killing of a brother or father, a violent past as an outlaw, the betrayal of a fiancée or friend — these are the secrets and conflicts that drive Mann's hero. At this point in the Mann/Stewart series, the audience can just assume that the hero is running from something, that he is haunted by a specter of his past. There's no need to explain it explicitly; he just tells his current love interest, Renee (Corinne Calvet), "I trusted a woman ... once." That's all we need to know. In an earlier scene, while walking alone in the woods, Renee tells Jeff: "He [Ben] said you don't even like people." Jeff answers: "Is there any reason why I should?" "Of course...." she tells him, and then refers to the sound of a lone wolf howling in the distance, "...you'll be lonely ... like him." Jeff replies: "Maybe he likes to be lonely, did you ever think of that? He never asks any favors because he can take care of himself. He never trusts anybody so he doesn't get hurt. That's not a bad way to live." Of course, Jeff will have to learn to trust and ask favors in order to become a complete man — a man who is able to love a woman and live amongst other men. By the end, Jeff must become the lone wolf who returns to the pack.

Jeff's first self-reflective moment comes when he and his companions witness a group of travelers getting buried under an avalanche. He feels bad for the travelers, but insists that they move along, while Ben (his mentor/conscience) and Renee (his anima) insist that they go and help. Renee: "We've got to go and help those people." Ben: "You're wrong, Jeff, ya gotta help." Jeff asks, "Why?" Renee responds with surprise: "Why? If you don't know why...." Jeff looks inwardly for a moment, realizes that there is a social element within him that hasn't been completely denied, and changes his mind. He rescues the survivors of the avalanche.

Mann often uses the metaphor of the external healing of a physical wound to represent the inner healing of a psychological wound. In *Bend of the River*, Glyn's disgraceful past is represented by the rope scar on his neck, which he is too ashamed to show anyone until the end. In *The Naked Spur*, Howie must recover from a leg injury before he can complete his journey of self-redemption. In *The Far Country*, Jeff is shot in the right hand during an ambush in which Ben is killed. The injury to his shooting hand is symbolically emasculating, and it is also the representation of his psychological handicap — his inability to trust anyone — which leaves him isolated and alone. The elimination of Ben, Jeff's only friend and his only connection to society, exacerbates this sense of isolation. The healing of his hand requires that he not only trust someone else, but that he give himself over completely to a woman, Renee. In this way, he overcomes the trauma of his earlier betrayal in order to become whole again. As a result of this transformation, Jeff finally dedicates himself to the cause of saving the community, which means that he will have to put his life on the line by confronting the villains. The violent confrontation he initiates at the end of the film has a purpose beyond revenge for Ben's murder. Jeff kills the villains in order to bring peace and security to the community. In doing so, he forsakes his lone wolf status and rejoins the pack, immersing himself in the community and allowing himself to love and be loved by a woman.

The Man from Laramie

Mann and Stewart's fifth and final Western collaboration is a mythical tale that combines elements of the oedipal myth, the archetypal sibling rivalry plot, Shakespeare's *King Lear,* and the classic vengeance quest theme. The hero is Will Lockhart (Jimmy Stewart), "the man with a secret." As usual, his only companion is an older male friend, an old coot named Charley (Wallace Ford), who sticks close to his partner out of the immutable sense of loyalty and camaraderie that is intrinsic to his character type. He expresses this sentiment to Will in these words: "I'm a lonely man, Mr. Lockhart. So are you. I don't suppose we spoke ten words coming down here, but I feel that I know you, and I like what I know." The male bonding that develops between the hero and his sidekick, often but not always an old coot, is one of the more sentimental aspects of the Western genre.

Will's secret is that his brother was part of an army regiment that was wiped out by Apaches bearing repeating rifles. He is searching for the man who is selling these repeaters to hostile Indians. His quest brings him to the territory controlled by Alec Waggoman (Donald Crisp), an archetypal cattle baron with a trusted foreman, Vic (Arthur Kennedy), and an extremely wicked son, Dave (Alex Nicol). A sibling rivalry conflict is developing over the inheritance rights of the land. Vic believes that he deserves to inherit half the ranch, as he earned it through hard work and dedication and because, although he isn't Alec's real son, he loves Alec as much as any son could love a father. What's more, he's a much better son to Alec than Dave, who is selfish, reckless and spoiled. We get our first sense of the evil of Dave's character when Dave and his cowboys come upon Will, who is harvesting salt from a salt-flat. Though the salt is free to anyone who wants it, Dave accuses him of "stealing salt" and proceeds to emasculate and torture Will in a manner quite peculiar to the Western. First, he lassoes Will and drags him behind his horse. This is the way a steer is treated, not a man, hence the act of rope dragging is not only a brutal torture, but also a maneuver aimed at dehumanizing and humiliating the victim. To add insult to injury, Dave burns Will's wagons and shoots his mules. When, in a later scene, Will sees Dave in town, he must confront and fight Dave as a point of honor. Before Dave can get the beating he deserves, Vic interferes to help his "brother," and the fight becomes between Will and Vic.

Though Dave's deplorable actions incited the fight, and though Vic fought Dave's battle for him, Alec winds up angry at Vic for the whole affair. Like God's expectation of Cain, the father figure expects the older brother to be his younger brother's keeper. This is because of his contrasting parenting styles with Vic and Dave. With Dave, his biological son, he has always been indulgent, resulting in a son who is soft and undisciplined, a son who — to his own shame — cannot live up to his father's measure. He tells Dave: "I hate to tell you this, but you're not the man I was. Copy me, and you'll meet up with somebody who'll break you, so stop acting like a crazy colt and get a hold of yourself, or you won't get a chance to run this outfit at all! I didn't spend a lifetime building this up for you to fritter it away!" In his attitude towards Vic, Alec is more demanding: "I've been pretty hard on you, Vic, maybe harder than you deserve. Maybe I've been jealous because you're not my son too. Take care of my boy. Love him like a brother, and I'll love you like a son." To this, Vic replies: "All right, *Pa.*"

When Dave overhears this last bit of dialogue, he is driven into a jealous rage, which he takes out on his new nemesis, Will. In another torture peculiar to the genre, Dave perpetrates the most vile act one man can commit upon another in a Western, short of lynching. Dave has his cowboys hold Will by the arms as he puts his revolver flush against the inside of Will's palm and blows a hole right through the center of his hand. In destroying his victim's right hand, the villain takes away his ability to shoot a gun, thus leaving him unable to defend himself. It is a barbaric and sadistic means of robbing a man of his honor, dignity, and masculinity. The major flaw in this otherwise classic psychological Western is that this most cowardly and dastardly deed is never properly avenged. The fact that Dave is the man selling repeaters to Apaches, the same rifles that killed Will's brother, only adds icing to the cake. Though it makes dramatic sense for Vic to be the one who kills Dave, in fulfillment of the sibling rivalry theme, the psychological need for Will to kill Dave, in retribution for both his brother and his hand, is overwhelming. This need is left completely unfulfilled.

A leitmotif of dream symbolism provides a Biblical/psychoanalytic connotation to the film. Alec is going blind. As an apparent compensation for his visual disability, he has developed a "second sight" in the form of a recurring dream, which he describes to Will: "A stranger comes into my home. He's tall, lean, like yourself; has a voice like yours, even walks like you ... He comes with a gun in his hand. He comes to kill my boy." The dream prophecy adds a level of suspense and mythical weight to the plot. Both Alec and the audience assume that Will is the stranger in the dream who will kill Dave. Hence, both Alec and the audience are a bit surprised when it is Vic, not Will, who fulfills the prophecy. We are also confused by the fact that Vic is not a stranger (he'd been living on the ranch since he was a boy), that he's not particularly tall or lean, and that he doesn't walk or talk like Jimmy Stewart. We might explain the "stranger" element by saying that there was an aspect of Vic's character that was a stranger to Alec — i.e. his secret complicity in Dave's illicit arms trade — but the prophecy, in general, must be accepted as being misleading.

Another flaw in the film is revealed in the demise of the two brothers. Dave's final moments are a descent into paranoid psychosis. He declares that everyone's against him: "I can't trust nobody no more!" He vows to arm the entire Apache nation with repeaters and hire them to kill everyone in the territory at his behest. His psychotic need to destroy everything is clearly an act of overcompensation for his raging inferiority complex. Dave's last words are: "I'll show you who's weak and who's strong!" Vic draws on him and kills him, simultaneously delivering the psychiatric diagnosis: "You're crazy!" It was enough for Dave to be a nasty villain with psychopathic/sadomasochistic proclivities. Though his psychotic break ratcheted up the psychological intensity, he didn't need to become a raving lunatic. Dave's crack-up into total madness was psychological overkill. As for Vic, he not only kills his "brother," but in an attempt to hide his crime, he nearly kills his "father" as well. Once again, it would be enough for Vic to commit these acts of violence in keeping with the Biblical/mythical themes intrinsic to the genre. But the final twist, in which Vic is revealed to be a gun runner as well, does not make sense. Its only purpose seems to be to give Will a target for his vengeance quest, once Dave is out of the picture. When Will finds Vic preparing to sell a wagon of rifles to the Apache, he says: "I came a thousand miles to kill you." But when he aims his rifle at Vic's chest, Will experiences his self-reflective moment. He cannot murder an unarmed man, no matter how much he deserves it. "Get away from me," he tells Vic, who rides off unarmed, only to be killed by the Apache.

All in all, *The Man from Laramie* is a bit of a mixed bag. As Mann's first film in Cinemascope, the images are glorious and breathtaking. *Laramie* is perhaps Mann's most visually appealing movie. The film has wonderful mythical and Biblical overtones, as well as a great cast. The scene in which

Dave shoots Will in the hand is jarring and raw, and there are some other great scenes as well. However, the flaws in the plot draw away from the over-all effect of the film. Kitses refers to Mann as "The Overreacher," and this designation certainly makes sense when looking at *Laramie*. Mann seemed to be over-reaching, trying to do too much, forcing psychological complexity onto narratives and themes that are best left simple, and pushing characters and plots into the realm of psychological overkill.

The Last Frontier

This Western was a bit of a departure for Mann. It was his first and only cavalry Western. Rather than his usual hero character, this story featured the archetypal White Indian character as the protagonist, which may be why Mann chose to cast Victor Mature rather than Jimmy Stewart for the lead role. Mature's brawny, raffish physicality provides a much needed change from Stewart's willowy, pensive neuroticism. The hero, Jed Cooper (Mature), is a fur trapper who travels with two sidekicks: Gus (James Whit-more), an elderly frontiersman who plays a father figure to young Jed, and Mungo (Pat Hogan), an Indian who symbolizes Jed's spiritual brotherhood with the red man. The days of the wide-open frontier are drawing to a close, as Gus so eloquently puts it: "Civilization is creepin' up on us, lads. The Blue Coats aren't satisfied with gobblin' up all the lands east of the 'Sippi. No, they won't stop till they've pushed us over the Rockies and into the Pacific Ocean. It's a drownin' fate that awaits us all. These are calamitous times, Jed, calamitous times."

The three trappers wind up as cavalry scouts stationed at a remote fort. Jed, who is given over completely to impulse, develops an infatuation with the Colonel's wife, Corinna (Anne Bancroft), despite admonishments from Gus —"She's a fancy lady, and she needs a fancy gent." The cavalry commander, Colonel Marston (Robert Preston), is a perfect example of the Custer archetype. He is mad with ambition and tortured by self-doubt and feelings of inadequacy. He's cursed with a massive inferiority complex, for which he overcompensates, resulting in a superiority complex — a psychopathic and self-destructive obsession to exterminate the local Indians, whom he perceives as subhuman. When his subordinate officer calls into question his suicidal plan to attack Chief Red Cloud's camp, Marston replies: "Are you afraid of this ignorant savage?" While he minimizes the abilities of the enemies that he considers inferior, he amplifies his own abilities, as when he refers to his exploits in the Civil War: "I dared where cautious men stood still!" For this daring, in which he "lost 1,500 men in a single encounter," Marston was branded with the title "the Butcher of Shiloh."

In Mann's Westerns, the hero's underlying goal is always to reintegrate into the community, to become a normal, productive member of society. In each of the Jimmy Stewart films, the hero's long-term goal was to settle down and build a ranch once his short-term goal, his obsessive inner conflict over revenge or betrayal, was resolved. *The Last Frontier* is different, as the hero's goal of reintegration is his primary one — there is no murdered brother or jilting lover in his backstory to deal with. Jed's self-reflective moments focus on his desire to be with Corinna, the representative of feminine white civilization, and his desire to be a real member of the cavalry, the representative of masculine white civilization. After a furtive liaison with Corinna, Jed is depressed by the realization that she will never have him for a husband, but only as a secret lover. He confides in Gus: "Sometimes she looks at me like I was a bear." Ben replies: "There's some comfort in being a bear, when you live in bear country." "But I don't wanna be a bear!" Jed responds despondently. Later, when Marston discovers the affair between Jed and his wife, he employs his sergeant to assassinate Jed, but the plan backfires and Jed kills the sergeant in self-defense. As Jed is literally standing on the fence between the fort and the wilderness, Marston and his captain demand that Jed come down and accept his punishment for killing the sergeant — a court-martial and a hanging. Feeling betrayed and disgusted by the white hypocrites around him, he tears off the cavalry coat he's wearing and throws it to the ground: "I would've died for this. It's nothing but a dirty, filthy, blue rag!"

In addition to the romantic rivalry over Corinna, Marston's determination to attack the Indians brings him into direct conflict with Jed, who values the lives of both white and red men. In essence, Jed's conflicts with Marston symbolize the conflict between the savage and civilized elements within the hero's soul, the contrasting sides of the White Indian character. The film is progressive because the Indians, who are depicted as peaceful and honorable, seem less savage than the bloodthirsty colonel, who is interested only in war and mayhem and the military advancement he can attain through victory. Marston's ill-conceived attack on Red Cloud's camp results in the death of Gus, dozens of cavalrymen, and the colonel himself. Jed proves himself a courageous cavalryman by leading the retreat back to the fort, and in the final scene, we see that he eventually makes the transition from a White Indian scout dressed in buckskins to a full-fledged cavalryman, dressed in a blue coat and hat. He has given up the savage element of his personality for the civilized, presumably for the love of Corinna, though we're left to wonder if he's given up more than he's gained.

The Tin Star

In this film, Henry Fonda plays the lead role, which seems tailor-made for Jimmy Stewart. Nevertheless, Fonda's portrayal of Morg Hickman, "the man with a secret," offers a variation from Stewart's intensity. Fonda is at his laconic, laid-back best as a mysterious bounty hunter who comes to town carrying the corpse of an outlaw. The townspeople naturally mistrust the dangerous stranger with his ghoulish prize, despite the fact that Morg practices his trade with a basic sense of honor. He says of his bounty: "It was a fair fight. You won't find any bullet holes in his back." Nevertheless, the occupation of bounty hunter is a dishonorable one in the Western, typically motivated by vengeance or betrayal. In this case, the motivation is betrayal. Morg was once a legitimate sheriff, but the duplicity of the townspeople whom he risked his life to protect soured Morg on the ideal of civil service and drove him into a self-enforced social exile. As a nihilistic loner, he's interested only in himself and his own pocketbook.

Morg later explains the details of his moral regression to the young sheriff, Ben (Anthony Perkins), whom he's taken under his wing. When Ben asks him why he quit marshalling, Morg responds: "I found out I was a fool ... Sheriff I knew in Kansas years ago had it bad like you. Always took his prisoners alive, proud of it. Finally, his wife had a baby, got sick. Doctor said they'd die if they didn't move to a drier climate. They had to have a thousand dollars. So he went to his friend at the bank, but it seems like money and friendship didn't mix...." In this thinly veiled retelling of Morg's backstory, none of his "friends," the townspeople that he defended with his life, would lend him the money to relocate his family. Bounty hunting was the only way he could make a thousand dollars: "There was a man wanted — big reward, dead or alive — so he went after him. Took a long time, took him a long ways from home, but he tracked him down.... By that time, his wife and baby had died. Never had much use for that tin star after that."

As with all of Mann's heroes, Morg's path to redemption is accomplished via reintegration into the community. Morg takes on the role of master to his apprentice, teaching young Ben how to survive as a good sheriff. The master/apprentice relationship recapitulates the father/son relationship, as the training entails the mastery of the same masculine skills that a Western father traditionally imparts to his son. In teaching Ben how to be sheriff, he teaches him how to be a man. He shows him how and when to shoot: "A decent man doesn't want to kill, but if you're gonna shoot, you shoot to kill." He shows him how to drink: "That's your second shot of whiskey.... Gives you more confidence — the wrong kind of confidence." Ben responds,

"I'll get laughed at if I took beer." (In the Western, whiskey is a man's drink; beer is tantamount to milk or water.) As Morg drinks his beer, he replies dryly: "See anyone laughing at me?" Most importantly, Morg shows Ben how to believe in himself, which involves the ability to read other men and ascertain when deadly force is called for: "To have confidence, you gotta keep a cool head. Don't take any chances you don't have to, but wait, and end the fight with one shot." To Ben's argument — "The law says a man ain't to be shot without his chance to surrender" — Morg replies: "Or make his fight. As long as you're wearing that badge, you gotta walk up, tell him to throw 'em up, and then watch which way his hands move. If they go up, you got yourself a prisoner. They go down, he's dead ... or you are."

In addition to the fatherly role he takes on with Ben, Morg also develops a relationship with a local widow, Nona (Betsy Palmer), and her son, Kip (Michel Ray). When he first arrives, Morg in not welcome in town, because of his dubious occupation. He's forced to take a room outside of town, with the widow, who is also an outcast. Nona's deceased husband was an Indian, and her son is a halfbreed. The taboo of miscegenation is too much for the "decent" townspeople to bear, so she is ostracized. When Nona realizes that Morg is not prejudiced, that he doesn't hold her past against her, and that he accepts Kip completely for who he is, she begins to love him. In Morg, she sees redemption — a husband for herself and a father for her boy. In Nona and Kip, Morg sees the wife and son he lost years ago. By the end of the film, Morg has helped Ben pass his initiation into the adult male role of sheriff, by defeating the various outlaws and bad men in town. He has also accepted Nona and Kip into his life. In the final scene, he and Nona and Kip ride out of town together to start a new legitimate life somewhere else. In dialogue somewhat reminiscent of *Shane*, Ben, Morg's figurative son, begs Morg to stay: "Morg, don't go! Stay here and be sheriff. Let me be your deputy till I learn." Morg replies: "You got nothin' more to learn. Maybe I learned from you. A man can't run away from his job ... I'll find me a town needs a sheriff; you got one here." In keeping with his role, the mentor takes his leave once the apprentice hero has learned all he needs to learn. As Morg and his new family ride out of town, the same townspeople who shunned him when he first came wave at him cheerfully and offer fond farewells: "So long, Hickman! Good luck!"

Man of the West

In Mann's most brutal western, Gary Cooper plays Link, a reformed outlaw who has been leading a secret life as an anonymous citizen in a quiet, isolated town. He's taking a trip on a train, secretly carrying a sack of gold coins, on a mission to find a schoolteacher for his town. But the train is stopped by a band of outlaws, who coincidentally turn out to be his former gang. He's held hostage by his uncle and former bandit compadres. As a function of this savage environment, Link degenerates into a specter of his former self. His regressed behavior pattern features intense violence and sadism. Unlike the villains in most of Mann's previous Westerns, the outlaws in this film are not glorified in the least. They are dirty, bestial, brutal, perverse, and repulsive, a portent of the villains to come in the anti–Westerns of the 1960s and '70s.

All of the basic elements of Mann's hero are present. He is a "man with a secret," running away from his shadowy past, and desperate to start anew, to reintegrate into decent society. But in *Man of the West*, these elements are intensified. Link's shadow is not a vengeance quest or betrayal, it is himself. He himself was an outlaw, just as brutal and debased as the villains holding him captive. In order to save himself and the woman in his care, he must pretend to be one of them. In doing so, he allows a dark part of himself to reemerge after years of suppression. What he sees himself becoming terrifies him, yet at the same time, he realizes that the only way he can survive is by using this dark power within him to kill his former gang members, his figurative brothers and father. In doing so, it is clear that he is attempting to kill a part of himself.

Kitses writes of Mann's films: "The hero, his sanity at stake, enters the world of ordinary mortals only through a kind of metaphysical suicide, destroying the mirror of his magic, the incarnation of his pride and ambition. The villain finds his release only through madness and death." Nowhere is this statement more true than in *Man of the West*. A distinct oedipal relationship is evoked between Link and his uncle, Dock Tobin (Lee J. Cobb), the elderly leader of the gang and Link's symbolic father figure. In his outlaw days, Link was Dock's most beloved "son," his "right arm," the heir apparent to the role of gang leader. Dock took Link's departure from the gang as a personal affront, and he mistakenly takes Link's coincidental reappearance as a desire to rejoin the gang, a clear sign of Dock's waning sanity. His demeanor towards Link is a perpetual display of intense ambivalence. He clearly loves Link, but hates him for leaving. He wants so desperately for Link to stay that he threatens to kill him if he tries to escape. Nowhere has there ever been a more overbearing father figure — constantly threatening his son with violence and death, threatening his son's woman with rape, forcing his sons to commit murder and robbery, and loving his son so much that he would rather kill him than let him go.

Though Link is married and has children with a woman in the little town he now calls home, he becomes attached to an attractive fellow hostage, Billie (Julie London), who just happens to be a lady of ill repute. He pretends to be her man in order to protect her from being raped by the other gang members. Coaley (Jack Lord), Link's cousin, forces Billie to strip in front of Dock and the gang, as he holds a knife to Link's throat. The next day, Link provokes a fistfight with Coaley. The fight scene is long and nasty. Link beats his cousin, then strips his pants off as payback for forcing Billie to strip. The forced de-pantsing is more brutal than the fight. Coaley is left emasculated and humiliated in front of the gang. But when Link tries to finish the job he started, when he fastens his hands around Coaley's neck and tries to choke him to death, he experiences a moment of self-reflection. "I can't do it.... I can't...." His descent into darkness stops short at killing a defenseless man. Dock enjoyed the show: "I never saw anything like that in all my life! Link, that was somethin' to make an old man's blood boil!" As Dock praises Link for destroying his cousin, Dock's other nephew, Coaley, crawls to his gunbelt. In a fit of anguish, he grabs his gun and aims at Link. "You can't make fun of me!" he cries over and over again, like a schoolboy whipped in a playground. The fact that Dock is praising Link for beating him adds insult to injury, as he is their shared uncle and figurative father. He fires, but hits an innocent hostage (Arthur O'Connell) who steps in the way. Dock draws and kills Coaley.

In the final act, Link leads the remainder of the gang into town to rob the bank. He leaves Billie temporarily in the care of his uncle, who promises upon his honor to protect her from harm. But of course, there is no honor among these villains. It turns out that the town has no bank — it is a ghost town, a symbol of the loss of potency and sanity in Dock's gang. Link takes advantage of this opportunity to kill off the remaining gang members in a savage gunfight. He returns to find Billie beaten and raped by his uncle, which sets up perfectly the oedipal showdown between Link and Dock. The ambiguous ending of *Man of the West* is very atypical for a Western. After having killed all of the outlaws, including Dock, Mann leaves our hero riding west with Billie. She declares her love for him, but he remains ambivalent and undeclared. Will Link go home to his wife and kids and resume his life as a reformed man, a simple farmer and citizen? Or will he forsake them for the sexy dance-hall girl? Will he take the sack of gold coins (which doesn't rightfully belong to him), give up his reformed life, and return to his wild, uncivilized nature, which he was forced to resume as a means of defeating his captors? What will it be for our hero, the peaceful path of the straight and narrow, or the libidinous excitement of the lawless wild side? For once, Mann leaves it up to the viewer to decide.

Cimarron (1960)

Mann's last Western was a transitional film for the director, who was clearly looking ahead to his next great leap as a filmmaker, from Westerns to epics. *Cimarron* would be a stepping stone for Mann, an epic Western in the tradition of *Duel in the Sun, Giant* (1956), and *The Big Country*. It would be his last contribution to the genre before moving on to period epics — *El Cid* (1961) and *The Fall of the Roman Empire* (1964) — and then a final foray into the spy thriller genre — *The Heroes of Telemark* (1965) and *A Dandy in Aspic* (1968) — before his untimely death in 1967, at the age of 61, during the production of his last film. As such, *Cimarron* is a departure from Mann's typical take on the Western. The focus is on grand social issues and family dynamics rather than psychological conflict and mythical themes of heroism. The hero, Yancey Cravat (Glenn Ford), whose nickname is Cimarron, is not a haunted, conflicted loner. Yancey is gregarious, outgoing, cheerful, and civilized. He starts out married and has a definite plan to build a ranch. There is no dark shadow in Yancey's past, other than a premarital affair with a lady of ill repute (Anne Baxter).

The first part of the film is centered around a spectacular set piece, the Oklahoma Land Rush, in which thousands of settlers make a mad dash to claim their own piece of two million acres of free land. Unfortunately, the build-up to this sequence is so great, and the sequence itself is so exciting, that it makes the rest of the film that follows, nearly two more hours, seem rather dull in comparison. Though the film was taken out of Mann's hands in postproduction and severely butchered by drastic cuts, it still feels way too long. There are many great scenes other than the land rush sequence, such as the atrocious lynching of an Indian, a brutal scene of anti–Semitic violence, a great sequence in which a Billy-the-Kid-like outlaw is killed, and a heartbreaking scene in which a little Indian girl is denied entry into school because of her race. But after the first hour and a half, the film drags on way too long, without much action. The plot is stuck in town, and we see little of Mann's specialty, characters moving against landscapes. What's worse, there are long stretches in which the hero, the only really engaging character, is not even in the movie. The main problem with the picture is that the story focuses more on Yancey's wife, Sabra (Maria Schell), than on him.

The recurring themes of the film — social prejudice, anti–Semitism, racism against Indians — are interesting, but nothing is ever resolved. Like many of the so-called "civil rights Westerns" that were made in the late 1950s and 1960s, the film has its heart in the right place, but civics lessons and ethical dilemmas aren't necessarily engaging or entertaining, especially in a genre that generally promises audiences a lot of action, excitement, and a decisive conclusion. Though Anthony Mann's last Western was his least satisfying, his work as a whole stands out in the genre as some of the most entertaining, powerful, and thought provoking Westerns ever made. The evolution of the genre in the 1950s and '60s, a time which saw the advent of the more gritty anti–Westerns and the socially conscious civil rights Westerns, owes much to Mann's influence. The development of the Western hero into a vastly complex character, torn by inner conflict and contrasting drives, is perhaps the single most important contribution that Anthony Mann made to the genre.

8

John Ford's
Ritualistic Westerns

"A myth that ceases to evoke this religious response, this sense of total identification and collective participation, ceases to function as a myth...."

— Richard Slotkin, 1985

If, as Charles Silver contends, John Ford is the "Shakespeare" of the Western genre, he may also be called its high priest. His films consistently display the traditions and customs of the Old West, ritualizing them and creating a spiritual sentiment that equates the old ways of the frontier with the ancient ancestral rites of mythical times. More than any other filmmaker, Ford's films depict the rites of passage that were key to the formation and regeneration of the American national identity. In each picture, we see the new generation learning from the old, the passing of the mantle of leadership from patriarchs to young men, the assimilation of immigrants into the American culture, and the ritual ceremonies that afford meaning to life and death, which gain added significance when performed in the perilous setting of the wild frontier. As John Cawelti notes:

> The Western, with its historical setting, its thematic emphasis on the establishment of law and order, and its resolution of the conflict between civilization and savagery on the frontier, was a kind of foundation ritual. It presented for our recurrent contemplation that epic moment when the frontier passed from the old way of life into the present. By dramatizing this moment, and associating it with the hero, the Western ritually reaffirmed the creation of America and explored not only what was gained, but what was lost in the movement of American history.

In a modern society bereft of initiating rituals such as the traditional puberty rites, blood rites, and vision quests of older societies, the Western depicted an imaginary realm of initiation in which young males proved their merit, demonstrated their masculinity, and established their cultural identities through ritualistic ordeals and trials of violence. The rite of passage, in which a pubescent male encounters danger, overcomes physical obstacles or painful ordeals, and proves himself worthy of initiation into the company of men, is the psychologically transcendent moment that the Western film provides. Although boys and men experience this transcendence vicariously, via identification with the hero figure, the psychological resonance of the act is no less profound, and by no means less necessary as a process of acculturation. It must be admitted, however, that if the Western did play a part in the acculturation of American boys into manhood, it no longer does so. The Western, for reasons to be discussed in the subsequent chapter, has lost its place in American culture. It is no longer relevant. But in the heyday of the genre, from the late 1930s through the 1960s, going to the movie theater on Friday nights or Saturday afternoons must have been a transcendent experience, much like attending church or temple, especially for the boys who went to the theater specifically to see their favorite B-Western serials.

Fans who experienced the B-Western during its "Golden Age" recall the communal experience of viewing the films as part of an audience — boys shooting cap guns, dressed up as cowboys for the Saturday afternoon matinees, each one earnestly attached to one of the many Western heroes of the silver screen. The experience recapitulates all of the elements of a cultural ritual: congregating at a specific time and place, donning distinctive costumes, using specialized instruments (capguns), and most importantly, engaging in communal expressions of emotion — cheering for the hero, booing the villain, applauding a good ending, etc. As every good ritual does, the cinematic experience of the Western appealed to all of the senses: the sight of the film projected onto the screen, the sound of the film — its music and dialogue — as well as the sounds of the audience, the smell of capgun smoke in the air, the taste of popcorn, and the feel of the velvet-covered seats. Even if the Western were still a vital film genre, the experience of it as a communal ritual could not exist in modern America, as young boys are more likely to spend their Saturday afternoons alone in their living rooms, eyes plastered to the television screen, rather than grouped together in a theater for the matinee.

Beyond the communal experience of the Western, the essence of ritual is experienced through the films themselves. As scholars such as Lord Raglan and Sir James Frazier have pointed out, ritual can be understood as a reenactment of myth. By replaying its foundational stories, legends, and hero sagas through the telling or reenactments of myth, a culture re-experiences its own birth and development and gains a stronger and more resonant sense of its own national identity. Americans have a variety of socio-cultural rituals, such as Thanksgiving turkey, Independence Day fireworks, days of recognition and parades for veterans, fallen soldiers, former presidents, and national heroes. The experience of the Western as a socio-cultural ritual was in one sense less significant — it was experienced vicariously by watching it on a screen, rather than firsthand. But in another sense, it was even more significant, as the individual films were experienced in the exact same way by millions and millions of viewers and because, at the genre's peak, so many films were made each year, featuring, for the most part, the same actors playing the same character types, with the same settings, plots, costumes, and scenery. Modern viewers complain that the old-style Westerns were too repetitive — they all seem the same — but it is this faithful repetition, this charm of ritualized convention and tradition, that fulfills the psychosocial function of the Western film. Certain ritualistic aspects of the genre can be seen in nearly every Western, from beginning to end.

The visual theme of the traditional opening sequence is one of the most recognizable features of the Western genre. The first shot opens on a rugged landscape, the Western frontier in any of its manifold forms. A lone rider or pair of riders appears in the distance, diminutive figures within the awesome endless background of the untamed Western wilderness. They traverse an uninhabited landscape, representing the sacred silence and solitude of the lost frontier. The traditional closing sequence is equally familiar. The hero or pair of heroes rides away from the camera, away from town, away from civilization, back into the desolate wilderness, riding forever westward into the setting sun. It may only be a coincidence that many of the great myth-making cultures, the Egyptians, Greeks, Romans, and Northern Europeans, imagined the western lands to be the home of the spirits and gods, the place where the sun spirit died, only to be reborn the next morning in the east. So too did the frontier heroes ride off into the west, fading away at the end of each replaying of their myth, only to reappear in the beginning of the next film, riding with the sun at their backs, ready to face the same challenges and embark with courage on the same adventure.

Between the conventional opening and closing sequences, the Western is filled with other ritualized reenactments of the frontier myth. The most infamous is the violent climax, in which the tension of the plot is resolved through the shootout or showdown between hero and villain, a depiction of the traditional gentlemen's duel, which itself represents a cultural ritual dating back to the age of chivalry. Filmmakers who understood the psychosocial function of the genre made sure to create a long suspenseful build-up to the showdown, as it is this moment in which the primal force of the Western — the viewer's identification with the hero and his vicarious catharsis of emotional tension — is achieved. The showdown is preceded by a scene of preparation, in which the hero arms himself, methodically loading and cocking his guns. There is the slow and deliberate walking approach between the conflicting figures, the exchange of words leading to a mutual demand for satisfaction, and the tacit enforcement of the rules for the quick-draw showdown.

The Western is also filled with rituals that designate specific meaning to both life and death in the regenerative landscape of the frontier. Funeral scenes are particularly important, especially in John Ford's films, as they not only recognize the sacrifices made by our nation's pioneers, but also provide motivation for the cathartic retributive violence to come. The ritual of scalping gives us a sense of the element of wildness and savagery on the frontier, which still lingers in the modern psyche. When performed by the Indian, the ritual evokes consternation and fear. When performed by white men, the effect is that of dubious self-questioning and shame. Similar feelings are evoked by the act of lynching, while the act of hanging is more or less accepted as just punishment when preceded by a fair trial. The ritual of indulging the victim in his last words (usually a prayer) and a last request (usually tobacco) is perceived as being solemnly appropriate at a hanging, but grossly hypocritical at a lynching.

Communal singing of traditional hymns such as "Shall We Gather at the River" and "Rock of Ages" are common at hangings, but also at weddings, camp meetings, and church services. John Ford was particularly fond of depicting traditional folk and square dances, which not only provide a glimpse of old-time Americana, but also reaffirm the national ideals of community, family, and cultural tradition. Fistfights were a mainstay of the Western genre, conspicuous in nearly all of Ford's Westerns. While the showdown is a moment of awe and solemnity, a fatal encounter, the fistfight provided emotional catharsis via non-lethal violence and was typically played for laughs.

The music of the Western was particularly ritualized. Traditional frontier ballads, cowboy songs, folk songs, hymns, and cavalry ditties were often sung by the characters themselves. Other times, the songs were played over the opening and closing credits. The melody of the particular theme song for each film became intertwined with the musical themes in the soundtrack. In the 1950s and early '60s, it was customary for an original title song to be created based on the title and plot of the film (e.g., *High Noon, The Searchers,* and *The Man Who Shot Liberty Valance*). These songs were always traditional in style, sounding like an old folk or frontier song performed by a contemporary crooner. Bugle calls, cavalry shouts, and army commands were particularly important in cavalry films, giving the viewer an auditory sense of the military tradition. Cowboys and cavalry scouts were always adept at making and recognizing bird calls, as this skill was necessary in locating the presence of hiding Indians and deciphering their communications. The Western dialogue itself, a distinct vernacular or "lingo," was a ritualistic manner of speech, not necessarily historically accurate, but peculiar to the Western scenario and evocative of the feel of the Western setting. The Western costume — blue jeans, boots, spurs, chaps, gunbelts, holsters, guns, bandannas, and ten-gallon hats — all add an element of tradition to the Western character. The conventional pastime (poker), the invariable beverages (whiskey and coffee), and the ubiquitous oral fixations (cigarettes and chewing tobacco) all provide a ritualized sense of connection and harmony between the Western characters in all of the genre's films.

Stagecoach (1939)

Though *Stagecoach* doesn't feature any formal ritual ceremonies — there are no weddings, funerals, or dances — the film is packed full of the archetypal themes and characters that would make the Western itself a ritualistic aspect of American culture. And while it wasn't among Ford's first Westerns — he made a number of Westerns in the silent era, including one of his greatest early films, *The Iron Horse* (1924) — *Stagecoach* was the first film that John Ford shot in Monument Valley, the setting which would become Ford's outdoor "cathedral," in which he would set nearly all of his subsequent Westerns. In this way, *Stagecoach* could be seen as the first in a sequence of a dozen Westerns made in the latter half of Ford's career (1939–1962) that embody the classical themes and motifs that would become identified with his work as a director.

Each character in *Stagecoach* is a fully developed archetype. The only original aspect of the film is the way in which these archetypes interact. The opening shot, after the credits, is traditional — two lone riders in the mythical landscape of Monument Valley. They ride into a cavalry camp to report that Geronimo and his hostile Apaches are on the warpath. In *Stagecoach,* Indians are portrayed in the traditional way, as wild forces of nature, faceless threats in a savage environment, an image that would persist for the next

decade of Westerns. After the brief prelude informing us of the encroach-
ing danger, we go to the town of Tonto, where we're introduced to the cast
of characters. Dallas (Claire Trevor) is the whore with the heart of gold, and
we meet her in a very traditional scene, in which she is being run out of
town by a gang of stuffy old ladies, representatives of the "Law and Order
League."

Being simultaneously exiled is Doc Boone (Thomas Mitchell), the
drunken town doctor, another recurring Western character. Saunders noted
on this archetype: "There seems to be a convention that the more educated
elements of society — doctors, newspaper editors, actors — need to anesthetize
themselves against the rigours of the West." This may be true, but perhaps
a more down-to-earth, less poetic interpretation would be that these characters' weakness in vice was what led them in the first place to their ignominious exile in the wilds of the western wasteland. In either case, it is a
basic truism or cliché that the western doctor is always a drunk. Other examples of the educated lush in Ford's Westerns include the drunken newspaper editor in *The Man Who Shot Liberty Valance* and the drunken Shakespearean actor in *My Darling Clementine*. In the Western, our sympathies
are generally drawn to the white outcasts of white society (as opposed to the
red or brown outcasts). The hero is an outlaw, his woman a whore, and his
friend a drunk. Dallas complains to Doc: "Haven't I any right to live?" Doc
responds eloquently: "We're the victims of a foul disease called social prejudice." The Western was progressive in its treatment of "social prejudice"
towards outsiders. Its treatment of racial prejudice would remain retrograde
until the 1950s and '60s.

The next character in the ensemble that we're introduced to is Mr. Peacock (Donald Meek), a timid whiskey drummer from Kansas City whom
Doc befriends in order to sample his wares. Peacock is out of place in the
wild frontier, representing the weakness of the civilized town folk. In the
bank we meet the villain, Mr. Gatewood (Berton Churchill), the greedy
bank manager who is leaving town with a sack full of embezzled money. In
the saloon, we meet another archetype, the tinhorn gambler, Hatfield (John
Carradine), a former Confederate soldier and southern gentleman now fallen
into disgrace and given to vice, his life filled with poker, whiskey, and gun-
smoke. He takes the stagecoach in order to accompany the southern belle,
Lucy Mallory (Louise Platt), the gentle lady from the East, who easily fits
the archetypal role of the schoolmarm. She is joining her husband, a cavalry commander, in Lordsburg, taking the arduous journey despite her late
stage of pregnancy. Driving the stagecoach is Buck (Andy Devine), the
chubby, whiney, and cowardly man-child who provides comic relief. Rid-

Disparate Riders. George Bancroft as Marshal Curly Wilcox, John Wayne (middle) as the Ringo Kid, and Louise Platt as Lucy Mallory in John Ford's *Stagecoach* (1939, United Artists).

ing shotgun is the marshal, Curly (George Bancroft), the tough and rugged Westerner who dutifully enforces the law in his territory, while occasionally bending the letter of the law in favor of a more honorable tradition, the Code of the West.

Not far from town, the stagecoach comes upon the Ringo Kid (John Wayne), whose horse has gone lame. Ringo is a traditional Western hero, the good badman, who was in jail for defending his family's honor with violence and who busted out in order to complete the job: to kill the three Plummer boys, the men who killed his father and brother. Vengeance, of course, is an honorable motive in the Western, despite its illegality and dubious morality. McGrath summed up both the character of Ringo and the archetype he represents with these words:

> The Ringo Kid is a product of the frontier, the natural man with a pure heart, uncorrupted by civilization. He has an intuitive sense of right and wrong, of justice, and of love that is not distorted by artificial norms imposed by society. He is guileless, has courage in abundance, and, despite his youth,

has a world of experience in the things that count—riding, shooting, and fighting Indians. He exemplifies the Code of the West: A man's word is his bond; great deference is paid to women; a man is expected to stand and fight; death is preferable to dishonor.

Curly, interested mainly in keeping the young Ringo from getting himself killed, takes Ringo into custody on the stagecoach. Almost all of the major characters in the stagecoach are seeking redemption in one way or another. Redemption in itself is an archetypal theme in the Western, as the frontier represents the environment of moral and spiritual rebirth. Dallas, haunted by her promiscuous past, is seeking reintegration into society. Ringo is seeking reintegration as well, but he cannot relinquish his vengeance quest until it is complete. His honor depends on the inevitable fatal encounter that awaits him. Hatfield is drawn to Lucy because he sees in her his lost honor and nobility. Doc is unaware of his need to overcome his alcoholism and regain his personal pride in his profession, but the situation will arise in which he is called to heal himself in order to heal another. The meek Mr. Peacock will become empowered, the cowardly Buck will show bravery, and the rigid Curly will show flexibility. All of the characters will change except Lucy and Gatewood, the representatives of Eastern society. Their snobbish codes of conduct are out of place in the West and inherently contradictory to the Western code of ethics.

Tension soon arises between the disparate classes of people on the stagecoach. The upper class folk—Lucy, Hatfield, and Gatewood—shun the lower-class folk—Dallas and Ringo. Though at first, we suspect that Ringo's acceptance of Dallas is due to his youthful ignorance of her profession, we eventually learn that his acceptance is a natural part of his character. Like the West himself, he is open to people who want to change and start anew. He doesn't hold their past deeds against them. When he proposes marriage to Dallas, she tells him: "But you don't know me. You don't know who I am!" Ringo responds: "I know all I wanna know." In short, he knows that she's a good, strong, kind, and decent woman who's had some bad luck (the Indian massacre of her family as a girl, forcing her into the flesh trade). Ringo experienced the male version of this bad luck (the killing of his family by gunmen, forcing him into a vengeance quest that led to imprisonment). Both the kind-hearted whore and the noble outlaw deserve a chance at redemption. The uppity Easterners don't accept this notion of social mobility, which is why they don't fit in.

Along the way, we briefly meet a few more archetypes: a gallant young cavalry officer (Tim Holt), a dimwitted but helpful Mexican (Chris-Pin Martin), and his halfbreed wife (Elvira Rios), who betrays the white folks to her Apache brethren. The central crisis of the film occurs when Lucy goes into labor. The birth of her child allows for the spiritual rebirth of several characters. Doc Boone sobers up long enough to deliver the baby, proving to himself and everyone else that he is still a viable member of his most honorable profession. Dallas helps Lucy and the Doc, staying up all night to take care of the baby. Ringo notices her kindness and maternal devotion, especially in light of the snobbish way that Lucy had treated her previously. He begins to fall in love with her. After the birth, when the men belly up to the bar to drink to Doc and the newborn, Peacock, the quintessential family man, stands up to all the other men by telling them to be quiet, as Lucy needs to sleep. This is his first flash of boldness. Later on, he will be hit by an Apache arrow, but will survive. In the end, when Lucy thanks Dallas for her help but gives her a final snub, Peacock gives Dallas full social acceptance. He invites her to visit his family at his home in Kansas City, displaying the possibility for social renewal, at least within the middle class, if not among the social elite.

In the only action sequence in the film, the Apaches attack the stagecoach. All of the men except Gatewood show their bravery in fighting off their attackers. When they've run out of ammunition and all seems lost, Hatfield spins the last bullet in his revolver under the firing pin, and places the barrel up to Lucy's head. As usual, the last bullet theme — honor before outrage for the white woman — is called into play, but not used. An Apache bullet hits Hatfield before he can pull the trigger. A moment later, a bugle call heard off-screen signals the cavalry charge, riding in at the last minute to save the day. After a valiant fight, Hatfield finds redemption in a noble death, the most honorable end he could hope for.

Upon arriving in Lordsburg, Gatewood gets his comeuppance, when he is arrested for embezzlement. A grateful Lucy, bound by her social status and caste-snobbery, snubs Dallas. A moment later, an injured Mr. Peacock accepts her. Curly allows Ringo to resolve his vengeance quest by seeking out the Plummer boys for a showdown. The pace of the film slows down to a crawl as mythical elements of the Western scenario add depth to the denouement. Luke Plummer (Tom Tyler), the elder of the villainous gunmen, draws the "dead man's hand" in poker — aces and eights — just as he's told that Ringo is in town. As he and his brothers step out of the saloon, a black cat crosses their path, another portent of imminent death. Meanwhile, Ringo accompanies Dallas on a long walk into the dark and dismal red light district of town. On each saloon porch is a sad, old whore for Dallas to gaze at, projections of her future life of degradation. Upon arriving at the rickety footbridge that leads to the entrance of the bordello, which looks as dark and foreboding as a haunted house, Ringo repeats his proposal. His devotion to her is twice as significant now, as their can be no doubt about her shameful profession, but Dallas assumes that he'll die in his showdown with the Plummers. He asks her to wait for him on the bridge, literally stuck in the middle between two potential futures. She waits.

After a long walking approach between the lone Ringo and his three adversaries, Ringo kills the three Plummer boys with three shots from his rifle. He returns to Dallas, to rescue her from her fate. Curly and Doc Boone ride up in a wagon. To Ringo's surprise, Curly gives him his freedom, appealing to a higher sense of justice than the one written down in the law books. Ringo and Dallas ride off to start a new life together. Doc says in an ironic tone: "Well, they're saved from the blessings of civilization." Free from the ghosts of their pasts and the rigid boundaries and snobberies of town society, Ringo and Dallas can build their own paradise on their remote ranch, the Adam and Eve of a new America, built on the Western frontier.

Drums Along the Mohawk (1939)

Drums Along the Mohawk is a colonial-era Western, focusing on a pair of newlyweds who move to the dangerous frontier, upstate New York, to build a new life and a new country. To do so, they must learn to survive among the hostile Indians. The film begins with a wedding, the ritual that binds together Gilbert (Henry Fonda) and Lana (Claudette Colbert), who represent the founding pioneers of America. The minister prays: "O Almighty God, look down upon and bless these two young people, as they go forth this day into the wilderness to make themselves a new home." As they drive their wagon out west, the minister comforts Lana's weeping mother: "It's always been like this, since Bible days. Every generation must make its own way, in one place or another." The westward voyage is portrayed as a Biblical passage to a new promised land. Gil and Lana are the Adam and Eve of the American Eden. Their pain, suffering, and sacrifice paved the way for this nation, and their blood, tears, and sweat irrigated the land for its future generations. This is the tale of their trials and ordeals.

Once Gil and Lana are settled on their farm, Ford brings the next level of the narrative into play with the rituals of a military roll call and drill for the local men, who are all required to serve in the militia, which will be called in to fight the Indians allied with the Tories in the Revolutionary War. In Ford's Westerns, the building and settling of the land is secondary in importance to the defense of it, casting the military tradition as superior to the settler's traditions. Directly after the roll call and drill, Ford shows the settlers' ritual of a communal ground clearing, in which all of the locals help the newcomers clear their fields of trees and boulders. The same men who bore muskets on their shoulders now bear axes and saws, but to the same general purpose: the conquering of the land. Hostile Indians, led by a villainous Tory (John Carradine), attack the farm and burn it down. While Gil is off with the militia driving back the attackers, Lana has a miscarriage. This is just the beginning of their trials and sacrifices. The homeless couple is forced to take jobs in the house of an old widow, Mrs. McKlennar (Edna May Oliver). The first major scene in this new chapter of their lives is another communal ritual, a Sunday church service. Ironically, the preacher's sermon becomes a call to arms, as all local men are pressed into service to fight in the war. In Ford's Westerns, religion and politics go hand in hand, as service to one's God is equated with service to one's country. In 1939, with the tides of war stirring around the world, the tearful scene in which Lana sends Gil off to battle was surely quite resonant among contemporary audiences. Upon Gil's return from the grisly battle, two scenes shown back to back provide juxtaposition. First, the death of the militia's general from a war wound. He is carried out somberly by his men, who recite a prayer over him while the drummer beats the death march. Next, Ford jump-cuts to a few months later, with Lana giving birth to her first son. The symbolism is clear — death and life are all part of the same regenerative cycle. The community, the people, endure and live on.

Directly after the birth scene, Ford takes us to yet another ritual, a harvest festival and dance. The dance scene appears in almost all of Ford's Westerns, giving the audience a taste of traditional American music, costume, and dance and establishing the vitality of the community as the central force within the story — the thing worth fighting and dying for. In the climactic sequence, the Tories and their Indian allies attack, forcing the settlers to take shelter in their newly built fort. The raiders burn down all of the farmhouses as they approach the fort. After a variety of sacrifices and heroic acts performed by Gil and his comrades, the town is saved from the savage attackers. Lana and the baby are safe. The people will live on. The war is over, and in the wake of sacrifice, destruction, and death, a new nation is born. In the final scene, another ritual, the raising of the new American flag onto the church steeple, offers a solemn moment of reflection. While "My Country 'Tis of Thee" plays on the soundtrack, various people — white settlers, a black servant, a friendly Indian — all look up at the flag with reverence for what it represents: the promise of a bold new beginning. Gil turns to Lana, and in Henry Fonda's trademark "simple folk" style, says: "Well, I reckon we better be gettin' back to work." The people have their victory, and the eternal struggle goes on.

My Darling Clementine (1946)

Ford's first Western after the war is the definitive version of the most frequently depicted artifact in the mythology of the Western frontier — the legend of Wyatt Earp and the infamous shootout at the O.K. Corral. What distinguishes Ford's version is the mythical feeling to his film, born through the beauty and simplicity of his shots and the masterful way in which Ford coordinates the different archetypal elements of the Western myth. The film opens in Ford's cathedral, Monument Valley, with Wyatt (Henry Fonda) and his brothers driving their cattle across the rough terrain. While the older brothers visit the town of Tombstone, the villainous Clantons rustle their cattle and murder the youngest brother, James (Don Garner), who was left behind to mind the herd. Forsaking a formal funeral scene, Ford opts for a quiet moment of solemnity, with eldest brother Wyatt placing a marker on his youngest brother's grave and speaking to him gently, with the majestic buttes of Monument Valley looking on impassively in the background: "...maybe when we leave this country, young kids like you will be able to grow up and live safe." Wyatt makes it clear that in taking the position of marshal of Tombstone, his aim is not just to avenge his brother's death, but to bring law and order to the Wild West.

The contrasting archetype to Wyatt's honorable marshal in the tinhorn gambler, Doc Holliday (Victor Mature). As with Wyatt Earp, the character of Doc Holliday has been depicted many times by many notable actors. Cesar Romero played the role in *Frontier Marshal* (1939), Kirk Douglas in *Gunfight at the O.K. Corral* (1957), Jason Robards in the sequel, *Hour of the Gun* (1967), Dennis Quaid in *Wyatt Earp* (1994), and Val Kilmer in *Tombstone* (1993). In many ways, the character of Doc is a juicier role than that of Wyatt. Doc is the healer turned destroyer, the Easterner turned Westerner, the Southern rebel turned outlaw gambler, the disgraced gentleman seeking honor and redemption in a violent death. He is full of conflicts and self-hatred. Welcoming death, he treats his consumption with a steady diet of booze and cigarettes, epitomizing the tragic drive towards self-destruction characterized in all gamblers, drunkards, and gunslingers. In *Clementine*, his inner turmoil is represented by the two women vying for his affections: the halfbreed showgirl, Chihuahua (Linda Darnell), and the Southern-belle schoolmarm, Clementine (Cathy Downs). As a disgraced

Southerner, Doc symbolizes the shadow of the Western hero, his unconscious motivations and darkest impulses. He also embodies the post–Civil War melancholia felt for the lost era of Southern chivalry, the mythical antebellum era in which whites were rich and honorable and the slaves were well-mannered and happy with their lot, a fairytale time romanticized in films such as *Gone with the Wind* (1939) and *Jezebel* (1938). Like other displaced Southerners in Western scenarios (such as the title character in *Shane*, Ethan Edwards in *The Searchers*, Lin McAdams in *Winchester '73*), the ex-rebel outlaw is an anathema, a relic from a time that's "lost and gone forever," just like the title character in the song, "My Darling Clementine."

Despite their differences, both Wyatt and Doc are bound by honor to a mission of vengeance and death. Wyatt must kill the men who killed his brothers; Holliday must kill the man who seduced and killed Chihuahua. At the climactic shootout, Holliday becomes the Old South's prodigal son. He redeems his long-lost honor after a sinful and wasted life, via a noble and gallant fight to the death. Before the end, Ford treats his viewers to a variety of Western archetypes and rituals. The Shakespearean actor, Granville Thorndyke (Alan Mowbray), comes to town, another example of the educated lush. His comical entrance and exit add depth and irony to the film, reminding us that what we are seeing is an American frontier version of a mythical tale of chivalry and honor. His recitation of Hamlet's famous soliloquy is especially significant for both Wyatt and Doc, who observe the actor with intense interest. Like Hamlet, Wyatt knows the identity of his loved one's murderer, yet he remains curiously inactive, stoically biding his time. Similarly, Doc knows that death is near, yet, like Hamlet, he lacks the courage or the inclination to take his own life: "Thus, conscience does make cowards of us all."

The centerpiece of the film is the traditional square dance, held on the floor of the church, which is just being built. As Wyatt escorts Clementine through the center of town, towards the wooden frame of what will be the church, with a bell ringing in its hollow steeple, we get the sense of a budding community, the frontier nation at its infancy, with Wyatt and Clementine as its eventual matriarch and patriarch. The church dedication and dance is the only formal ritual in the film, but it is the emotional heart of the picture. It is the grand purpose behind the violence, the thing worth fighting for, and the positive, promising side of romance and love, as opposed to the dark, doomed relationship between Doc and Chihuahua. As Wyatt and Clementine spin around the dance floor, we can't help but be reminded of a similar scene in Ford's *The Grapes of Wrath* (1940), in which Fonda's character dances with his mother and the same sense of community and family is established.

Fort Apache (1948)

By the time he made the first film in what would become known as Ford's "Cavalry Trilogy," the mythical landscape of Monument Valley was firmly established as John Ford territory. Filmmakers who used that setting ran the risk of being called imitators or even counterfeiters of the master. Within the U.S. Cavalry tradition, Ford found a plethora of rituals that portrayed the history, customs, and culture of the American forefathers who conquered the West. The army dance sequences are ritualized ceremonies that represent the establishment of Eastern and European traditions within the white man's civilized enclave of the savage frontier. More importantly, the cavalry was an environment in which sacred rites of passage were afforded to immigrants, especially Irishmen and Swedes, who earned their advancement from foreigner status to American citizenship via service in the army. In other Ford Westerns, such as *The Man Who Shot Liberty Valance* and *The Searchers*, the same theme is applied, only the rite of passage involves settling on the frontier land, civilizing the wilderness via homesteading. In essence, the West for Ford can be seen as a melting pot for the Americanization of various immigrant populations via the shared cultural experiences and trials of taming the West. In addition, the Western film can sometimes be seen as a healing rite, in which disenfranchised ex–Confederate rebels are reintegrated into American society via service in the U.S. Cavalry, or by homesteading on the western plains.

The key rite of passage in Ford's cavalry Westerns is the initiation of young soldiers into the realm of adult manhood, so that the mantle of leadership can be passed from the older generation to the young. In *Fort Apache*, the representation of the older generation is embodied in Colonel Thursday (Henry Fonda), who provides the definitive characterization of the Custer archetype in the Western genre. Because the film uses the alias "Thursday," and the dubious leader is technically not Custer, Ford is able to deconstruct the character and show him for all of his weaknesses and faults without necessarily demythologizing or debunking the heroic status of Custer himself. Like Custer, Thursday found much glory in the Civil War. He had held the rank of general, but due to some undisclosed disgrace or conflict, he'd been demoted to Lt. Colonel and sent off to the remote frontier outpost, Fort Apache. Thursday regards this assignment as a shameful exile, as it carries very little chance for glory or advancement. The Custer archetype's narcissistic obsession with glory and military distinction are treated as flaws in *Fort Apache*. Thursday is an ultra-officious military martinet. He is too much of the East and of the European military tradition to fit in with the frontier cavalry. He doesn't respect, understand, or fit in the West. By far his worst attribute is his racism — a complete lack of regard for the honor of the Indian peoples. He considers them to be ignorant, barbaric savages. Thursday's racism is a subtext to his caste-snobbery, his belief that enlisted men are a subordinate class to officers in all aspects of life. He is also clearly prejudiced against the Irish Catholic soldiers who compose a large part of his regiment.

The fort's sergeant major, O'Rourke (Ward Bond), is a Medal of Honor winner, a mark of distinction that won his son (John Agar) the right to attend West Point by presidential appointment. Young Lieutenant O'Rourke comes to Fort Apache as a commissioned officer. Nevertheless, Thursday is still unwilling to allow his daughter, Philadelphia (Shirley Temple), to be courted by Lt. O'Rourke. He tells the young officer's father: "Sgt. Major

Trading Honor for Glory. From left to right: Grant Withers as Silas Meacham, the treacherous Indian agent, Victor McLaglen as Sgt. Festus Mulcahy, the Irish Catholic cavalryman, John Wayne as Capt. Kirby York, the man who knows Indians, Henry Fonda as Lt. Col. Owen Thursday, the embodiment of the Custer archetype, George O'Brien as Capt. Sam Collingwood, the faithful officer, Miguel Inclan as Cochise, the noble savage, and Pedro Armendariz as Sgt. Beaufort, the obedient translator, in John Ford's *Fort Apache* (1948, Argosy Pictures/RKO).

O'Rourke, you'll pardon me for speaking bluntly, but as a noncommissioned officer, you are well aware of the barrier between your class and mine." Thursday's rigidity points out not only his caste-snobbery and prejudice against the Irish, but also Thursday's self-defeating obsession with decorum and propriety. In these character traits, Thursday is seen to be, to a certain extent, anti–American, as his views reject the notion that a man can become whatever he dreams of becoming, as a function of hard work and determination. In contrast, the Westerner is invariably a self-made man. He is the Horatio Alger story incarnate, the democratic ideal, while Thursday is emblematic of the Old World, the aristocratic elite, fixed classes, and social immobility. Thursday simply has no place on the western frontier.

Thursday's ultimate downfall arises from his lack of respect for the Apache leader, Cochise, which is a clear sign of his incompatibility with the frontier setting. Furthermore, his obsession with military glory is anathema to the Western code of personal honor. Military glory is won through brazen acts of courage that must be noticed by others and are performed for the purpose of recognition, advancement, and ego aggrandizement. In contrast, the Westerner's code of honor is interested only in the individual application of one's personal sense of justice. His acts are not meant to be publicized and are not performed for any ulterior purposes. For example, Tom Doniphon (John Wayne), the Western hero in *The Man Who Shot Liberty Valance*, exemplifies the Westerner's code of honor by killing the villain (Lee Marvin) without taking any of the credit for his own, while Ransom Stoddard (James Stewart), the greenhorn Easterner who is given credit for the killing, is seen as the antithesis of the Westerner, partly because he uses his legacy as "the man who shot Liberty Valance" towards the purpose of fame, glory, and political prestige.

As a contrast to Thursday, Captain York (John Wayne) is seen as the archetypal man of the West. Because York has respect for the Indian, he is able to convince Cochise to return his people to the reservation and seek peace. When Thursday betrays him by insulting Cochise and then attacking him in a vain and ultimately suicidal quest for personal glory, York is enraged. Thursday's act of forcing York to break his word to Cochise is final evidence of his lack of honor, at least in terms of the Western code. For a Westerner, a word given to an Indian is just as binding as if it were given to a general or a senator. When York argues against fighting Cochise, Thursday calls him a coward, prompting York to throw down his gauntlet (demanding satisfaction for the offense). Thursday refuses to pick up the gauntlet, not accepting York's challenge to a duel and once again displaying his lack of Western honor. He does, however, redeem his honor on a military level.

After leading his regiment into a suicidal charge that is quite reminiscent of Custer's charge at Little Big Horn, Thursday is injured and then rescued by York. But instead of riding away to safety, Thursday goes back to the last remaining survivors of his regiment, leading them in their last stand, though it means certain death. His self-sacrifice in this instance is emblematic of military glory, and like Custer, it earns Thursday much posthumous fame, but from a Westerner's perspective, his actions are tragic at best.

In the end, our feelings about the protagonist are ambivalent. Thursday was a conflicted character. His inappropriately strict management of his daughter's love life was suggestive of a taboo psychosexual attachment, the flip side of the Electra Complex, in which the father cannot bear to see his sexually maturing daughter in the arms of another man. His holier-than-thou attitude towards everyone else led to an unmitigated military disaster. *Fort Apache* may be the only cavalry Western in which the climactic battle scene features an Apache force completely wiping out a troop of U.S. cavalrymen. Yet, in retrospect, our feelings towards Thursday are similar to our feelings for Custer. He was a man who led other men into battle and died for his country. He was proud, brash, stubborn, and vainglorious. Though he died, and many men died with him, the regiment lives on, and in the words of York, the man who took command of the regiment when Thursday died: "They're better men than they used to be. Thursday did that. He made it a command to be proud of." Perhaps the need for a hero overpowers the lesser requirements of truth and historical accuracy. Ford will revisit this same theme in one of his last Westerns, *The Man Who Shot Liberty Valance*.

In the final scene, we're introduced to "Michael Thursday York O'Rourke," the toddler son of Lt. O'Rourke and Philadelphia Thursday. In his name and heritage we see all of the contrasting elements of cavalry society — the upper class officer, the working-class Irish Catholic, and the classless Westerner. The little boy represents both the past and future of America, as well as the reconciliation between its rival classes. Most significantly, as the product of a union that was forged and defended on the frontier, the child represents the sanctity and vitality of the community and the family unit, the all-important thing worth fighting for.

3 Godfathers (1948)

Filmed directly after *Fort Apache*, *3 Godfathers* is not a part of the cavalry trilogy and not a traditional Western. In a sense, the movie could be considered a sequel to Ford's religious parable, *The Fugitive* (1947), which was filmed directly before *Fort Apache*. While *The Fugitive* is a parable of the betrayal and martyrdom of a Christ-like figure, a saint whose fidelity to his beliefs transforms him into an outlaw, *3 Godfathers* is a religious fable in which the birth of an infant heralds the spiritual redemption of an outlaw, whose dedication to the baby transforms him into a saint. The film opens with a lone cowboy riding up a desert ridge at sundown, the dedication: "To the Memory of Harry Carey. Bright Star of the early western sky..." appears on the screen. Harry Carey was one of the first great Western icons, a close friend and collaborator of John Ford in the director's early years. When Carey died in 1947, Ford decided to remake one of his greatest early Westerns, *The Marked Men* (1919), which starred Harry Carey. Ford's remake, titled *3 Godfathers,* featured Carey's son, Harry Carey, Jr., in his debut performance. The film's star, however, is John Wayne, the contemporary Western icon of his day. As a supporting player, Carey, Jr. would become a central member of Ford's stock company of actors. This family approach to making pictures gives a sense of history and tradition that is unique to Ford's canon of Western films.

Though Ford uses religious symbolism in many of his films, *3 Godfathers* is exceptional in its explicitness. The film is clearly a religious parable. Three outlaws on the run in the desert come upon a stranded pioneer woman in labor. The woman (Mildred Natwick) dies, but her baby lives. In her dying words, she asks the three men, Bob (John Wayne), Bill (Harry Carey, Jr.), and Pedro (Pedro Armendáriz), to save her son. She makes them all the baby's godfathers, and names him after them. The hardened criminals are immediately softened by the heartbreaking death of the pioneer mother. A strong paternal instinct takes hold of all of them. Following a solemn funeral, in which Bill sings "Shall We Gather at the River," the three godfathers, likening themselves to the three wise men in the story of the birth of Jesus, embark on the long journey through the wilderness to bring the baby to the town of "New Jerusalem." They are guided by passages from Bill's Bible and a bright star on the horizon. Bill exhausts himself to death, carrying his godson in the scorching desert sun. He dies reciting a prayer. Then Pedro falls and breaks his leg while carrying the baby. He can't go on, so Bob must take the baby and leave Pedro behind. Pedro says a prayer before he takes himself out of his misery with a pistol. On death's door, Bob finds inspiration when the wind blows Bill's Bible open to a prescient passage: "...unto Jerusalem ... a donkey tied, and a colt with her...." Dehydrated and delusional, Bob stumbles on, accompanied by the ghostly apparitions of his dead compadres, until finally, a vision appears before him of a donkey and a colt —

but it's not a hallucination; the animals are real. Leaning on the miraculous donkey, Bob makes it to New Jerusalem, saving the baby and himself. He arrives at midnight on Christmas Eve.

Weeks later, at the familiar ritual of a frontier town trial, court is held in the town saloon, and the judge sits behind the bar, with law books in front of him and whiskey bottles behind him. The judge offers to suspend Bob's 20-year sentence if he transfers the right of permanent guardianship of his godson to the boy's aunt and uncle. Bob refuses: "You can throw the book at me, Judge, but I ain't gonna do her. I ain't breakin' my promise to a dyin' woman." Of course, the judge's offer was just a ruse, a final test to see if the former outlaw has truly been transformed by his love for his godson. The judge says, "That's just what I been waiting to hear you say, son." He sentences Bob to the minimum prison term under the law, one year and one day, then bangs his gavel on the bar and says quickly: "Court's closed, bar's open, double bourbon, bartender, if you please." All the cowboys immediately belly up to the bar for a drink.

To the sound of the town ladies singing "Bringing in the Sheaves," Bob heads off to do his penance in jail, leaving little Robert William Pedro in the temporary custody of his aunt. Jane Darwell, Ford's quintessential frontier mother, sends Bob off with a note of encouragement: "Goodbye and good luck, boy. A year in jail will do you real good." By the time Bob rolls away on the train, the townsfolk have moved on to "Shall We Gather at the River." "All is calm, all is bright," in the little frontier town. The hope of a new America is saved by the Western hero, who is an outlaw turned savior, a gunfighter turned godfather.

She Wore a Yellow Ribbon (1949)

The second film in Ford's cavalry trilogy and the only one filmed in color, *Yellow Ribbon* does the most to demonstrate Ford's mastery in filming the beauty and majesty of Monument Valley. His cinematographer, Winton C. Hoch, won an Academy Award for his work. At this point, Ford's stock company was fairly set, resulting in the feel of a ritualized reenactment within the identifiable canon of Ford Westerns. Wayne's character, now named Captain Brittles, carries the same persona as Wayne's character in *Fort Apache*, but is significantly older — on the brink of retirement. The role of the young soldier who knows Indians, previously played by Wayne, is taken over by Ben Johnson, as Sgt. Tyree. He also fills the position of the ex–Confederate Southerner who is now loyal to the U.S. cavalry, though he still refers to his commanding officers as "Yanks." Joanne Dru, who had just starred opposite Wayne as the love interest in *Red River*, is cast as the love interest in this film. She is the one who wears the yellow ribbon, a token which signifies that a maiden has a sweetheart in the U.S. Cavalry. Once again, John Agar is cast in the role of the male romantic lead.

The opening words of the narrator — "Custer is dead"— could be interpreted as a reference to Ford's previous cavalry film, which ended with Thursday's death. The death of Custer is represented as the precipitant of an alliance among the Indian nations in preparation for a great war against the U.S. cavalry. As expected, there are moments of reconciliation with the South. When an elderly Southern cavalryman, who looks a lot like Robert E. Lee, is killed in action, a cavalry wife makes an impromptu Confederate flag out of red petticoats, so that the troop may lay the "Southern Cross" over his coffin as the bugler plays "Dixie." There's the usual crew of hard-drinking and rowdy Irish cavalrymen, as well as the traditional villain — a corrupt sutler and Indian agent (Harry Woods) — who sells repeating rifles to hostile Indians.

Though historically inaccurate, many Westerns contend that the only reason Custer was defeated at Little Big Horn was that the Sioux had repeating rifles, while Custer's cavalrymen carried single-fire Springfield rifles. Hence, the selling of Winchesters to Indians is often depicted as the most treacherous crime imaginable on the Western frontier. In a scene directed with wonderful subtlety and tact, Brittles, Tyree, and young Lieutenant Penell (Harry Carey, Jr.) spy from behind the sagebrush as the sutler and his gun runners sell Winchesters to Indians. The deal goes awry, and the Indians attack their suppliers. The three cavalrymen witness one gun runner being roasted alive over a campfire. Brittles turns to Tyree: "Sergeant?" Tyree offers him his rifle and replies: "It's cocked, sir." He incorrectly assumes that his captain wants to shoot the man being tortured, to take him out of his misery. "No, your knife," Brittles replies. He uses Tyree's knife to cut himself a piece of chewing tobacco. In Brittles's eyes, the gun runner is getting his just desserts, and even if he wanted to help him, the shot would betray their presence to the Indians. "Join me in a chaw of tobacco?" Brittles offers Tyree, over the sound of the gun runner screaming in agony. Tyree declines. "Chawin' tobacco's a nasty habit," Brittles continues. "It's been known to turn a man's stomach." He admits that the atrocity they're witnessing is sickening, but in the same breath declares that he's man enough to take it, and he'll even chaw tobacco to boot. Harry Carey, Jr., who's always cast by Ford as the young innocent looking to prove himself, asks the captain for a chaw. His character, Penell, is a greenhorn from the East planning to resign from the army, tired of the rough life. Up to this point, his captain has been disappointed with him. Now Brittles gives him an approving glance, indicating that the boy is finally showing signs of becoming a man. A moment later, after they remount, Brittles asks him: "Still figuring on resigning?" Penell replies, "No, sir." Witnessing the Indian atrocity has steeled his nerves and stiffened his resolve to fight the savages and protect the progress of white civilization. The notion of passing on the essence of manhood from patriarch to progeny via the encountering and withstanding of intense violence is an ancient rite of passage, expressed beautifully in this short scene with very little dialogue and, by today's standards, little graphic violence.

Even more so than its predecessor, *Yellow Ribbon* is about depicting traditional rites of passage. It's the story of young men learning to become leaders and of older men handing over the mantle of leadership to their successors. There is a memorable scene in which Brittles, upon addressing his regiment for the last time, is given a silver watch as a retirement gift. Before he reads the "sentiment" on the back, he puts on a pair of spectacles, making him look like an old man. The passage from active service to passive retirement is a stage of life that everyone must face, even brave cavalrymen, but the ritualization of this passage gives it a form and structure of its own, which eases the transition for the initiate and helps him pass from one life phase to the other. The scene in which Brittles retires is sad, but not tragic, because a sense of accomplishment and appreciation is expressed through the ritual that Ford depicts.

Like *Fort Apache*, *Yellow Ribbon* ends in a manner that is contrary to the typical cavalry Western. There is no battle scene. Brittles's last-minute maneuverings, in which he shows an intimate knowledge and understanding of the Indian sense of honor, allows his troops to avoid a bloody battle with the local tribes. In a sense, the film ends in the way that Wayne's character wanted the conflict to end in *Fort Apache*. The difference is that now, Wayne's character has the confidence to defy orders and follow his own instincts. He follows his own code, the Western code, rather than military protocol, to achieve the goal that he personally believes to be the most honorable. Wayne's character is the ideal cavalry officer: brave, strong, resolute, disciplined, and more interested in peace and honor than war and glory. As the film moves towards its end, the narrator's voice returns, as we watch Brittles ride off into the sunset: "*So Nathan Brittles, ex-captain of the U.S. Cavalry, started westward for the new settlements in California. Westward toward the setting sun, the end of the trail for all old men.*" The ritualized ending, riding into the sunset, and even the conventional destination, California — the Westerner's Valhalla — are evoked. The film should end here, with this wistful conclusion, but unfortunately, there is a tacked-on happy ending, typical for Hollywood movies in those days, in which Brittles is promoted to the position of chief of scouts, at the rank of Lt. Colonel (the same rank as Thursday and Custer). His return to the fort coincides with a formal dance, which, at this point in Ford's work, has become an obligatory scene in all of his Westerns. The denouement of Brittles's storyline could still be seen as a rite of passage, in which he passes from the active life of a young soldier to a more sedentary life of a senior commanding officer, but the taste is more saccharine than bittersweet. Just as John Wayne's character couldn't die in *Red River*, he cannot retire into anonymous old age in *Yellow Ribbon*.

Rio Grande (1950)

By the third installment of the cavalry trilogy, the repetition of characters, setting, and themes truly instill the sense of a cohesive and homogenous canon of films on the same subject. Even the names become repetitious, as if Ford no longer saw the need to hide the fact that the characters in each film are essentially the same. Wayne plays Lt. Col. York, clearly taking over, though some years later, where the character by the same name left off at the end of *Fort Apache*. His trusty Irish cohort from the first two films, played by Victor McLaglen, is present, bearing the same name, rank, and persona as he did in the previous film, Sgt. Maj. Timothy Quincannon, as McLaglen plays essentially the same character in all three films. The Southern soldier who knows Indians, Tyree, is again played by Ben Johnson. Once again, Harry Carey, Jr. plays the innocent greenhorn, Sandy, who will become an experienced cavalryman by the end of the film. (Harry Carey, Jr.'s character was also named Sandy in Ford's previous Western *Wagon Master*.) As with all three films in the cavalry trilogy, Ford's major concern is with the intertwined institutions of the American family and the U.S. cavalry, both of which represent the foundational and regenerative forces of life on the frontier. In *Rio Grande*, the family melodrama takes the front of the stage.

Col. York, rather than just being a symbolic father figure, is an actual father in this film. His adolescent son, Jeff, short for Jefferson (Claude Jarman, Jr.), is a baby-faced youth determined to prove to his father that he could be a good soldier. After being expelled from West Point for failing math, he lied about his age and enlisted in the army, finding himself by great coincidence as a trooper in his father's regiment. His mother, Kathleen (Maureen O'Hara), comes to the fort to bring him back home. She is a Southern belle, a representative of the Old South and the Eastern aristocracy. Kathleen is estranged from her husband because of an old grievance, dating back fourteen years to the Civil War, when York, a Yankee officer, burned down her family's plantation. She wants her son to return east with her, where she can enroll him in another military academy and ensure his proper education as a gentleman. However, she needs both her husband's and her son's acquiescence, and she will get neither. Both York and Jeff believe that the real passage to manhood is achieved via service in the army, not through attending some fancy military academy. The film deals with Jeff's rite of passage into manhood by becoming a cavalryman, which parallels the reunification of his family, in which the broken bonds between father and son and husband and wife are mended.

As with most of Ford's Westerns, the postwar reconciliation between North and South is an explicit subtext. The son, who represents the new nation coming of age during the Reconstruction, has one Yankee parent and one Southern. His name, Jefferson York, attests to this. The first name was no doubt chosen by his mother in homage to Jefferson Davis, while the surname brings to mind the town of New York, the home of the Yankees. The reconciliation of Jeff's parents symbolizes the reconciliation of the fractured elements of American culture and the emergence of a new nation, which takes place — significantly — on the Western frontier.

There are so many moonlight serenades and marching songs in this film, provided by the "Sons of the Pioneers" troupe of traditional songsters, that the film could almost be considered a musical. Ford's previous two Westerns each had moonlight serenades and marching songs, but not nearly as many as in *Rio Grande*. The use of American folk and traditional music to add to the ambience of the frontier setting will be repeated by Ford in all of his Westerns from this point forward. Interestingly, there is no formal dance scene, as one would expect in a Ford Western, but there is a very significant staging of a traditional Indian dance ritual. In the third act of the film, Apache renegades take the children of the fort captive, as (ironically) they are being transported to a safer area. The Apaches hold them in an old Spanish village across the Rio Grande, in Mexican territory. Tyree spies on the Apaches and reports to York that the children are being held in an abandoned church and that the Indians are drinking and dancing. "Vengeance dance," York explains. "They'll dance until dawn, and then...." York trails off, leaving the viewer to understand that the culmination of the dance will be a savage and bloody vengeance taken on the children.

Jeff and Sandy prove their mettle by going with Tyree on the extremely dangerous mission of protecting the children in the church, while the cavalry charges the village at sun-up. The fact that the children are being held in an old Spanish church has bipartite religious significance. First, the atrocities committed on Christian children by heathen savages is the oldest justification for warfare against the Indian peoples. The juxtaposition of the innocent white babes imprisoned in the sanctuary of the church, while the wild red Injuns drink and dance themselves into a ritualized frenzy in preparation for their massacre, evokes the most primal fears and associations in the frontier mythology. Secondly, in a quick but telling scene, as the children are being rescued, Quincannon finds his niece, Margaret Mary (Karolyn Grimes), in the church bell tower. As they dash for the door, they stop briefly to kneel before the altar. The Irish Catholic sergeant and girl, though running for their lives, still find time to fulfill the ritual required of a Catholic upon leaving a Catholic church. Ford's intention, more than just a nod to his fellow Irishmen, is to purvey the notion of cultural diversity among the 18th-century pioneers, a quick reminder that a variety of cultures were involved in the settling and capturing of the Western frontier.

As in the previous films, Wayne's character must defy military regulations in order to take the most honorable action. In this case, he must cross the Rio Grande into Mexican territory and engage the Apaches outside American soil — an action that he was expressly forbidden to take. In the battle, York is hit in the chest with an arrow. He asks his son to pull out the arrow. This final act of masculine fortitude, pulling out the bloody arrow while neither one of them cries out or winces, cements the newly reformed bond between father and son. In the end, the children are saved, symbolizing the safe regeneration of American life after the war and on the frontier. Similarly, the idealized American family, York, his wife, and his son, are reunited. The cavalry is victorious. And even the North and South are reconciled, both within the family unit and within the army itself, as the regiments' ceremonial parade — to Kathleen's delight — is accompanied by the military band playing "Dixie."

Wagon Master (1950)

Wagon Master is the least remembered of John Ford's Westerns from his classic period, 1939–1962. This is probably because the film did not feature John Wayne. The star had become so associated with Ford's Westerns that audiences may have turned a blind eye to any John Ford Western without "the Duke" cast in the lead role. Ben Johnson, an actor who would become a favorite of the genre, carries the lead role and does it well. In fact, the film is a must-see for any true fan of the Western, merely for the experience of seeing Ben Johnson in a lead role, as he always played supporting roles in his many films, almost all Westerns. The great thing about Johnson was that he was a natural cowboy. A ranch hand and rodeo performer from Oklahoma, he spoke in the same thick Southern drawl in every film and seemed always to play the same character — a laid-back cowboy with a devilish sense of humor and a disarming grin. His ease with horses and natural athleticism made him a born cowboy. His extreme good looks got him work in front of the camera. As for his acting, he played the one character type quite well, but had no range beyond that. As Johnson himself admitted: "Everybody in town's a better actor than I am, but none of them can play Ben Johnson." He certainly did a wonderful job playing Ben Johnson and did so in some of the best Westerns ever made, including *She Wore a Yellow Ribbon* (1949), *Rio Grande* (1950), *Shane* (1952), *One Eyed Jacks* (1961), *Major Dundee* (1965), *Will Penny* (1968), *Hang 'Em High* (1968), *The Wild Bunch* (1969), and *Junior Bonner* (1972). He was also a frequent performer on television Westerns.

Though *Wagon Master* is not necessarily on many people's top-ten lists of all-time best Westerns, it remains an inside favorite among the genre's faithful, due mainly to the fact that it was Johnson's only significant lead role and that the film has the classic John Ford touch. The actors in *Wagon Master* were members of John Ford's stock company at the time: Ben Johnson (whom Ford discovered), Harry Carey, Jr. (the son of the great silent Western film star of the same name), Jane Darwell (the great American mother figure, as per her role in Ford's *Grapes of Wrath*), Ward Bond, Hank Worden, and Francis Ford (John's older brother). There is a sense of ritual that arises from seeing the same actors over and over again, playing almost exactly the same parts in each of the rather similar films. This sense of the familiar and almost traditional is amplified in Westerns, as the genre calls for character types who are well suited to this particular setting, but were not necessarily well suited to other genres. Johnson, Carey, Jr., Bond, John Wayne, Randolph Scott, and other Western staples were examples of this "Western character" type.

The soundtrack for *Wagon Master* was provided by The Sons of the Pioneers. Though the soundtrack comes off as overbearing to a modern viewer, the music in its day was probably experienced more as a part of the ritualistic aura of the Western film. The pioneer songs were reverent hymns, sung as the Western film depicted the heroic acts of the mythological figures who were such an integral part of the American ethos. The ritualistic themes in *Wagon Master* play upon the notion that the pioneers on the wagon train were following a religious calling that led them out west. As Buscombe (1988) described the film, "Society's outcasts journey across country and settle in the West after a rite of passage comprising internal and external dangers." In this sense, the pioneers of the Western frontier in the 19th century were linked historically to the Puritan pilgrims of the 17th century. Both groups saw the new frontier as a "promised land," a new Eden within which they would find spiritual fulfillment, economic independence, and political freedom. Furthermore, both groups had to undergo much hardship and face great dangers as a "rite of passage" in order to capture, settle, and occupy the land. Hence, the underlying sociopolitical argument of the Western genre — that the settlement of the continent by white Europeans was a "manifest destiny," based on historical, racial, and spiritual grounds — was confirmed by presenting the 19th-century homesteaders as a continuation of the pioneering process begun by the 17th-century pilgrims. John Wayne's infamous and often imitated use of the epithet "pilgrim" when referring to Jimmy Stewart's Eastern neophyte character in *The Man Who Shot Liberty Valance* embodies this association.

Jane Darwell is typecast in the role of the all–American frontierswoman and mother, Sister Ledeyard. Even before her signature role as Ma Joad in John Ford's *The Grapes of Wrath*, Darwell had established herself as the definitive American mother, especially in Westerns. In Henry King's *Jesse James* (1939), she played Jesse and Frank's mother, and it was her death at the hands of the railroad bully that motivated Jesse and Frank to avenge her death and embark on their subsequent lives of crime. In *The Ox-Bow Incident* (1941), she played a strong-headed frontierswoman who, like most of the other characters in this very atypical Western, was way too eager to lynch the three men accused of murder. In *Wagon Master,* Sister Ledeyard is a strong, determined, wholesome woman who represents a frontier version of the earth goddess archetype. Whenever the wagon train needs to get moving, the Mormon leader (Ward Bond) shouts out "Wagons west!" signaling Sister Ledeyard to blow upon her ram's horn. This mythological symbol is clearly a link between the American pioneers on the Western frontier and the Israelite tribes en route to the Promised Land. The fact that the frontierswoman earth mother is the one chosen to blow the sacramental horn, as opposed to the wagon master or the Mormon leader, signifies the nation-building connotation of the female character. While the wagon train brings seed grain and religion and other elements of civilization and domestication into the wild frontier, the most important thing it brings is women. With women come children and families, necessitating the establishment of law and order for their safety, the building of schools for their education, the creation of towns and churches, etc. While single men like the frontiersmen heroes and their outlaw counterparts can live on the frontier and allow it to remain wild and open, women entering the frontier always represents the domestication of the wilderness and the establishment of civilized society.

A sense of history and culture is provided in the traditional dance scenes. The Mormons put on an old-fashioned square dance one night, where we get a sense of frontier-era Americana through the old-time music and folksy dance steps. The presence of Jane Darwell leads the viewer to recall the memorable square dance scene in *The Grapes of Wrath*, which establishes a sense of family and community. In addition to the square dancing, the Mormons on the wagon train engage in the frequent singing of hymns (another John Ford trademark). Later on in the film, after the wagon train and Indians have made peace, both parties join in an Indian "squaw dance," symbolizing the dream of peace and tranquil coexistence that, at least for the Mormons, was a legitimate wish of the pioneering homesteaders.

A final element of ritual in *Wagon Master* is the use of ritual punishment. When one of the outlaws rapes an Indian squaw, the wagon masters, the Mormons, and the outlaw leader all agree that the offender must be punished, in order to avoid a massacre at the hand of the Indians. As the outlaw is a white man, he must be punished in the tradition of the white man. He is tied to a wagon wheel and whipped. This tradition of flogging dates back to pre–Biblical days, but is most associated with British discipline, especially in the army and navy, and therefore found its way into American usage, both in the military and — most resonantly — as the standard form of discipline in the Southern plantations. The use of ritual punishment is significant in Westerns because it represents the attempt to control the savage or lawless element of the frontier. It also reveals the fact that, at times, the long arm of the law can act just as savagely as the lawbreakers themselves. And finally, the offender who is punished is made to feel pain in accordance with his victim's pain and in step with society's need for "justice," which in its most basic form is arguably a formalized ritual of societal vengeance.

The Searchers (1956)

After making six Westerns in four years, from 1946–1950, Ford took a hiatus from making Westerns, returning to the genre in 1956 with a film that many people say is not only Ford's best Western, but the best Western ever made. The film is a series of arrivals and departures to and from a pair of homesteads in post–Civil War Texas, though the actual location of filming was in Monument Valley. Ethan Edwards (John Wayne) is the most psychologically complex hero that Wayne would ever play or that Ford would ever direct. A product of their long and fruitful collaboration, Ford and Wayne were able to take the Western hero to places that he had never been before. Showing him for both his strengths and weaknesses — his courage and his savagery, his loyalty and his prejudice, his constancy and his obsessiveness, his love and his hate — *The Searchers* forces us to accept our beloved Westerner for who he truly is, an incredibly complex and conflicted figure, who could be called both heroic and villainous, depending on your point of view.

The film opens with one of Ford's signature shots, the camera looking out from a dark interior through the frame of a doorway, onto a wide-open desert landscape. This is civilization, the civilization represented by the homestead and also the civilized folks in the movie theater, looking out in wonder at the majesty and danger of the wild frontier. Out of this foreboding landscape emerges a lone rider, Ethan Edwards, a man of the wilderness. An ex–Confederate soldier who never surrendered, he comes home after years of savage warfare as a raider and several more years as an outlaw and wanderer. He is finally returning home to his brother's ranch to live quietly and peacefully with his brother's family, to hang up his sword and gun for good. But the truth of his nature is foreshadowed in Ford's opening shot. Ethan can never stay at home. His true nature is of the wilderness, to which he must always return. Ethan will never find peace.

The secret of Ethan's forbidden, repressed love for his brother's wife, Martha (Dorothy Jordan), is expressed only through glances and facial expressions, a subtlety no longer found in most modern films. Upon entering the ranch house, he lifts his nine-year-old niece Debbie up into the air in an avuncular gesture of affection. He gives her his Medal of Honor: "Oh, let her have it ... doesn't amount to much." To his 13-year-old nephew he gives his saber. He's surprised to see that his older niece, Lucy, has grown into a mature young woman. Ethan is also taken aback when he sees the dark-skinned Martin Pawley join the dinner table as one of the family. "A fella could mistake you for a halfbreed," he tells him, only slightly hiding his disdain. "Not quite," Martin replies, somewhat offended. "I'm eighth Cherokee and the rest Welsh and English." The exact proportion of Martin's Indian blood will be a matter of contention between him and Ethan for the rest of the film, as is their relationship. Martin first addresses him as "Uncle Ethan," a title that Ethan is clearly uncomfortable with. Later on, Ethan tells him, "Don't call me 'Uncle,' I ain't your uncle." To Ethan, blood is everything, and Martin is not his blood relation. Furthermore, Martin's blood is tainted. But their relationship goes deeper, as Ethan's brother explains: "It was Ethan who found ya squallin' under a sage clump after your folks had been mas-

The Fate Worse Than Death. Natalie Wood as Debbie Edwards, displaying Chief Scar's prize scalps to her uncle, Ethan Edwards (John Wayne), and adoptive brother, Martin Pawley (Jeffrey Hunter). With their backs to the screen are the Comanche chief, Scar (Henry Brandon), and the Comanchero, Emilio Gabriel Fernandez y Figueroa (Antonio Moreno), in John Ford's *The Searchers* (1956, Warner Bros.).

sacred." Ethan tries to minimize this fatherly connection to Martin: "It just happened to be me; no need to make more of it."

In the first act of the film, Ethan's brother and nephew are killed in a Comanche massacre on the homestead. Martha is mutilated and raped to death — these facts are only disclosed through Ethan's reaction to the sight of Martha's remains, another subtlety that seemingly no longer exists in today's cinema. The Comanche raid destroys not only Ethan's last hope of a civilized life, a family and a home, but also his deepest love. The Comanche abduct Lucy and Debbie. The next morning, Ethan commits one of the gravest sacrileges in a Ford film — he cuts short a solemn ritual, a funeral scene, in order to commence the rescue mission for Lucy and Debbie: "Put an amen to it! There's no more time for praying!" Eventually they discover that Lucy met the same fate as her mother, but since Debbie is just a child, she will be raised among the Comanche until she comes of age as a woman and is taken as a bride by a "buck."

Ethan and Martin decide to continue their search for Debbie. Slotkin notes that the pair of searchers recalls the traditional pairing of the White Indian and his noble savage companion, dating back to Cooper's Hawkeye and Chingachgook and finding its most familiar variant in the Lone Ranger and Tonto. But in *The Searchers*, the traditional roles are reversed: Ethan is the godless savage, the one who knows the Comanche ways, while Martin is the civilized, Christian character, whose actions are always tempered by love and compassion. After years of fruitless searching, the objective of the search begins to diverge between the companions. Martin is still interested in rescuing Debbie; he wants to take her home. But Ethan's goal has become a dark one. He knows that Debbie has reached puberty. She will have had sex with Indian men; she will have lived among them, as one of them, for too long. To Ethan, Debbie has already suffered a fate worse than death. Her body and blood have been tainted. She is no longer white. If he had been present at the massacre, he would have saved three last bullets to put into the brains of Martha, Lucy, and Debbie. It's too late to save Martha and Lucy from the fate worse than death, but he can still deliver a last bullet to Debbie. His search is a mission of mercy, to release Debbie from her fallen state of depravity and degradation, even if she, as an acculturated Indian, doesn't see it that way. This film asks the question: How resilient is the archetypal last bullet theme? How far does it extend? Does it extend till after the raid? For days after the raid? For years after? Even 10 years after? The answer for Ethan is that it never ends: "An Indian will chase a thing till he thinks he's chased it enough, then he quits. Same way when he runs. Seems like he never learns there's such as thing as a critter who'll just keep coming on. So we'll find 'em in the end. I promise you. We'll find 'em, just as sure as the turnin' of the earth."

Ethan's savagery grows as the search goes on. When the original rescuers fight off a band of Comanche at a riverbank, Ethan keeps on shooting at their backs, eager to kill as many as he can, just for the sake of killing. A few scenes later, he shoots a trio of robbers in the back. And later on, Ethan empties his rifle into a herd of buffalo, just to kill as many as he can so that the Indians will have less resources for the winter. At a cavalry station, the searchers see several white women rescued from Indian captivity. Ethan's look of disgust at the fallen women signifies that he'd like to put a bullet in each of their heads. Surely, he'd believe that it would be the merciful thing to do. "They ain't white," he says. "Not any more. They're Comanche."

The focal point of the search is the Comanche leader, Scar (Henry Brandon), but again, there are divergent reasons. Both searchers believe that Scar still has Debbie in his custody, but only Ethan has a personal score to settle with him. Aside from wanting to find and kill Debbie, Ethan wants to wreak vengeance on Scar for raping and killing the only woman he ever loved. Ethan and Scar can be seen as two sides of the same coin. They're both savage warriors, fierce racists, and leaders of men. In Ethan we see the embodiment of the hunter-hero archetype, the man who at the same time hates and reveres his prey and who finds existential meaning in the pursuit of a creature as fierce and powerful as himself. The search and hunt find resolution in the scalping ritual. The Indians believed that the purpose of scalping was to shame your enemy, so that they enter the spirit world incomplete. Being scalped symbolizes defeat in battle, disgrace, and emasculation.

Before the violent climax to the film, there is a dance and wedding scene, but once again, these rituals that affirm family and community are cut short. Scar's camp has been located nearby, and the men are enlisted to attack it. In the raid, Ethan finds Scar's body, already killed, but that doesn't matter. He scalps him, injuring his spirit even after his body is dead. He chases down Debbie, intent on killing her. He fights off Martin, who is trying to stop him. Debbie runs into a cave. He rides in after her, grabs her, and holds her up in the air. Two contrasting images are evoked. The first, an image of savagery, the often-told tale of Indians lifting up white babies and bashing their heads against tree trunks and rocks. The second image is a memory from the beginning of the film, when Ethan affectionately held his beloved little niece up in his arms in the same way that he's holding her now. The audience is torn. What will he do?

In Alan Le May's novel, from which he and Frank Nugent adapted the screenplay, Amos (the character who would become Ethan), attempts to trample Debbie under his horse. She runs. Then, when she is finally in sight and range of his pistol, he lifts her onto his saddle, rescuing her rather than killing her. But he is mistaken. In the mayhem of battle, he mistook a young Comanche girl for Debbie. The girl shoots Ethan at point-blank range in the chest, and he dies. As usual, while the novel stays true to its mythic themes and the essence of tragedy, the Hollywood adaptation depicts a more sterile version, in which the hero is allowed to live. However, unlike *Red River*, in which the tacked-on happy ending seems blatantly forced and out of place, the ending of *The Searchers* works very well. There are several reasons for this, all relating to Ethan's character development. Ethan's final acceptance of Debbie as a white woman is linked to his acceptance of Martin as a white man. A few scenes back, Ethan tells Martin that he is leaving him all his property in his will. Though Martin doesn't completely understand the importance of this, Ethan is saying, in the only way that he knows how, that he has come to love and respect Martin for the man that he is, that he has accepted him as an equal despite his mixed blood, and that he has finally accepted him as a full-fledged family member — not just as an adoptive nephew, but as his son and heir. In doing so, Ethan has shown that he has softened. There are limits to his prejudice, and therefore there can be reasons for acceptance, even when Indian blood or miscegenation is involved. Furthermore, in scalping Scar, Ethan has fulfilled his vengeance quest and satiated his bloodlust. Having exorcised his psychological demons, he no longer needs or desires to shed the blood of his niece. Having killed her captor and corrupter, he can finally accept Debbie as the niece he once adored: "Let's go home, Debbie."

Since Ethan doesn't resolve his mission by killing Debbie, he doesn't have to die in penance for this act. We can understand Ethan's change of heart as a natural development of his journey, a transformative passage through the wilderness that softened his hatred and rekindled the desperate need for personal connections that brought him back to his brother's homestead in the first place. And finally, though there is a happy ending for Debbie and Martin, the ending for Ethan is bittersweet. It doesn't feel fake or tacked on, like the endings of *Red River* and *Yellow Ribbon*. In the final scene, the opening shot of the film is recalled. From the interior of a ranch house, through the frame of a wide door, we see Debbie return to civilization. She is taken in by her neighbors, the Jorgensens. Martin also enters the house, led by his fiancé, Laurie Jorgensen (Vera Miles). But Ethan cannot enter. He's shut out of the house by some unseen force-field. As he tugs his arm, a gesture borrowed from the silent Western film star, Harry Carey, we see the conflict within him. In the closing shot of the film, perhaps the most famous in film history, the solitary figure turns his back on home and walks away into the wilderness, as the door shuts behind him.

The Second Cavalry Trilogy

After *The Searchers*, Ford focused on non–Western projects for the rest of the 1950s. Though *The Horse Soldiers* looks a lot like a Western — it stars John Wayne, everyone rides horses, it's set in the mid–19th century — the film is a Civil War picture and doesn't deal with any of the key themes found in Westerns. His first real Western after *The Searchers* was *Sergeant Rutledge* (1960), a film that could also be considered the first entry in Ford's second cavalry trilogy. The second trilogy — *Sergeant Rutledge, Two Rode Together* (1962), and *Cheyenne Autumn* (1964) — are not nearly as well known or as well loved as the first trilogy. This is because the films are much darker and pessimistic in tone. One could say that *The Searchers* was a turning point for Ford. No longer was he satisfied with simple ideals and flag-waving sentiments. Now he wanted to fix his camera on complex issues. He was no longer afraid to criticize the country he loved and the national mythology he helped to create. The second trilogy deals with issues of racism and genocide in a bold and progressive manner.

If we look at Ford's career, we can see him contributing films to all three periods of mythical development. His mythopoeic Westerns, such as *The Iron Horse* and *Drums Along the Mohawk*, draw from the original artifacts of the old West and deal with the establishment of the archetypal themes and characters in the genre. His romantic Westerns, such as *Stagecoach, My Darling Clementine*, his first cavalry trilogy, and *Wagon Master*, embellish on the established archetypes and take them to greater levels. His consummatory Westerns, such as *The Searchers, The Man Who Shot Liberty Valance*, and the second cavalry trilogy, are aimed at deconstructing the archetypes and revealing the true artifacts behind the myth.

Sergeant Rutledge focuses on racism, using the treatment of a black cavalryman in the 19th century as an allegory for the treatment of blacks in contemporary America. The rituals of justice, as represented by the rigid procedures and officious trappings of a military court-martial, are seen as tools that could be used for good or bad, just as the Constitution itself could be used for good purposes, such as Civil Rights, or bad purposes, such as segregation laws. The second film in the trilogy, *Two Rode Together*, focuses on social prejudice. The ritual that Ford always used as a symbol of communal harmony, the dance, is turned on its head. When the woman who had lived as a captive among the Indians is excluded and snubbed by the white settlers, the social ritual is transformed into a showcase for caste-snobbery and hypocritical conceit. In the third film in the trilogy (and Ford's last Western), *Cheyenne Autumn*, Ford censures the artifact of the Western myth which he'd previously glorified to epic proportions — the U.S. Cavalry. In depicting the U.S. Cavalry's genocidal treatment of the Native Americans, as well as the disenfranchised Cheyenne's noble but doomed effort to survive, Ford offers a rare glimpse of the other side of the cavalry Western, a side filled with tears of despair rather than cheers of glory.

The Man Who Shot Liberty Valance (1962)

Considered Ford's last "classic Western," with the possible exception of his brief contribution to the epic *How the West Was Won, Liberty Valance* is a self-reflective, elegiac Western, looking back sentimentally on the bygone age of the Wild West. It begins with an elderly senator, Ransom Stoddard (James Stewart), returning to Shinbone, a town that he once knew as a frontier outpost, but which is now home to a railroad, telephone wires, electricity, and all the other dubious harbingers of civilization and progress. He is attending the funeral of an old friend, Tom Doniphon (John Wayne), but on a symbolic level, he is not just mourning the death of one man, but the death of what this one man represented — the frontier hero, the old West, and the days when legends were born.

Rans recalls the day when he came to Shinbone as a young man, and the film follows his narrative. His first is encounter is with a villainous outlaw with the provocative name of Liberty (Lee Marvin). Though Liberty Valance is a villain, he also represents the freedom and wildness of the old West, which is lost and mourned for. Rans, on the other hand, is an Eastern lawyer. His presence represents the approach of civilization. Liberty, sensing the threat of the approach of the modern world, reacts to Rans with vicious savagery: "I'll teach you the law ... western law!" Liberty tears up Rans's law books and whips him nearly to death. The villain's sadism is clearly beyond what John Ford has showed us before. Liberty is not content to beat his victims with his fists or shoot them with his gun; he must whip them, finding a perverse and sadistic pleasure in the gruesomeness of the act and prolonging the act itself in order to extend the satisfaction he gains from his own depravity.

Rans, for his part, seems unfitted to his new environment. The Eastern neophyte is too meek and timid for the West. Tom takes Rans under his wing and tries to show him the ways of the West. When Rans says of Liberty, "I don't wanna kill him, I wanna put him in jail," Tom replies, "Out here, men settle their own problems." To that, Rans argues: "You're talking just like Liberty Valance!" In truth, Tom is more like Liberty than he is like Rans. Tom is a frontiersman, a man who is interested more in honor than in law and willing to use violence to defend his honor. Liberty is the same kind of man. But while Tom's personal sense of honor is matched by a compassionate and reasonable disposition, Liberty's is besmirched by sadism, greed, and cruelty. However, both hero and villain are destined to be replaced by representatives of civilization, thus fulfilling the Biblical prophecy: "The meek shall inherit the Earth."

After he is whipped, tortured, and beaten by Liberty, Rans's emasculation continues. He is forced to become a kitchen worker in the town restaurant, wearing an apron as he washes the dishes and serves cowboys their dinners. To add to Rans's feminine qualities, he also becomes the town schoolmarm, as he decides to bring education as well as law and order to the town of Shinbone. The feminization of Rans sets up the conflict for a character who, once feminized, must then prove his masculinity by fighting and killing. Significantly, within his classroom, whites, Indians, Mexicans, and black people are all treated equally and with respect. This is shown in stark contrast to the way that Tom treats his black servant, Pompey (Woody Strode), who is spoken to like a slave rather than like a free man. It is significant that Strode also played the title character in *Sergeant Rutledge*. Ford was clearly using Strode as a symbol of the history of white oppression against black people, especially in the West.

While the Westerner represents the three Is of independence, individualism, and isolationism, his foil, the Easterner, represents the three Ls: literacy, legislature, and liberalism. And within this contrast between East and West, we also see some remnants of the contrast between North and South, as the Easterner is the representative of liberal and progressive attitudes towards women and minorities, while the Westerner wants to cling to the

Prelude to a Showdown. Lee Marvin (left) as Liberty Valance, the savage outlaw, James Stewart (middle) as Rans Stoddard, the liberal easterner, and John Wayne as Tom Doniphon, the noble westerner in John Ford's *The Man Who Shot Liberty Valance* (1962, John Ford Productions/Paramount).

old ways, in which women are supposed to remain submissive and blacks are to do what they're told. This conflict is depicted in the schoolroom scene, in which Rans tries to teach Hallie (Vera Miles)—the woman whom Tom loves—how to read, as he also tries to teach Pompey—Tom's servant—the same skill. Tom is unhappy with the education of both of these characters, as it may lead to unwanted uppity behavior. He tells Pompey: "What have you been wastin' your time around here for? Get on back to work. Your schoolin's over." He tells Hallie: "Go on back to where you belong." Tom wants his black man in the stable, his woman in the kitchen, and his justice in his own hands. Rans is there to change all of that. To add to the depiction of Rans as the representative of Eastern liberalism, Rans forms an alliance with the town's newspaper editor, Dutton Peabody (Edmund O'Brien), who is the only man brave enough to publish editorials condemning the brutal tactics of the cattle barons and their principal roughneck, Liberty Valance. In the tradition of depicting educated men as drunkards, Dutton is a lush, as is the town doctor (Ken Murray). And in keeping with the ubiquitous vengeance motif, it is Liberty's savage whipping of Dutton in response to his unfavorable editorial that provokes Rans into his climactic showdown with Liberty.

Liberty is killed, but it is Tom who kills him, furtively shooting from out of the shadows to make it look like Rans was the shooter. This is an act of sacrifice for Tom on various levels. If Rans were to die, he would have no rival for Hallie, his true love, so in killing Liberty and saving Rans's life, he gives up his only chance for a life with Hallie. He demonstrates this loss by getting blind drunk directly after the shootout and then burning down the house he was building for himself and Hallie while he's still inside. His attempt at suicide is forestalled when Pompey pulls him out of the burning house. On another level, by killing Liberty and allowing Rans to get the credit, Tom sacrifices his own ego, withholding from himself any of the fame and praise for this act of heroism. The humility and selflessness of this act are very much reflective of the archetypal character traits of the Western hero, who not only sacrifices himself for the sake of the community, but who usually does it in an extremely blasé fashion, always unwilling to take the glory and recognition he deserves. And finally, in a larger sense, by giving Rans the title of "the man who shot Liberty Valance," Tom sets the stage for the inevitabilities to come. Rans will become a hero based on this legend of glory, and he will use his reputation as political credit to spearhead the statehood movement, which will end the days of the open range and thereby destroy the freedom of the frontier, ending the freedom of the Western hero along with it. Though it is a stretch, there is a sense in the film that Tom knowingly sacrifices himself when he kills Liberty Valance, as the death of Liberty will directly lead to the death of the frontier and the death of men like himself in its wake. In this act of sacrifice, like the ritual sacrifice of the divine king, we see the Westerner's voluntary death as a symbolic and essential act of heroism, in which the idealized man — representative of the land itself— allows himself to die in order for the land to be revitalized and in order for the transition of power to flow smoothly from one man to another. Tom Doniphon, representative of the old West, kills Liberty, representative of both the freedom and savagery of the Wild West, and in doing so, symbolically kills himself, allowing the land itself to pass from wilderness to civilization and allowing the helm of leadership to pass from the wild frontiersman to the civilized politician.

John Ford's contribution to film in general and the Western in particular is immeasurable. In his Westerns, we see the American myth being born, coming of age, and, in his later Westerns, the beginning of its decline. His earlier films are celebratory rituals of America coming to life. As Hallie in *Liberty Valance* said of the frontier: "It was once a wilderness; now it's a garden." In his later films, Ford saw it necessary to peel off the veneer of the myth that he was so instrumental in creating. He began debunking the legends, deconstructing the heroes, and demystifying the nostalgic and romantic aura that surrounded the mythology. In *Liberty Valance*, he even exposes the legerdemain of mythmakers like himself, who made divine heroes out of ordinary men. When Rans tries to explain to a newspaperman that he was not actually the man who shot Liberty Valance, the reporter replies flatly: "This is the West, sir. When the legend becomes fact, print the legend."

Conclusion:
The Western...
Dead or Alive?

*"I am not far from believing that, in our own societies, history has
replaced mythology, and fulfills the same function...."*
— Claude Lévi-Strauss

Starting with *The Great Train Robbery* (1903), the Western genre established itself in the years that saw the birth of the medium of film. The great
visual appeal of the Western, in its open landscapes, rustic locations, distinctive costumes, and opportunities for action sequences, offered early directors an ideal canvas for their cinematic art. Many of the very early Westerns
produced before 1920, when the film industry was still based on the East
Coast, were Indian subjects. These films played on audiences' fascination
with the Native American and were well suited to the Hudson River Valley
locale, as they were generally set in the Colonial Era. By the 1920s, the film
industry had moved to Hollywood, so the look of the Western changed irrev-
ocably from the lush mountain woodlands of New York State to the desert
plains of the West. And while the Indian characters remained a crucial part
of the genre, their role changed from leading parts to background characters. The Western hero — typically an outlaw, cowboy, cavalryman, or marshal — became the central figure in the genre. Though still popular in the
1920s, the Western was just one of many kinds of films being made and was
by no means a dominant force in the medium. Some significant epic Westerns, such as James Cruze's *The Covered Wagon* (1923) and John Ford's *The*

Iron Horse (1924), were made in the early 1920s; but interest in the genre was beginning to wane by the time Gary Cooper starred in *The Virginian* in 1929 and John Wayne made his debut as a leading man in Raoul Walsh's *The Big Trail* (1930). But even though the Western epic *Cimarron* (1931) was a popular hit, winning the Academy Awards for best picture, writing (adaptation), and art direction, the genre itself was at a low point. Westerns were being produced mainly as B-picture serials, and by the early 1930s, the genre had become so firmly associated with the B-picture market that A-picture producers, directors, and actors did not want to make Westerns, for fear that it would hurt their careers.

Few big-budget Westerns were made in the 1930s. But suddenly, in 1939, the Western experienced a grand revival. A slew of big-budget Westerns produced by A-list directors and starring the biggest stars in the industry burst out of Hollywood like a stampede of cattle. The most significant of the 1939 big-budget Westerns include *Dodge City*, directed by Michael Curtiz and starring Errol Flynn and Olivia de Havilland, *Union Pacific*, directed by Cecil B. DeMille and starring Joel McCrea and Barbara Stanwyck, *Destry Rides Again*, directed by George Marshall and starring James Stewart and Marlene Dietrich, *Jesse James*, directed by Henry King and starring Tyrone Power and Henry Fonda, and of course *Stagecoach*, directed by John Ford and starring John Wayne. After a dozen years of acting in Hollywood, John Wayne became an overnight success as an A-list movie star. More than any other actor, audiences would identify Wayne as the prototypical Western movie hero. Along with Wayne's rise to superstardom, the Western would become the most popular, successful, and dominant film genre in Hollywood. This dominance lasted, with a few minor lags, for three decades, ending in 1969, with the very different but extremely successful epics, *Butch Cassidy and the Sundance Kid* and *The Wild Bunch*. There are a variety of explanations for the Western revival of 1939. It is often claimed that *Stagecoach* reinvigorated the genre single-handedly, though this is clearly not the case. Multiple A-list Westerns came out that year that as a group, reestablished the Western film as a marquee headliner, rather than as a perennial second bill tacked on for the kids. A better explanation for the revival is that one studio decided to make a big-budget Western, and the other studios, always interested in blocking the other studios' moves, decided to offer competing big-budget Westerns in their theater chains, resulting in a bandwagon effect in which every Hollywood studio entered an A-list Western into the competing market.

Another factor at work in 1939 was the end of the Depression, due to the increased demands for U.S. raw materials and industrial goods, sparked by the tides of war in Europe. The wartime economy put extra dollars in the pockets of the New York executives who owned the Hollywood studios, so they may have been more generous in allotting their film budgets for that year. Indeed, 1939 was a renaissance year for all films, not just Westerns. 1939 was the year of *Gone with the Wind, The Wizard of Oz, Wuthering Heights, Mr. Smith Goes to Washington,* and many other classic films. And on a sociopolitical level, the Western may have touched a sentiment in the contemporary American subconscious. The U.S. was rising out of the Depression, just coming into its own as a true world power, and being steadily drawn into the war in Europe. The pride of national growth and independence was mingling with the fear of getting involved in another costly world war and rising sentiments of isolationism. The Western hero, with his ideals of independence, individualism, and isolationism, may have struck a chord with an American public that cherished its traditional independence from European diplomatic turmoil. Americans, as always, craved individual control over their own political concerns, and many desired to isolate themselves from the imminent bloodbath that would soon engulf Europe and Asia. The Western offered Americans a shared sense of national identity. The Western character was cut off from the political turmoil of the Old World empires. He was a nation builder, a frontiersman, always looking forward. He needs nothing from his European past. The existence of a shared mythology helped Americans feel at home with their own distinctive culture and heritage and made them less reliant on Europe for their cultural and historical roots. The notion that America was its own nation, completely independent and, if necessary, isolated from its European ancestors, may have been a comforting notion to many Americans living in those troubled times.

The main difference between the straightforward, simplistic Westerns, typical of the first half-century of the genre, and the more complex "adult" or "psychological" Westerns which arose in the late 1940s and 1950s is in the placement of what Cawelti calls the "central conflict" of the Western film — the conflict between the savage and the civilized. The earlier Westerns depicted this conflict as an external struggle between a civilized hero and a savage villain. The psychological Westerns depicted this conflict as an internal struggle within the hero, between the contrasting forces of savagery and civilization within himself. In Freudian terms, the hero in the psychological Western represents a conflict between id and superego. In Jungian terms, it is a conflict between persona and shadow.

To repeat a gross oversimplification of unknown origin: "A Western is a movie in which a man kills someone. A psychological Western is a movie in which a man kills someone, and then feels bad about it." Hence, at the ending scene of earlier Westerns, the hero typically stays in town, marries the schoolmarm, and becomes a townsman — presumably ready to beat his six-gun into a plowshare. This is because the hero, even if he starts out as an outlaw, is at heart a good, honorable, and civilized person. At the ending scene of later Westerns, the hero typically rides off into the sunset, heading west into the frontier, away from town and civilization. The conflict within him, the savage elements of his character, restrict him from settling down. He cannot be tamed or domesticated.

By 1962, the Western was showing signs of decline. Fewer movies and TV shows were being made. The Western icons — John Wayne, Gary Cooper, James Stewart, Henry Fonda, Randolph Scott, Joel McCrea, and Clark Gable — were getting older, retiring, or dying. In the 1960s, many Westerns took an autumnal or elegiac approach to their heroes. They dealt in a self-reflective, almost postmodern way with the death of the genre itself, allegorized in the end of the frontier era, as the heroes faded away into death or disregard. Anti-Westerns reflected on the genre in a bleak way, focusing on the gritty and realistic aspects of frontier life and deconstructing the classical Western hero, showing him for his faults and weaknesses. And civil rights Westerns looked back on the treatment of Native Americans with a modern perspective, introducing a new political sensibility to the genre. These subgenres represent the dominant themes in the consummatory stage of the frontier mythology.

Elegiac Westerns

Also referred to as autumnal Westerns, elegiac Westerns deal with the end of the frontier era and the subsequent demise of its hero. Many of these films are set in 20th-century America, a time in which only the remnants of the wild frontier remained and the Wild West was understood as a symbol rather than as a real place in time. The modern-day Western generally falls into the category of the elegiac Western. It mourns the loss of the frontier and its denizens via the retrospective viewpoint of its relics — the modern-day cowboys, rodeo performers, Wild West showmen, and other contemporary atavists or misfits. The modern-day Western is filled with men who still cling faithfully to the long-gone spirit of the old West. It looks back upon the frontier days with maudlin 20th-century spectacles, with nothing but the myth itself to refer to.

The modern-day Western lies on the margins of what can be considered a Western film. It does not take place on the frontier, nor is it set during the frontier era. The standard themes of savagery versus civilization, the establishment of law and order, and the honor or vengeance quest, are generally not the standard themes in the modern-day Western. Also, while there are clear-cut heroes in the modern-day Western, there are rarely any clear-cut villains or antagonists for him to shoot it out with. The modern age itself is at odds with the hero, a foe over which he couldn't possibly prevail. The films are typically about an anachronism, a Western hero character living in a modern era, a man out of sync with his time and place. The modern-day Western hero invariably has difficulty adjusting, resulting in trouble with the law, trouble holding a job, or trouble maintaining an intimate relationship. And while most Westerns, especially those made before the 1960s, were stories about victories and triumphs, the modern-day Western is almost always about a defeated character, who must either learn to somehow live with defeat or learn to die with some sort of self-respect.

Many of the heroes in modern-day Westerns are rodeo riders or disenfranchised cowboys, such as in *The Lusty Men* (1952), *The Misfits* (1961), *Junior Bonner* (1972), *The Electric Horseman* (1979), and *Bronco Billy* (1980). The rodeo is a symbol of the old-time West, making the riders the last remnant of the mythical cowboy hero. These "saddle tramps" are at once glorious and pathetic. They believe that won money is always better than wages, that honor is more important than security, and that the frontier is not completely gone — as long as they can remember it. It is easy to sympathize with the fate of the cowboy hero in the modern-day Western. In this modern world, where you can't buy a can of corn without getting a parking ticket, where the landscape is obscured by telephone poles, power lines, skyscrapers, and interstate highways, and where each lungful of air is filled with smog, engine exhaust, and toxic fumes, one could easily aspire to the same heartfelt desires of the modern-day cowboy — the desperate need for breathing space, elbow room, fresh air, untarnished wilderness, and the freedom of the open plains.

Lonely Are the Brave (1962)

Probably the most self-conscious of all the modern-day Westerns is *Lonely Are the Brave*. As the opening credits of the film roll, we see John "Jack" Burns (Kirk Douglas) cutting barbed wire so he can ride through the range, thus enabling the traditional opening scene of the lone horseman riding across the Western landscape. But this landscape, of course, is obstructed by barbed wire, the symbol of the death of the frontier, and the quiet is disturbed by the blasts of jet planes flying above and the clamor of highway traffic in the distance. Presently, the open territory ends, and now Jack and his horse must navigate across treacherous highway traffic, weaving through speeding cars and trucks, trying to somehow get by in the modern age. When Jack goes to his friend Paul's house, he learns from Paul's wife, Jerry (Gena Rowlands), that Paul is in jail, serving a two-year stint in the pen for "helping wetbacks across the border." Jerry is naturally embittered by her husband's absence, failing to see why he chose to broke the law to help some Mexicans. It is up to Jack to explain to her the Western hero's mentality: "A westerner likes open country; that means he's gotta hate fences, and the more fences there is, the more he hates 'em!" Jerry replies with a call to reason, the hallmark of the modern age: "The world that you and Paul live in doesn't exist — maybe it never did." Jack recognizes this truth and laments it: "Y'ever notice how many signs they got: No Hunting, No Hiking, No Admission, No Trespassing, Private Property, Closed Area, Start Moving, Go Away, Drop Dead!" The last few signs he mentioned are more than a little bit of foreshadowing for Jack Burns. It is not just him who is being told to drop dead — it is everyone like him, the entire Westerner creed. Their days are over, and modern society wants nothing to do with their independent-minded, law-breaking, nonconformist ways.

Unwilling or unable to wait until visiting day, Jack tries to get himself jailed so he can spend some time with Paul. After getting into a drunken fistfight and getting arrested, the booking sergeant decides not to put him in jail, so Jack is forced to punch out a policeman in order to complete his goal of getting into prison. This impulsive act, however, means that his stay in jail won't just be a couple of days for drunk and disorderly behavior; he will now be charged with assaulting a police officer and face a year in prison. Realizing that his wild nature precludes the possibility of being locked up that long, he decides to escape. To his chagrin, he discovers that Paul will not escape with him. Paul has his wife and kids to think about. He cannot live the rest of his life as a fugitive, simply to avoid a two-year sentence. Jack realizes that he is on his own — the last of his kind, the last of the wild cowboys. He stops off at Paul's house to retrieve his beloved horse. In his last exchange with Jerry, she tells him: "Either you go by the rules or you lose everything!" Jack replies hopefully: "Ya always keep something...." With the police in pursuit, he rides off towards the border.

At the end of a long manhunt, Jack is in a position where he could get across the border if he abandons his horse and continues up the rocky terrain on foot, but he can't leave her behind. As he drags her up the slope, fatefully aware that he may be destroying his chances of escape by taking her, he tells his mare: "You're worse than a woman!" For the cowboy hero, his horse is often representative of a woman — that is, the anima, or his feminine side. The cowboy, who is typically without a mate, retains the company of his horse, his sole companion on the barren plains. He is married to his horse just as the sea captain is married to his ship. There is a twist at the end, though it was well foreshadowed from the beginning of the film. After escaping from the police and the air force, Jack and his horse are hit by a truck while crossing the highway. The truck is hauling toilets. The death of the cowboy hero is depicted neither as irony or tragedy, but rather as fate. He wasn't killed by man, but by time. Like his horse, who couldn't navigate through highway traffic, the cowboy hero couldn't navigate through modern times. The creature who cannot adapt is doomed to die, and so the truck full of toilets that killed Jack and his horse was sent by providence, to flush out the relics of yesterday's world.

Ride the High Country (1962)

There are also many elegiac Westerns that are set at the end of the frontier era — any time between the end of the 19th century and the end of the first world war. Sam Peckinpah's *Ride the High Country* is one of the best elegiac Westerns and arguably Peckinpah's greatest film. Peckinpah uses the aging stars Randolph Scott and Joel McCrea as living symbols of the ending age of both the Western frontier and of the film genre that mythologized it. Randolph Scott was strongly associated with audiences as a Western star, even more so than other actors of his generation such as John Wayne and Jimmy Stewart. While Wayne and Stewart found success in other genres, Scott only found real success in the Western genre. Joel McCrea, on the other hand, had worked in a variety of genres, but he had done his share of Westerns as well.

Ride the High Country begins with Steve Judd (Joel McCrea), an aging Westerner, riding into town. The people are lined up along the street, and Steve mistakenly believes that they are gathered about to welcome him. However, they are actually just waiting to see the end of an endurance race between a camel and a horse. The symbolism is clear. The quixotic Western hero in this setting is seen as retrograde and out of date. No longer admired, he is scorned and laughed at, pushed out of the way to make room for more modern heroes. Steve, riding his trusted mare, must move aside for the sputtering "Tin Lizzie" automobile rushing past him. The cop shouts at him: "Get outta the way, old-timer!" There's no room in this new world for an old cowboy and his antique code of honor and self-respect. The scene is very reminiscent of *Lonely Are the Brave*, which begins and ends with Jack trying to navigate on horseback across highway traffic. The central theme of *Ride the High Country* is symbolized in the race between camel and horse. While the horse is prettier and flashier, representative of youth, the camel is sturdier and has more longevity. The camel is representative of the aging hero. Though he is not as stylish as the younger men around him, he will last longer, because his character carries the reserves of honor and self-respect, which are eternal. Though Steve is old and tired, no longer a legendary lawman, he still carries himself like a hero. Though he is reduced to working for wages as a gold courier for a bank, he maintains the code of honor that defines the Western hero's character.

Steve's counterpart, Gil (Randolph Scott), is found in an even lowlier state of degradation at the beginning of the film. Dressed up in a costume reminiscent of Buffalo Bill, wearing a tasseled buckskin jacket, a fake wig, and long curly moustache, he is running a sideshow shooting challenge. As the infamous "Oregon Kid," he cheats rubes out of their hard-earned nickels by using buckshot in his pistol. Gil has clearly lost his self-respect and honor. Though Steve is poor, at least he is honest. But Gil has become a trickster, and even worse, he scorns himself, making a mockery out of the Western character he once embodied, for a paltry profit. So, while Steve must only remain himself to find honor in the end, Gil must redeem himself in order to regain his lost sense of pride.

Steve enlists Gil as a partner in his job transporting gold from Coarsegold, a mountain mining camp, back to the bank. It is implied that Steve is trying to help his old friend regain his self-respect by offering him honest work. But Gil has less than respectable intentions in accepting the job. His plan is to convince Steve along the way to turn crooked, and then split the gold. Gil brings in his partner Heck (Ron Starr), a reckless youth. Since the road to the mining camp is littered with bandits, they'll need the third gun for protection. For Gil, Heck's allegiance is crucial, if his plan to enlist Steve into his crooked scheme doesn't work. Heck's youth and hotheadedness are immediately at odds with Steve's even-tempered and stoic nature. Heck is the reckless young horse to Steve's steady old camel. The three partners stop for the night at a farm along the way. The farmer's daughter, Elsa (Mariette Hartley), is a young beauty who immediately catches young Heck's lustful eye. Encouraged by Heck's flirting, Elsa runs away from her abusive, clinging, overprotective, and overly pious father. (It is implied subtly that her father is also sexually molesting her.) She catches up with the three partners in the wilderness, asking for safe passage to Coarsegold, where she will meet her fiancé, Bill Hammond (James Drury). Since they're traveling in dangerous territory, the partners are obliged to take her along. Displaying the folly and passion of youth, Heck tries to force his hand with Elsa. She screams for help, and Heck is quickly corrected by Steve and Gil, via two stiff right crosses to his jaw. It's clear at this point that Steve and Gil have become the twin father figures to these adoptive children, Heck and Elsa. Heck is a juvenile delinquent who needs discipline and a proper role model. Elsa, an innocent, abused, and confused runaway, needs a mature and gentle father figure to guide and protect her.

When the party of four enter Coarsegold, the film decidedly changes tone from that of an elegiac Western to an anti–Western. The town is filled with dirty and depraved people whose characters are dark and disturbing. The tone is in keeping with the feel of the anti–Western, in which everything is corrupted and base, violence and depravity are the rule, and innocence is quickly defiled. Billy Hammond's father and three brothers construe Billy's marriage to Elsa as an acquisition benefiting the whole family. Each Hammond intends to share Elsa as if she were a bottle of whiskey to be passed around. Poor unwitting Elsa has escaped a presumably incestuous situation with her father only to find herself entering an exponentially worse situation with the depraved Hammond clan. In the 1960s, the Western became darker and films in general became more overtly sexual. As such, the feral brothers archetype became more twisted and degenerate. As the psychological Western morphed into the anti–Western, the feral brothers devolved from outlaws and rapists into incestuous, psychopathic sexual deviants.

In earlier Westerns, the whore archetype was generally euphemized as a "dance-hall maiden" or a "showgirl," or else her shady occupation was never directly mentioned at all. In this film, there is no doubting that the only structure in town made of wood rather than tent canvas is a whorehouse called "Kate's Place" and that Kate and her employees are whores. The sign outside of Kate's Place reads: "Men taken in and done for." To prove that poor innocent Elsa has entered a den of iniquity tantamount to the Biblical Sodom and Gomorrah, the marriage ceremony is held in the whorehouse. The drunken judge (another Western archetype) presides over the ceremony. It appears that Elsa should have taken her pious father's advice about the evils of men, because as soon as she says "I do," the Hammond brothers are on her like a pack of wild dogs, one after another, forcing inappropriately intimate kisses on her, as Billy drinks and cavorts with the whores. Drunken Billy brings Elsa to a back room of the whorehouse to consummate the marriage. She is unwilling and unready to submit in such a sordid location. Billy forces his hand, becoming as brutal and abusive as her father. But before he can deflower her, Billy passes out. His brothers enter the room, intending to complete the job that Billy has started. Elsa's screams are heard across the camp. Steve and Heck come to her rescue. They take her away from the camp, intending to return the wayward runaway to her father. Steve takes on this burden, knowing full well that the Hammond clan will come after them, but his chivalrous honor demands no less than the rescuing of a maiden in distress, no matter what the risks. As Heck's love for Elsa deepens, he begins to respect Steve more and Gil less. Steve is a proper father figure, arguing that Elsa must be protected from the Hammonds. Gil is not a proper father figure, as he argues from a self-interested perspective that Elsa should be left behind. The transference of Heck's allegiance from Gil to Steve is the central shift in this character's development. He finally understands that honor and self-respect demand sacrifice and courage. Self-worth cannot be found in a bag full of stolen gold. As his love for Elsa redeems his soul, his gradual transference of allegiance from Gil to Steve will redeem his character and transform him from outlaw to hero.

The party of four rides back to town, but the vengeful Hammonds are on their trail. Gil finally realizes that his plan to enlist Steve in his plot to steal the gold is futile. Gil asks him: "Partner, you know what's on the back of a poor man when he dies? The clothes of pride ... and they're not a bit warmer to him dead than when he was alive. Is that all you want, Steve?" Steve replies stoically: "All I want is to enter my house justified." Steve is too honorable to break his word for a sack of gold. When Gil and Heck make their move and try to sneak off with the gold, Steve catches them. While he is disappointed with Heck, Gil's betrayal clearly cuts Steve to the bone. In a manner reflective of the Southern code of honor, he slaps Gil across the face and demands satisfaction, challenging him to "draw," the Western version of the gentleman's duel. Gil abjures, showing that he's yellow as well as crooked. Steve ties up his ex-partners, intending to turn them in to the sheriff when they get back to town.

When the Hammonds confront Steve, threatening to take back Elsa by any means necessary, Steve accepts Heck's word of honor that if he is given a gun to fight with, he will give it back afterwards. But Steve doesn't give Gil his gun. Gil's word of honor is no good any more. Heck proves his mettle by fighting courageously, killing two of the Hammond brothers by himself. He proves his honor by keeping his word and returning his gun to Steve. The three remaining Hammonds retreat to the woods. Before bedding down for the night, Gil asks Steve to unbind his hands. Steve asks "Why?" Gil replies contritely: "Because I don't sleep so good any more." The notion that

Gil is being tortured by his guilty conscience is enough to allow Steve to take pity on him. He cuts his hands loose. That night, Gil escapes and steals a gun off a dead Hammond.

In the climactic sequence, Steve and Heck bring Elsa back home. They are unaware that the three remaining Hammonds have killed Elsa's father and are waiting inside the house to ambush them. Gil redeems himself by rejoining his ex-partners at their moment of greatest need. Steve and Gil, the quintessential quixotic cowboys, decide to end this conflict in an honorable fashion. Using a slew of verbal insults, they challenge the Hammond family honor and call them out into the open, so they can face each other like men. The Hammonds accept the challenge. Because Heck is shot in the leg, only Gil and Steve walk across the open field, two elderly relics of the Old West, swaggering towards the inevitable Western ritual, the showdown. The Hammonds, of course, are cut down. Both Gil and Steve are shot, but only Steve's wound is mortal. In traditional fashion, Gil, the disgraced outlaw, has redeemed his honor through violence, sacrifice, and a display of courage. Steve, the man who never lost his honor, dies a hero's death. Left alone on the field of battle, he turns his head to the west and gazes at the setting sun, then enters his house, "justified."

The Wild Bunch

Peckinpah's other great Western, *The Wild Bunch* (1969), was both extremely successful and highly influential. It blended the wistful themes of the elegiac Western with the gritty realism and self-conscious violence of the anti–Western. The protagonists in *The Wild Bunch* are true anti-heroes — desperate and savage outlaws — with little moral value to redeem themselves, save the courage to honor their bond of comradeship with one of their own. In the end, that courage is more than enough. The ultraviolent climax in *The Wild Bunch*, in which the heroes use the villain's machine gun to kill hundreds of Mexican soldiers, can be seen as both a sacrifice and a suicide. The machine gun itself symbolizes the end of the frontier era. The Bunch's willingness to use the machine gun reflects their awareness of their imminent demise. By the end of the film, the Bunch have become tragically conscious of the fact that they've outlived their time. The frontier no longer exists, not even in Mexico. They could either go out in a blaze of glorious gunfire, or fade away in a squalid haze of tequila and dirt. The desperadoes decide to go out fighting, and grasp on to the last chance of honor they've got, a bold and suicidal showdown with the corrupt Mexican general who

A Final March to Glory. Left to right: Ben Johnson as Tector Gorch, Warren Oates as Lyle Gorch, William Holden as Pike Bishop, and Ernest Borgnine as Dutch Engstrom in Sam Peckinpah's *The Wild Bunch* (1949, Warner Bros.).

has imprisoned and tortured their friend. Though they die in the end, their final bloody battle frees the poor Mexican village of its tyrannical oppressor. In the closing shot, Peckinpah recalls an earlier scene in the film, in which the Bunch rides out of a Mexican village as conquering heroes, imparting a sense of honor and glory in death that the Bunch never actually had in life.

The Anti-Western

Antecedents of the anti–Western can be seen early on in the genre. Silent Westerns such as *The Vanishing American* (1920) depicted the unjust and genocidal treatment of Native Americans at the hands of the white man. *The Ox-Bow Incident* (1943), with its anti-lynching theme, its impotent heroes, and its condemnation of many of the Westerns archetypal characters, could certainly be seen as the first anti–Western. Anthony Mann's dark, conflicted hero was an important predecessor to the anti-heroes in the anti–Western subgenre, as was his depiction of the depraved, degenerate outlaw clan in *Man of the West* (1958). Though by strict interpretation not a true anti–Western, Henry King's *The Bravados* (1958) was a significant film that was extremely influential in establishing the Western anti-hero in the quickly darkening genre. In the film, the hero's vengeance quest ends with his discovery that the men he's been hunting and killing, though guilty of many heinous crimes, are not the actual men who raped and murdered his wife. The hero (Gregory Peck) is left with a guilty conscience and a dubious sense of uncertainty in himself.

While this untraditional resolution provides a much more psychologically complex character to observe, it is ultimately unfulfilling. The denouement provides no cathartic release for both the hero and the audience, who experience catharsis vicariously through the hero's acts of violence and vengeance fulfillment. This lack of primary gratification is anticlimactic in a Western, hinting that the more psychologically complex the plots became in the latter days of the Westerns, the less satisfying they were than the simpler, more basic plots of the Westerns that preceded them. As the psychological Westerns became more prone to morbid self-reflection than simple cathartic resolutions, they evolved into the deconstructivism of the anti–Western.

Sergio Leone

Undeniably, the central figure in the anti–Western is Clint Eastwood, the man who came to embody the Western as actor, director, and producer since the initial decline of the genre in the early 1960s. Sergio Leone's postmodern "Spaghetti Westerns" of the mid–1960s established Eastwood as a movie star and icon of the newer, darker Westerns. His persona — "The Man with No Name" — was a marketing tool used on the movie posters. In his three Westerns made by Leone, Eastwood's character always had a name, but the designation of "Man with No Name" seemed to fit. The man he played had no honor, at least not in the traditional sense of the Western hero. His word meant nothing. His motivation was money. Having been extracted from the American film industry, the Western hero in the "Spaghetti Western" was cut off from his Old South roots, stripping him of his gentility, grace, and charm. In Italy, the Western hero was symbolic of violence and egotism and had little to do with the Anglo-Saxon traditions of chivalry, honor, and the Code of the West.

Leone's vision of the West fit in well within a postmodern age, in which established genres had to become self-reflective in order to survive. Violence became a central focus of these films, the killing scenes extended and artistically rendered, rather than the short, abrupt shootouts in the older Westerns, in which violence was only a functional part of the plot. Leone used an arsenal of stylistic artifices to create an otherworldly, surreal feel to his scenes of violence, including but not limited to: expressionistic sound effects, peculiar angles, extensive use of close-up shots, slow motion, and illogical actions by his actors. The fact that the original dialogue, according to Italian filmmaking laws, had to be overdubbed in Italian for the initial European release meant that the American actors, though they delivered their lines in English before the camera, had to overdub their own lines for the English version of the films. The overdubbing creates a bizarre sense of disconnection between the characters and their own voices, adding to the surreal quality of the Italian Westerns. The soundtracks, composed by master movie composer Ennio Morricone, are also extremely idiosyncratic, intrusive, and overblown, creating another element of distance between Leone's films and American audiences. Morricone's music for Leone's Westerns has become as associated with the Italian Western as Clint Eastwood and Leone himself. One has only to hear Morricone's distinctive music and the image of the Italian Western comes to mind, a world much different from the Western that audiences had come to know so well, yet somehow oddly familiar as well. Though the hero displays a somewhat different persona, he is still the rugged individualist that the Americans idealize, and he is still the redemptive force of the wilderness, though his skill with a pistol has become hyperbolic as opposed to functional, and his purity has become stained with dirt and blood. Nevertheless, we can see the new Western hero, epitomized by Eastwood's "Man with No Name" character, as a natural development of the darker, more conflicted Western heroes of the psychological Westerns from the 1950s.

Clint Eastwood

Hang 'Em High (1968), Eastwood's first American-made Western, can almost be seen as a sequel to *The Ox-Bow Incident*, in which the wrongly lynched man rises from the dead (so to speak) to wreak vengeance on his killers. *High Plains Drifter* (1973) functions in pretty much the same way, though the protagonist appears to be a real ghost as opposed to a metaphorical one, and his killers, while presenting themselves as upright townspeople, were not even pretending to be upholding the law. The subject of lynching is a curious matter in the Western. In *The Virginian* (1929), the act is indicative of heroism and honor; in *The Ox-Bow Incident*, it is an atrocity, and in other films, it is simply accepted as a part of frontier life. In Raoul Walsh's *The Tall Men* (1955), when Clark Gable's character comes upon a dead man dangling from a tree bough, he remarks nonchalantly, "Looks like we're close to civilization."

Hang 'Em High not only depicts the act of lynching as a horrific abomination of the principle of justice, but also questions the moral legitimacy of "legal hanging" as well, suggesting that all capital punishment is just another version of lynching. The film itself, however, cannot be seen as an ethical allegory, as the hero is on a typical vengeance quest, leaving a trail of bullet-riddled bodies behind him as he searches for the men who wrongfully lynched him. In the first act, Ben Johnson appears as an old-time marshal, the representative of the traditional Western heroes. In a strange scene, he kills a raving madman (Dennis Hopper) by shooting him in the back. The madman dies in a crucifixion pose, symbolizing the passing of the old Western hero and the emergence of the new Western anti-hero, in the persona of Eastwood's "Man With No Name" character.

The Outlaw Josey Wales (1976)

The Outlaw Josey Wales blends elements of the anti–Western with the more sentimental themes of the elegiac Western. The result is an epic film that many fans consider to be Eastwood's finest Western, with the possible exception of *Unforgiven* (1992). After Yankee "Redlegs" slaughter his wife and son, Josey Wales (Eastwood) joins Bloody Bill Anderson's band of ruthless Confederate raiders. In this way, the title character is linked historically with Jesse James, the quintessential outlaw hero, who also rode with Bloody Bill. After the war, the rebels have lost their cause, but Josey remains an outlaw, unwilling to give up his vengeance quest. He declines the amnesty offered by the army, as he refuses to swear loyalty to the U.S. Like Jesse James and other outlaw heroes of Southern origin, such as Ethan Edwards in *The Searchers*, he remains true to his oath to the Confederate flag. This constancy and dedication to a cause long dead provides a romantic element to this brand of outlaw hero. He is an anachronism, a remnant of an earlier age, reminiscent of the glory days of the Old South, an age in which honor and a man's word meant something, an age when an oath once taken could not be rescinded. Like the outlaw heroes in *The Wild Bunch*, though he may steal and kill, the distinctive code of the outlaw hero does not allow him to break his word of honor. Such is the peculiar yet romantic nature of the code of the West and the men that clung to it.

The amnesty, however, is a ruse — a brutal trap set by the dishonorable Yanks. After his former comrades declare loyalty to the U.S., the army slaughters the ex-raiders with a machine gun, the instrument of mechanized killing and modern destruction that symbolizes the death of the Old West. Observing the massacre from a distance, Josey rides in and takes control of the machine gun, turning it on the Yanks and giving them a taste of their own cold, bloody medicine. After killing numerous soldiers, he escapes, rescuing one wounded former raider, who, like him, refused to rescind his oath to the Confederacy. The young comrade he rescues, Jamie (Sam Bottoms), becomes a figurative son to him, giving us the first clue that the film is about Josey reconnecting with the family he lost before becoming a killer. When Jamie dies, we also realize that this is a forlorn hope. Josey can never rejoin the society of peaceful men. He has killed too many times, both as a raider and as an outlaw, and he will never be forgiven for the evils that he has done. Josey is condemned to live in exile, a lone rider in the wilderness, forever running from the law and his shadowy past.

Jamie's death is also a poignant reminder of the lost generation of American boys, on both sides of the Mason-Dixon, who fell in the bloodiest and most tragic of American wars. In particular, his death is representative not only of the death of the Southern soldier, but of the death of the Old South and its culture of honor and chivalry. And, of course, as Josey's symbolic son, Jamie's death at the hands of the cowardly Yanks is just another painful reminder of the cold-blooded killing of his own little boy and wife. Both crimes were perpetrated by the same man, Terrill (Bill McKinney), the psychopathic Yank who is in hot pursuit of the desperate outlaw. He is the shadow figure that Josey must ultimately encounter in order for his vengeance quest to be complete and for him to find peace in his soul. Aiding Terrill is Fletcher (John Vernon), Josey's former Confederate comrade, who has become a turncoat and is now not only loyal to the U.S. army, but dedicated (though conflicted) to the cause of hunting down the outlaw Josey Wales, dead or alive.

As the pursuit goes on, various characters flock to Josey, seeking protection from the dangers of the Western frontier under the shelter of his supernatural killing ability. In this way, a ragtag band of misfits comes together, figuratively replacing the family Josey once had and lost and teasing the viewer with the false promise that Josey could once again become a normal man. The first to join him is Lone Watie (Chief Dan George), an elderly Cherokee who, like Josey, lost his family to the treacherous U.S. army on the Trail of Tears. By identifying the outlaw hero with the betrayed Indian, we see him as a sympathetic character. He is a man of the frontier who is lost in time, oppressed and pursued and pushed to the edge of existence by the hypocrites and cold-blooded tyrants who have taken over the West and marginalized all of its native inhabitants.

As the last of the raiders to stay true to the Confederacy, Josey recalls Cooper's archetype of the last of the Mohicans, who in turn is evoked in Watie's character, who is the last of his branch of the Cherokee tribe. They are both the last members of rare and honorable breeds of men, forced into extinction by a cold and soulless modern age. The Indian harkens back to a mythic American age, in which the land was a virgin wilderness, an open frontier, a natural paradise before the entrance of civilizing white men, an Eden before the entrance of the serpent. In turn, the outlaw hero hearkens back to a mythic American age of the antebellum South, a lost era of honor and chivalry, that was destroyed forever in the holocaust of the Civil War.

The next to join this unlikely band of heroes is a Navajo woman whom Josey rescues from a pair of white devils who were brutally raping her. She becomes Watie's woman, thus giving Josey a figurative Indian mother as well as an Indian father. A "mangy redbone hound" joins his crew, providing a mascot for the misfits under the banner of the underdog hero. Next, Josey rescues two Kansas pilgrims, Laura Lee (Sandra Locke) and Grandma Sarah (Paula Trueman), from a gang of Comancheros operating as white slavers. It is clear at this point that Josey has become a knight errant, a Lancelot of the American frontier, riding from adventure to adventure and rescuing any helpless elders or maidens in distress that he encounters along the way. He is the Western desperado cast as chivalrous knight.

Laura Lee, the pretty Southern Belle, replaces Josey's lost anima/wife. Grandma, the tough, frontier-hardened pioneer woman, represents a link to the old frontier spirit that brought folks like Josey out West to begin with. Of all the characters in the film, she is the only one who stands up to Josey and pushes him around, as his manners as a Southern boy do not allow him to disrespect an old woman. Hence, Josey has replaced his parents with Indians, his wife with another woman, and has even rediscovered his old connection to a more peaceful, gentle, and domestic way of life, through his relationship with Grandma.

Josey's affiliation with Indians, his outlaw status, and his basic sense of honor, allow him to make peace with the chief of the Comanche Indians. The band of refugees can settle in Comanche territory, finding a modicum of safety under the protection of their Indian hosts. But Terrill and Fletcher eventually catch up with Josey. The outlaw hero encounters his shadow, Terrill, and kills him, thus finally bringing his vengeance quest to fruition. Fletcher, however, remains alive and on Josey's trail. In the end, Josey is not allowed to settle down with his surrogate family. He must stay true to his outlaw nature and return to his path of wandering. In the final scene, and in traditional fashion, Josey rides off alone into the sunset.

New Frontiers

In 1974, Pauline Kael wrote in the New Yorker: "...the Western is dead." This had been said before. In 1911, a film critic for *The Nickelodeon* wrote: "...the Western photoplay has outrun its course of usefulness and is slated for an early demise." In the 1930s, nobody expected the genre to rise again from the depths of B-picture status. And in the 1980s, after nearly two decades of waning interest and ticket sales and the catastrophic flop of one of the biggest film fiascos of all time, Michael Cimino's Western epic *Heaven's Gate* (1980), it was claimed once again that the genre was dead. But to everyone's surprise, the Western keeps showing sporadic signs of life, even if it's on its deathbed. Lawrence Kasdan's modern classical Western, *Silverado* (1985), was a huge hit, as was Kevin Costner's revisionist epic, *Dances with Wolves* (1990), and Clint Eastwood's masterful anti–Western, *Unforgiven* (1992). Other big-budget Westerns of note, such as *Tombstone* (1993), Kasdan's *Wyatt Earp* (1994), Ron Howard's *The Missing* (2003), and Costner's *Open Range* (2003), have kept the genre breathing, if not actually reviving it. Recently, Ang Lee's *Brokeback Mountain* (2005), a gay love story set in the contemporary West, was a critical and commercial success. And recently, a big-budget feature, *3:10 to Yuma* (2007), a remake of Delmer Daves's classic 1957 psychological Western, has done extremely good business in theaters.

Television is also keeping the genre alive. Classic Westerns are getting a second life on cable movie channels such as American Movie Classics and Turner Classic Movies. The Encore cable network has an entire channel dedicated solely to Westerns, giving a second life not only to classic Western films, but also to the many not-so-classic Western television shows of the 1950s and '60s and the B-movie serials of the 1930s and '40s. Television miniseries such as *Lonesome Dove* (1989) and *Broken Trail* (2006) as well as television shows such as *Dr. Quinn, Medicine Woman* (1993) and *Deadwood* (2004–2006) have even introduced the genre to new generations of viewers. Nevertheless, the question remains, if the Western is not quite dead, will it ever experience even a shadow of its former glory, when it was the dominant force in American popular culture? My instinctive response to this question is "no." Mass audiences no longer seem to respond to the plots and iconography of the Western. The classical Westerns' stereotypical representations of people of color — Native Americans, Latinos, and Asians — are abhorrent to modern viewers. To feminist viewers, the classical Western is irredeemably masculinist. Furthermore, Westerns appear to legitimize outdated political values that accepted imperialism and colonialism. Present-day audiences view the Western clichés as racist and sexist. And finally, there is no doubt that the decline of the Western also has something to do with its pacing. The long silences and panoramic shots are not appealing to a modern film audience's MTV-formed attention span, which requires a cut every two seconds, a million edits a minute, and a cluttered frame.

The Westerns of the past are long gone. They are only appreciated by those old enough to have lived during their creation, as well as serious film buffs, academics, and the occasional oddball fan. New Westerns are being made for the screen as well as for television. They are much different from the old Westerns, and they will not revive the genre to any of its former grandeur. Yet they are keeping the genre alive, just barely, and modernizing it for new generations. The old motifs of Western expansionism, alcoholism, violence, and racism are giving way to stories about gay cowboys (*Brokeback Mountain*) and independent single mothers (*The Missing*). Nevertheless, the archetypal themes that the Western setting represents — independence, isolationism, and individualism — remain the primary forces behind the genre. The frontier still holds a mythic significance for Americans. It is still the place where the American character is reborn. The longing for a land where the individual is free to determine his own goals, pursue his own definition of happiness, and live according to his own code of honor, is as strong today at it was a century ago. The Western still stands as the principal American mythology.

Filmography

Apocalypse Now (1979). *Directed by* Francis Ford Coppola. *Writing credits:* John Milius, Francis Ford Coppola, and Joseph Conrad (novel). *Starring:* Martin Sheen, Dennis Hopper, Robert Duvall, and Marlon Brando.

Arizona (1940). *Directed by* Wesley Ruggles. *Writing credits:* Claude Binyon and Clarence Biddington Kelland (novel). *Starring:* Jean Arthur and William Holden.

Arrowhead (1953). *Directed by* Charles Marquis Warren. *Writing credits:* Charles Marquis Warren and W.R. Burnett (novel). *Starring:* Charlton Heston, Jack Palance, Katy Jurado, and Brian Keith.

Backlash (1956). *Directed by* John Sturges. *Writing credits:* Borden Chase and Frank Gruber (novel). *Starring:* Richard Widmark and Donna Reed.

Bad Girls (1994). *Directed by* Jonathan Kaplan. *Writing credits:* Ken Friedman and Yolanda Turner. *Starring:* Madeline Stowe, Mary Stuart Masterson, Andie MacDowell, and Drew Barrymore.

The Ballad of Little Jo (1993). *Directed by* Maggie Greenwald. *Writing credits:* Maggie Greenwald. *Starring:* Suzy Amis.

Bend of the River (1952). *Directed by* Anthony Mann. *Writing credits:* Borden Chase and Bill Gulick (novel). *Starring:* James Stewart, Arthur Kennedy, and Rock Hudson.

The Big Country (1958). *Directed by* William Wyler. *Writing credits:* William Wyler, Sy Bartlett, and Donald Hamilton (novel). *Starring:* Gregory Peck, Charlton Heston, Burl Ives, Chuck Connors, and Jean Simmons.

The Big Sky (1952). *Directed by* Howard Hawks. *Writing credits:* Dudley Nichols and A.B. Guthrie, Jr. (novel). *Starring:* Kirk Douglas, Dewey Martin, and Arthur Hunnicut.

The Big Trail (1930). *Directed by* Raoul Walsh. *Writing credits:* Jack Peabody, Mary Boyle, Florence Postal, and Hal G. Evarts. *Starring:* John Wayne.

Blazing Saddles (1973). *Directed by* Mel Brooks. *Writing credits:* Mel Brooks, Norman Steinberg, Andrew Bergman, and Richard Pryor. *Starring:* Cleavon Little, Gene Wilder, Madeline Kahn, Slim Pickens, and Harvey Korman.

The Bravados (1958). *Directed by* Henry King. *Writing credits:* Frank O'Rourke (novel) and Philip Yordan. *Starring:* Gregory Peck and Joan Collins.

Brokeback Mountain (2005). *Directed by* Ang Lee. *Writing credits:* Larry McMurtry and Annie Proulx (short story). *Starring:* Heath Ledger and Jake Gyllenhaal.

Broken Arrow (1950). *Directed by* Delmer Daves. *Writing credits:* Michael Blankfort and Elliott Arnold (novel). *Starring:* James Stewart and Debra Paget.

Broken Lance (1954). *Directed by* Edward Dmytryk. *Writing credits:* Richard Murphy, Philip Yordan, and Jerome Weidman (novel). *Starring:* Robert Wagner, Spencer Tracy, Katy Jurado, and Richard Widmark.

Broken Trail (2006). *Directed by* Walter Hill. *Writing credits:* Alan Geoffrion. *Starring:* Robert Duvall, Thomas Hayden Church, and Greta Scacchi.

Buffalo Bill (1944). *Directed by* William Wellman. *Writing credits:* Aeneas McKenzie, Clements Ripley, Cecile Kramer, and Frank Winch. *Starring:* Joel McCrea, Maureen O'Hara, Linda Darnell, and Thomas Mitchell.

Cat Ballou (1965). *Directed by* Elliott Silverstein. *Writing credits:* Walter Newman, Frank Pierson, and Roy Chanslor (novel). *Starring:* Jane Fonda and Lee Marvin.

Cheyenne Autumn (1964). *Directed by* John Ford. *Writing credits:* James R. Webb and Mari Sandoz (novel). *Starring:* Richard Widmark, James Stewart, Carroll Baker, Edward G. Robinson, Sal Mineo, Ricardo Montalban, Arthur Kennedy, Dolores Del Rio, Ben Johnson, and Karl Malden.

Cimarron (1960). *Directed by* Anthony Mann. *Writing credits:* Arnold Schulman and Edna Ferber (novel). *Starring:* Glenn Ford and Maria Schell.

Comanche Station (1960). *Directed by* Budd Boetticher. *Writing credits:* Burt Kennedy. *Starring:* Randolph Scott.

The Comancheros (1961). *Directed by* Michael Curtiz. *Writing credits:* James Edward Grant, Clair Huffaker, and Paul I. Wellman (novel). *Starring:* John Wayne and Stuart Whitman.

The Covered Wagon (1923). *Directed by* James Cruze. *Writing credits:* Jack Cunningham and Emerson Hough (novel). *Starring:* J. Warren Kerrigan, Lois Wilson, and Alan Hale.

The Cowboys (1972). *Directed by* Mark Rydell. *Writing credits:* William Dale Jennings (novel and screenplay), Irving Ravetch, and Harriet Frank, Jr. *Starring:* John Wayne and Bruce Dern.

Dances with Wolves (1990). *Directed by* Kevin Costner. *Writing credits:* Michael Blake (novel and screenplay). *Starring:* Kevin Costner and Mary McDonell.

Dark Command (1940). *Directed by* Raoul Walsh. *Writing credits:* Grover Jones, Lionel House, F. Hugh Herbert, and W.R. Burnett (novel). *Starring:* John Wayne, Claire Trevor, and Walter Pidgeon.

Deadwood (2004–2006). Television series created by David Milch. *Starring:* Ian McShane and Molly Parker.

Decision at Sundown (1957). *Directed by* Budd Boetticher. *Writing credits:* Charles Lang, Jr., and Vernon L. Flaherty (novel). *Starring:* Randolph Scott.

Destry Rides Again (1939). *Directed by* George Marshall. *Writing credits:* Felix Jackson, Gertrude Purcell, and Max Brand (novel). *Starring:* James Stewart, Brian Donlevy, and Marlene Dietrich.

Devil's Doorway (1950). *Directed by* Anthony Mann. *Writing credits:* Guy Trosper. *Starring:* Robert Taylor.

Dr. Quinn, Medicine Woman (1993–1998). Television series created by Beth Sullivan. *Starring:* Jane Seymour.

Dodge City (1939). *Directed by* Michael Curtiz. *Writing credits:* Robert H. Buckner. *Starring:* Errol Flynn and Olivia de Havilland.

Drums Along the Mohawk (1939). *Directed by* John Ford. *Writing credits:* Lamar Trotti, Sonya Levien, and Walter D. Edmonds (novel). *Starring:* Henry Fonda, Claudette Colbert, John Carradine, and Ward Bond.

Duel in the Sun (1945). *Directed by* King Vidor. *Writing credits:* David O. Selznick, Oliver H.P. Garrett, and Niven Busch (novel). *Starring:* Jennifer Jones, Gregory Peck, Joseph Cotten, Lillian Gish, and Lionel Barrymore.

The Electric Horseman (1979). *Directed by* Sydney Pollack. *Writing credits:* Shelley Burton (story), Paul Gaer (story), and Robert Garland (screen story and screenplay). *Starring:* Jane Fonda and Robert Redford.

The Far Country (1954). *Directed by* Anthony Mann. *Writing credits:* Borden Chase. *Starring:* James Stewart, John McIntire, and Walter Brennan.

Fort Apache (1948). *Directed by* John Ford. *Writing credits:* Frank Nugent and James Warner Bellah (novel). *Starring:* Henry Fonda, Ward Bond, John Agar, Shirley Temple, and John Wayne.

The Furies (1950). *Directed by* Anthony Mann. *Writing credits:* Charles Schnee and Niven Busch (novel). *Starring:* Barbara Stanwyck and Walter Huston.

Giant (1956). *Directed by* George Stevens. *Writing credits:* Fred Guiol, Ivan Moffat, and Edna Ferber (novel). *Starring:* Rock Hudson, James Dean, Elizabeth Taylor, and Dennis Hopper.

The Grapes of Wrath (1940). *Directed by* John Ford. *Writing credits:* John Steinbeck (novel) and Nunnally Johnson (screenplay). *Starring:* Henry Fonda, John Carradine, and Jane Darwell.

The Great Train Robbery (1903). *Directed by* Edwin S. Porter. *Writing credits:* Edwin S. Porter. *Starring:* Bronco Billy Anderson.

The Gunfighter (1950). *Directed by* Henry King. *Writing credits:* William Bowers (screenplay and story), Andre de Toth (story), and Nunnally Johnson. *Starring:* Gregory Peck and Karl Malden.

Gunman's Walk (1958). *Directed by* Phil Karlson. *Writing credits:* Frank Nugent and Ric Hardman. *Starring:* Van Heflin, Tab Hunter, and James Darren.

Hang 'Em High (1968). *Directed by* Ted Post. *Writing credits:* Leonard Freeman and Mel Goldberg. *Starring:* Clint Eastwood.

Heaven's Gate (1980). *Directed by* Michael Cimino. *Writing credits:* Michael Cimino. *Starring:* Kris Kristofferson and Christopher Walken.

High Noon (1952). *Directed by* Fred Zinneman. *Writing credits:* Carl Foreman and John W. Cunningham (novel). *Starring:* Gary Cooper, Grace Kelly, Katy Jurado, Thomas Mitchell, Lloyd Bridges, Lon Chaney, Jr., Lee Van Cleef, and Otto Kruger.

High Plains Drifter (1973). *Directed by* Clint Eastwood. *Writing credits:* Ernest Tidyman. *Starring:* Clint Eastwood.

Hondo (1953). *Directed by* John Farrow. *Writing credits:* James Edward Grant and Louis L'Amour (short story). *Starring:* John Wayne, Geraldine Page, and Ward Bond.

The Horse Soldiers (1959). *Directed by* John Ford. *Writing credits:* John L. Mahin, Martin Rackin, and Harold Sinclair (novel). *Starring:* John Wayne, Constance Towers, and William Holden.

How the West Was Won (1962). *Directed by* John Ford, Henry Hathaway, and George Marshall. *Writing credits:* James R. Webb. *Starring:* George Peppard, Debbie Reynolds, John Wayne, James Stewart, Gregory Peck, Henry Fonda, Richard Widmark, Robert Preston, and Karl Malden.

The Indian Fighter (1955). *Directed by* Andre de Toth. *Writing credits:* Frank Davis, Ben Hecht, and Ben Kadish. *Starring:* Kirk Douglas and Elsa Martinelli.

The Iron Horse (1924). *Directed by* John Ford. *Writing credits:* Charles Kenyon. *Starring:* George O'Brien.

Jeremiah Johnson (1972). *Directed by* Sidney Pollack. *Writing credits:* John Milius, Edward Anhalt, David Rafiel, and Vardis Fisher (book). *Starring:* Robert Redford.

Jesse James (1939). *Directed by* Henry King. *Writing credits:* Nunnally Johnson and Hal Long. *Starring:* Tyrone Power, Henry Fonda, Randolph Scott, Nancy Kelly, Henry Hull, Brian Donlevy, John Carradine, and Jane Darwell.

Jubal (1956). *Directed by* Delmer Daves. *Writing credits:* Delmer Daves, Russell S. Hughes, and Paul Wellman (novel). *Starring:* Glenn Ford, Ernest Borgnine, and Rod Steiger.

Junior Bonner (1972). *Directed by* Sam Peckinpah. *Writing credits:* Jeb Rosebrook. *Starring:* Steve McQueen, Ida Lupino, and Robert Preston.

The Last Frontier (1955). *Directed by* Anthony Mann. *Writing credits:* Philip Yordan, Russell S. Hughes, and Richard E. Roberts (novel). *Starring:* Victor Mature, Anne Bancroft, and Robert Preston.

The Last Hunt (1956). *Directed by* Richard Brooks. *Writing credits:* Richard Brooks and Milton Lott (novel). *Starring:* Stewart Granger, Debra Paget, and Robert Taylor.

The Last of the Mohicans (1920). *Directed by* Clarence Brown and Maurice Tourneur. *Writing credits:* Robert Dillon and James Fenimore Cooper (novel). *Starring:* Wallace Beery, Barbara Bedford, and Alan Roscoe.

The Last of the Mohicans (1992). *Directed by* Michael Mann. *Writing credits:* John L. Balderston and James Fenimore Cooper (novel). *Starring:* Daniel Day-Lewis and Madeline Stowe.

Last Train from Gun Hill (1959). *Directed by* John Sturges. *Writing credits:* James Poe, Edward Lewis, and Les Crutchfield. *Starring:* Kirk Douglas and Anthony Quinn.

The Left Handed Gun (1958). *Directed by* Arthur Penn. *Writing credits:* Leslie Stevens and Gore Vidal (teleplay). *Starring:* Paul Newman and John Dehner.

Little Big Man (1971). *Directed by* Arthur Penn. *Writing credits:* Calder Willingham and Thomas Berger (novel). *Starring:* Dustin Hoffman and Faye Dunaway.

Lone Star (1952). *Directed by* Vincent Sherman. *Writing credits:* Borden Chase and Howard Estabrook. *Starring:* Clark Gable, Ava Gardner, and Lionel Barrymore.

Lonely Are the Brave (1962). *Directed by* David Miller. *Writing credits:* Dalton Trumbo and Edward Abbey (novel). *Starring:* Kirk Douglas, Walter Matthau, and Gena Rowlands.

Lonesome Dove (1989) (television miniseries). *Directed by* Simon Wincer. *Writing credits:* Larry McMurtry (novel) and William D. Wittliff (teleplay). *Starring:* Robert Duvall and Tommy Lee Jones.

Major Dundee (1965). *Directed by* Sam Peckinpah. *Writing credits:* Sam Peckinpah and Harry Fink, Jr. *Starring:* Charlton Heston and Richard Harris.

A Man Called Horse (1970). *Directed by* Elliot Silverstein. *Writing credits:* Jack DeWitt and Dorothy M. Johnson (story). *Starring:* Richard Harris.

The Man from Colorado (1948). *Directed by* Henry Levin. *Writing credits:* Borden Chase. *Starring:* Glenn Ford and William Holden.

The Man from Laramie (1955). *Directed by* Anthony Mann. *Writing credits:* Philip Yordan, Frank Burt, and T.T. Flynn (novel). *Starring:* James Stewart, Arthur Kennedy, Alex Nicol, and Donald Crisp.

Man of the West (1958). *Directed by* Anthony Mann. *Writing credits:* Reginald Rose and Will C. Brown (novel). *Starring:* Gary Cooper, Julie London, and Lee J. Cobb.

The Man Who Shot Liberty Valance (1962). *Directed by* John Ford. *Writing credits:* James Warner Bellah, Willis Goldbeck, and Dorothy M. Johnson (short story). *Starring:* John Wayne, James Stewart, Vera Miles, and Lee Marvin.

Man Without a Star (1955). *Directed by* King Vidor. *Writing credits:* Borden Chase, D.D. Beauchamp, and Dee Linford (novel). *Starring:* Kirk Douglas and Jeanne Crain.

The Misfits (1961). *Directed by* John Huston. *Writing credits:* Arthur Miller. *Starring:* Clark Gable, Marilyn Monroe, Montgomery Clift, and Eli Wallach.

The Missing (2003). *Directed by* Ron Howard. *Writing credits:* Ken Kaufman and Thomas Eidson (novel). *Starring:* Cate Blanchett, Tommy Lee Jones, and Evan Rachel Wood.

My Darling Clementine (1946). *Directed by* John Ford. *Writing credits:* Samuel C. Engle and Stuart N. Lake (book). *Starring:* Henry Fonda, Victor Mature, Walter Brennan, Ward Bond, Cathy Downs, John Ireland, Linda Darnell, and Jane Darwell.

The Naked Spur (1953). *Directed by* Anthony Mann. *Writing credits:* Sam Rolfe and Harold Jack Bloom. *Starring:* James Stewart, Robert Ryan, and Janet Leigh.

Night Passage (1957). *Directed by* James Neilson. *Writing credits:* Borden Chase and Norman A. Fox (novel). *Starring:* James Stewart and Audie Murphy.

North to Alaska (1960). *Directed by* Henry Hathaway. *Writing credits:* John Lee. *Starring:* John Wayne and Stewart Granger.

Northwest Passage (1940). *Directed by* King Vidor. *Writing credits:* Laurence Stallings, Talbot Jennings, and Kenneth Roberts (novel). *Starring:* Spencer Tracy, Robert Young, and Walter Brennan.

On the Waterfront (1954). *Directed by* Elia Kazan. *Writing credits:* Budd Schulberg and Malcolm Johnson (articles). *Starring:* Marlon Brando, Rod Steiger, Lee J. Cobb, Karl Malden, and Eva Marie Saint.

One Eyed Jacks (1961). *Directed by* Marlon Brando. *Writing credits:* Calder Willingham and Charles Neider (novel). *Starring:* Marlon Brando, Ben Johnson, Katy Jurado, Pina Pellicer, and Karl Malden.

Open Range (2003). *Directed by* Kevin Costner. *Writing credits:* Craig Storper and Lauran Paine (novel). *Starring:* Robert Duvall and Kevin Costner.

The Outlaw (1943). *Directed by* Howard Hughes. *Writing credits:* Jules Furthman. *Starring:* Walter Huston, Thomas Mitchell, Jane Russell, and Jack Beutel.

The Outlaw Josey Wales (1976). *Directed by* Clint Eastwood. *Writing credits:* Philip Kaufman, Sonya Chernus, and Forrest Carter (novel). *Starring:* Clint Eastwood.

The Ox-Bow Incident (1943). *Directed by* William A. Wellman. *Writing credits:* Walter Van Tilburg Clark (novel) and Lamar Trotti (screenplay). *Starring:* Henry Fonda, Henry Morgan, Jane Darwell, Anthony Quinn, and Dana Andrews.

Pat Garret and Billy the Kid (1973). *Directed by* Sam Peckinpah. *Writing credits:* Rudolph Wurlitzer. *Starring:* Kris Kristofferson, James Coburn, Bob Dylan, Jason Robards, and Katy Jurado.

The Plainsman (1936). *Directed by* Cecil B. DeMille. *Writing credits:* Waldemar Young. *Starring:* Gary Cooper and Jean Arthur.

Pursued (1947). *Directed by* Raoul Walsh. *Writing credits:* Niven Busch. *Starring:* Robert Mitchum, Teresa Wright, Judith Anderson, and Dean Jagger.

The Quick and the Dead (1995). *Directed by* Sam Raimi. *Writing credits:* Simon Stone. *Starring:* Sharon Stone and Gene Hackman.

Rancho Notorious (1952). *Directed by* Fritz Lang. *Writing credits:* Daniel Taradash and Sylvia Richards. *Starring:* Arthur Kennedy, Marlene Dietrich, and Mell Ferrer.

Red River (1948). *Directed by* Howard Hawks. *Writing credits:* Borden Chase (novel and screenplay) and Charles Schnee. *Starring:* John Wayne, Montgomery Clift, Walter Brennan, Joanne Dru, and John Ireland.

The Return of Frank James (1940). *Directed by* Fritz Lang. *Writing credits:* Sam Hellman. *Starring:* Henry Fonda, John Carradine, Gene Tierney, Henry Hull, Donald Meek, and Jackie Cooper.

Ride the High Country (1962). *Directed by* Sam Peckinpah. *Writing credits:* N.B. Stone. *Starring:* Joel McCrea and Randolph Scott.

Rio Bravo (1959). *Directed by* Howard Hawks. *Writing credits:* Jules Furthman. *Starring:* John Wayne, Walter Brennan, Dean Martin, Ricky Nelson, and Angie Dickinson.

Rio Grande (1950). *Directed by* John Ford. *Writing credits:* James Warner Bellah (story), James Kevin McGuiness (screenplay). *Starring:* John Wayne, Maureen O'Hara, Ben Johnson, Harry Carey, Jr., and Claude Jarman, Jr.

The Scalphunters (1968). *Directed by* Sidney Pollack. *Writing credits:* William W. Norton. *Starring:* Burt Lancaster, Shelley Winters, Telly Savalas, and Ozzie Davis.

The Searchers (1956). *Directed by* John Ford. *Writing credits:* Frank S. Nugent and Alan LeMay (novel). *Starring:* John Wayne, Jeffrey Hunter, Vera Miles, Hank Worden, Ward Bond, and Natalie Wood.

Sergeant Rutledge (1960). *Directed by* John Ford. *Writing credits:* James Warner Bellah (novel and screenplay) and Willis Goldbeck. *Starring:* Jeffrey Hunter, Woody Strode, and Constance Towers.

Seven Men from Now (1956). *Directed by* Budd Boetticher. *Writing credits:* Burt Kennedy. *Starring:* Randolph Scott.

Shane (1952). *Directed by* George Stevens. *Writing credits:* A.B. Guthrie, Jr., Jack Sher, and Jack Shafer (novel). *Starring:* Alan Ladd, Jean Arthur, Van Heflin, Brandon de Wilde, and Jack Palance.

She Wore a Yellow Ribbon (1949). *Directed by* John Ford. *Writing credits:* Frank Nugent, Laurence Stallings, and James Warner Bellah (short stories). *Starring:* John Wayne, Joanne Dru, John Agar, Ben Johnson, Andrew McLaglen, and Harry Carey, Jr.

The Shootist (1976). *Directed by* Don Siegel. *Writing credits:* Miles Hood Swarthout and Glendon Swarthout (novel). *Starring:* John Wayne, Lauren Bacall, James Stewart, Henry Morgan, and Ron Howard.

Silverado (1985). *Directed by* Lawrence Kasdan. *Writing credits:* Lawrence Kasdan and Mark Kasdan. *Starring:* Scott Glenn, Kevin Costner, Danny Glover, Kevin Kline, and Rosanna Arquette.

Soldier Blue (1970). *Directed by* Ralph Nelson. *Writing credits:* John Gay and Theodore V. Olsen (novel). *Starring:* Candice Bergen and Peter Strauss.

Stagecoach (1939). *Directed by* John Ford. *Writing credits:* Dudley Nichols and Ernest Haycox (short story). *Starring:* John Wayne, Claire Trevor, Thomas Mitchell and John Carradine.

The Tall Men (1955). *Directed by* Raoul Walsh. *Writing credits:* Heck Allen (novel) and Sydney Boehm (screenplay). *Starring:* Clark Gable, Jane Russell, and Robert Ryan.

The Texans (1938). *Directed by* James V. Hogan. *Writing credits:* Bertram Millhauser, Paul Sloane, William Wister Haines, and Emerson Hough (novel). *Starring:* Randolph Scott and Walter Brennan.

They Died with Their Boots On (1941). *Directed by* Raoul Walsh. *Writing credits:* Wally Kline and Æneas MacKenzie. *Starring:* Errol Flynn and Olivia de Havilland.

3 Godfathers (1948). *Directed by* John Ford. *Writing credits:* Frank S. Nugent, Laurence Stallings, and Peter B. Kyne (novel). *Starring:* John Wayne, Harry Carey, Jr., Pedro Armendariz, Ward Bond, Ben Johnson, and Mae Marsh.

3:10 to Yuma (1957). *Directed by* Delmer Daves. *Writing credits:* Halsted Welles and Elmore Leonard (short story). *Starring:* Glenn Ford and Van Heflin.

3:10 to Yuma (2007). *Directed by* James Mangold. *Writing credits:* Halsted Welles, Michael Brandt, and Elmore Leonard (short story). *Starring:* Christian Bale and Russell Crowe.

The Tin Star (1957). *Directed by* Anthony Mann. *Writing credits:* Dudley Nichols, Barney Slater, and Joel Kane. *Starring:* Henry Fonda, Anthony Perkins, Betsy Palmer, and John McIntire.

Tombstone (1993). *Directed by* George P. Cosmatos. *Writing credits:* Kevin Jarre. *Starring:* Kurt Russell and Val Kilmer.

Two Rode Together (1961). *Directed by* John Ford. *Writing credits:* Frank Nugent and Will Cook (novel). *Starring:* James Stewart and Richard Widmark.

Ulzana's Raid (1972). *Directed by* Robert Aldrich. *Writing credits:* Alan Sharp. *Starring:* Burt Lancaster, Jorge Luke, and Bruce Davison.

Unforgiven (1992). *Directed by* Clint Eastwood. *Writing credits:* David Webb Peoples. *Starring:* Clint Eastwood, Morgan Freeman, Gene Hackman, Richard Harris, Anna Thomson, and Jaimz Woolvett.

Union Pacific (1939). *Directed by* Cecil B. De Mille. *Writing credits:* Walter DeLeon and Ernest Haycox (novel). *Starring:* Joel McRea, Barbara Stanwyck, Robert Preston, and Brian Donlevy.

The Vanishing American (1925). *Directed by* George B. Seitz. *Writing credits:* Ethel Doherty and Zane Grey (novel). *Starring:* Richard Dix, Noah Beery, and Lois Wilson.

Vera Cruz (1954). *Directed by* Robert Aldrich. *Writing credits:* Borden Chase (story) and Roland Kibbee (screenplay). *Starring:* Gary Cooper and Burt Lancaster.

The Virginian (1929). *Directed by* Victor Fleming. *Writing credits:* Howard Estabrook and Owen Wister (novel). *Starring:* Gary Cooper, Walter Huston, and Mary Brian.

Wagon Master (1950). *Directed by* John Ford. *Writing credits:* Frank Nugent and Patrick Ford. *Starring:* Ben Johnson, Harry Carey, Jr., Ward Bond, Jane Darwell, and Francis Ford.

The Westerner (1940). *Directed by* William Wyler. *Writing credits:* Niven Busch (screenplay) and Stuart N. Lake (story). *Starring:* Gary Cooper, Doris Davenport, and Walter Brennan.

The Wild Bunch (1969). *Directed by* Sam Peckinpah. *Writing credits:* Sam Peckinpah and Walon Green. *Starring:* William Holden, Ernest Borgnine, Robert Ryan, Ben Johnson, Warren Oates, and Jaime Sanchez.

Will Penny (1968). *Directed by* Tom Gries. *Writing credits:* Tom Gries. *Starring:* Charlton Heston, Donald Pleasance, Ben Johnson, Lee Majors, Bruce Dern, and Joan Hackett.

Winchester '73 (1950). *Directed by* Anthony Mann. *Writing credits:* Stuart N. Lake (story), Borden Chase (screenplay) and Robert L. Richards (screenplay). *Starring:* James Stewart, Stephen McNally, Dan Duryea, Millard Micthell, and Shelley Winters.

Wyatt Earp (1994). *Directed by* Lawrence Kasdan. *Writing credits:* Dan Gordon and Lawrence Kasdan. *Starring:* Kevin Costner, Dennis Quaid, and Gene Hackman.

Bibliography

Adler, Alfred. *The Practice and Theory of Individual Psychology.* New York: Harcourt, Brace and World, 1927.

_____. *Understanding Human Nature.* New York: Fawcett, 1954.

Aquila, Richard, ed. *Wanted Dead or Alive: The American Western in Popular Culture.* Urbana: University of Illinois Press, 1998.

Basinger, Jeanine. *Anthony Mann.* Middletown, CT: Wesleyan University Press, 2007.

Bataille, Gretchen M., and Charles L.P. Silet, eds. *The Pretend Indians: Images of Native Americans in the Movies.* Ames: Iowa State University Press, 1980.

Bulfinch, Thomas. *Bulfinch's Mythology.* New York: T.Y. Crowell, 1947.

Buscombe, Edward, ed. *The BFI Companion to the Western.* New York: Atheneum, 1988.

_____, and Pearson, Roberta, eds. *Back in the Saddle Again: New Essays on the Western.* London: British Film Institute, 1998.

Cameron, Ian and Douglas Pye, eds. *The Book of Westerns.* New York: Continuum Publishing, 1996.

Campbell, Joseph. *The Hero with a Thousand Faces.* Princeton, NJ: Princeton University Press, 1949.

_____. *The Mythic Image.* Princeton, NJ: Princeton University Press, 1974.

_____, ed. *Myths, Dreams and Religion.* New York: E.P. Dutton, 1970.

Cawelti, John G. *The Six-Gun Mystique Sequel.* Bowling Green, OH: Bowling Green State University Popular Press, 1999.

Churchill, Ward. *Fantasies of the Master Race: Literature, Cinema, and the Colonization of American Indians.* San Francisco: City Lights Books, 1998.

Cooper, James Fenimore. *The Last of the Mohicans.* 1876.

Courtwright, David T. *Violent Land: Single Men and Social Disorder from the Frontier to the Inner City.* Cambridge, MA: Harvard University Press, 1996.

Coyne, Michael. *The Crowded Prairie: American National Identity in the Hollywood Western.* New York: I.B. Tauris Publishers, 1998.

Frazier, James George. *The Golden Bough.* New York: Simon and Schuster, 1922.

French, Philip. *Westerns: Aspects of a Movie Genre,* revised edition. New York: Oxford University Press, 1977.

Freud, Sigmund. *The Complete Psychological Works: Standard Edition* (24 volumes). J. Strachey, ed. London: Hogarth Press, 1956.

Garfield, Brian. *Western Films: A Complete Guide.* New York: Da Capo Press, 1982.

Hilger, Michael. *The American Indian in Film.* Metuchen, N.J.: Scarecrow Press, 1986.

_____. *From Savage to Nobleman: Images of Native Americans in Film.* Lanham, MA: Scarecrow Press, 1995.

Indick, William. *Movies and the Mind: Theories of the Great Psychoanalysts Applied to Film.* Jefferson, NC: McFarland, 2004.

_____. *Psychology for Screenwriters: Building Conflict in Your Script.* Los Angeles: Michael Wiese Productions, 2004.

Izod, John. *Myth, Mind and the Screen: Understanding the Heroes of Our Time.* Cambridge, UK: Cambridge University Press, 2001.

_____. "Westerns and global imperialism." A paper presented at the 2nd International Academic Conference of Analytical Psychology and Jungian Studies, 7–10 July, 2005.

Jung, Carl G. *Archetypes and the Collective Unconscious.* In *Collected Works,* Vol. 9, 1936.

_____. *Collected Works.* H. Read, M. Fordham & G. Adler, eds. Princeton, NJ: Princeton University Press, 1953.

_____. *The Portable Jung.* Joseph Campbell, ed. New York: Viking Penguin, 1971.

Kilpatrick, Jacquelyn. *Celluloid Indians: Native Americans and Film.* Lincoln: University of Nebraska Press, 1999.

Kitses, Jim. *Horizons West: Anthony Mann. Budd Boetticher. Sam Peckinpah: Studies of Authorship Within the Western.* Bloomington: Indiana University Press, 1970.

_____, and Gregg Rickman, eds. *The Western Reader.* New York: Limelight Editions, 1998.

Lawrence, D.H. *Studies in Classic American Literature, 3rd Edition.* New York: Viking Press, 1966.

Lyon, Peter. "The Six-Gun Galahad." *Time Magazine,* March 30, 1959.

May, Rollo. *The Cry for Myth.* New York: Norton, 1991.

_____. *Man's Search for Himself.* New York: Norton, 1953.

Maynard, Richard. *The American West on Film: Myth and Reality.* Rochelle Park, N.J.: Hayden, 1974.

McGrath, Roger D. "Gunfighters, Highwaymen, and Vigilantes: Violence on the Frontier," *Chronicles,* Vol. 10, 2005.

Mitchell, Lee Clark. *Westerns: Making the Man in Fiction and Film.* Chicago: University of Chicago Press, 1996.

Nash Smith, Henry. *Virgin Land: The American West as Symbol and Myth.* New York: Vintage, 1950.

O'Connor, John E. *The Hollywood Indian.* Trenton: New Jersey State Museum, 1980.

Parks, Rita. *The Western Hero in Film and Television: Mass Media Psychology.* Ann Arbor, MI: UMI Research Press, 1982.

Prats, A.J. *Invisible Natives: Myth and Identity in the American Western.* Ithaca, N.Y.: Cornell University Press, 2002.

Raglan, Lord. The Hero: A Study in Tradition, Myth and Drama. New York: Dover Publications, 2003.

Rank, Otto. *The Myth of the Birth of the Hero*. New York: Random House, 1914. Reprint: 1959.

Saunders, John. *The Western Genre*. New York: Wallflower Press, 2001.

Silver, Charles. *The Western Film*. New York: Pyramid Communications, 1976.

Simmon, Scott. *The Invention of the Western Film: A Cultural History of the Genre's First Half-Century*. Cambridge, UK: Cambridge University Press, 2003.

Slotkin, Richard. *The Fatal Environment: The Myth of the Frontier in the Age of Industrialization, 1800–1890*. Norman: University of Oklahoma Press, 1973.

_____. *Gunfighter Nation: The Myth of the Frontier in Twentieth-Century America*. Norman: University of Oklahoma Press, 1992.

_____. *Regeneration Through Violence: The Mythology of the American Frontier, 1600–1860*. Norman: University of Oklahoma Press, 1985.

Tompkins, Jane. *West of Everything: The Inner Life of Westerns*. New York: Oxford University Press, 1992.

Turner, Frederick Jackson. "The Significance of the Frontier in American History." A paper read at the meeting of the American Historical Association in Chicago, 07/12/1893, during the World Columbian Exposition.

Walker, Janet. *Westerns: Films Through History*. New York: Routledge, 2001.

Wheelwright, Philip. "A Semantic Approach to Myth." In *MYTH: A Symposium*, by Thomas Sebeok, ed. Bloomington: Indiana University Press, 1965.

Wright, Will. *Six Guns and Society: A Structural Study of the Western*. Berkeley: University of California, 1975.

Index